Census of Great Britain, 1851: Religious Worship in England and Wales

Horace Mann, Great Britain. Census Office

[BY AUTHORITY OF THE REGISTRAR-GENERAL.]

CENSUS OF GREAT BRITAIN, 1851.

RELIGIOUS WORSHIP

IN

ENGLAND AND WALES.

ABRIDGED FROM THE OFFICIAL REPORT

MADE BY

HORACE MANN, Esq.,

TO

George Graham, Esq., Registrar-General.

SEVENTEENTH THOUSAND,

(REVISED.)

LONDON:
GEORGE ROUTLEDGE AND CO., 2, FARRINGDON STREET.

PRINTED BY GEORGE E. EYRE AND WILLIAM SPOTTISWOODE,
PRINTERS TO THE QUEEN'S MOST EXCELLENT MAJESTY.

One Shilling.

1854.

CONTENTS.

PREFACE.

Religious parties of every denomination, in the estimates they have endeavoured to form of their comparative strength in this country, have hitherto felt the great disadvantage resulting from the absence of official returns on the subject of public worship. It has been attempted, by means of the information preserved by particular communities, in some measure to supply this deficiency, but the statistical information obtained by any one denomination has never been deemed authentic by any other; and, after all the efforts made by particular bodies, it has been found that the results have been of little practical value, not only because their accuracy was suspected, but also on account of their meagre and limited character. For the *first* time in the history of this country a Census of Religious Worship has been obtained by the Government. We are now able to ascertain the entire number of places of worship, the particular sects to which they respectively belong, the number of sittings provided by each sect, and the actual attendance on a given day.

In consequence of the deep interest known to be taken in the subject, and the general wish to possess impartial and authentic information upon it, arrangements have been made for placing within reach of the public generally all the more important parts of the Report, in which the results of the Census inquiry are embodied, at a price which should secure the object of its wide diffusion with the least possible delay. Appreciating this design, Major Graham, the Registrar General, has kindly sanctioned the publication of this abridgment, and has allowed it to go forth in the present cheap and popular form with his express authority.

To form a just estimate of the value of the following Tables, it is necessary to know the extensive and costly apparatus by means of which they have been obtained. This will best appear from the following statement of the "Mode of Procuring and Digesting the Returns," as given in the Appendix to the Report, from which will also be seen the great attention which has been devoted to the work of supplementing defective returns, and rendering them as nearly as possible an exact and faithful picture of the religious state of England and Wales :—

" For the primary object of the Census, that of simply numbering the
" people, England and Wales was divided into 30,610 separate plots
" or districts, each of which was the sphere of a single person called
" an Enumerator, who in his turn was under the direction of a Registrar
" of Births and Deaths, of whom there are 2,190 in England and Wales.
" To these 30,610 officers was assigned the additional duty of pro-
" curing the returns relating to public worship."

" The first proceeding was to obtain a correct account of all existing
" edifices or apartments where religious services were customarily per-
" formed. The enumerators, therefore, were directed each to prepare,
" in the course of the week preceding March 30th, 1851, a list of all
" such places within his district, setting out the name and residence of
" the minister or other official party competent to give intelligence. To
" each such party was delivered or transmitted a schedule of inquiries—
" chiefly respecting the accommodation furnished in the building, and
" the number of the congregation upon Sunday, March the 30th. The
" schedules were of two descriptions : one for churches connected with
" the Established religion, and the other for places of worship
" belonging to the various bodies not connected with the Establishment.
" For the sake of ready identification, the two descriptions of schedule
" had each a distinctive colour, the former being printed black, and the
" latter red. The difference in the questions was slight : in the Church
" of England form the additional queries had relation to the date of
" consecration—the agency by which, and the cost at which, the fabric
" was erected, and the amount and sources of endowment. But, in
" deference to expressed objections, this last question was abandoned
" after the forms were issued, and the clergy were informed that no
" reply to it was wished for. In the other form, the further particulars
" inquired about were—the precise religious denomination of the parties
" making the return—whether the service was conducted in a separate
" building or in a portion merely, as a room—whether it was used
" exclusively for public worship—the date at which it was erected or
" first appropriated to its present use—and (with exclusive reference to
" Roman Catholic chapels) the space allotted as *standing-room* for
" worshippers. In both of the forms a statement of the number of
" free, as distinguished from rented or appropriated, sittings, was
" requested ; and in both there was a column for the insertion of the
" *average* number of the congregation, to provide for cases where the
" church or chapel might be closed upon the Sunday of the Census, or
" where, from peculiar circumstances, the attendance might be less than
" usual."

" When delivering the schedules to the proper parties, the enume-
" rators told them it was not compulsory upon them to reply to the
" inquiries ; but that their compliance with the invitation was entirely
" left to their own sense of the importance and the value to the public
" of the information sought."

" The schedules were collected by the enumerators in the course of
" their rounds upon the Census day, viz., March the 31st, 1851. They

" were then transmitted to the registrar ; who, having previously
" received the list above referred to, would compare the number of
" returns collected with the number mentioned in the list, and would
" take measures to procure, if possible, the returns, if any, which were
" missing."

" Having finished his revision, the registrar despatched returns and
" lists together to the Census Office, London, where the 30,610 lists and
" about 34,000 returns were numbered in parochial order and collected
" into books. A further comparison of lists and returns was then pro-
" ceeded with ; the Clergy List being also used to check the complete-
" ness of the Established Church returns. The result of these com-
" parisons was the discovery of a still considerable number of defi-
" ciencies ; principally of returns from places of worship in connexion
" with the Church of England,—several of the clergy having enter-
" tained some scruples about complying with an invitation not proceed-
" ing from episcopal authority. In all such cases, a second application
" was made direct from the Census Office, and this generally was
" favoured by a courteous return of the particulars desired. The few
" remaining cases were remitted to the Registrar, who either got the
" necessary information from the secular officers of the church, or
" else supplied, from his own knowledge, or from the most attainable
" and accurate sources, an estimate of the number of sittings and of the
" usual congregation."

" By these means, a return was ultimately, and after considerable
" time and labour, procured from every place of worship mentioned
" in the enumerators' lists, viz., from 14,077 places belonging to the
" Established Church, and from 20,390 places belonging to the various
" dissenting bodies, making 34,467 in all."

" The returns, when thus made as complete as practicable, were tabu-
" lated in parochial order. It was then discovered that many of them
" were defective, in not stating the number of sittings, and that others
" which gave the sittings omitted mention of the number of attendants.
" Full information as to *sittings* seemed to be so very essential to a
" satisfactory view of our religious accommodation, that an application
" was addressed to every person signing a return defective in this point,
" requesting him to rectify the omission. The intelligence thus fur-
" nished was incorporated with the original return. There are still,
" however 2,524 cases where no information could be got : these,
" wherever they occur, are mentioned in the notes to the district which
" contains them. Where the number of *attendants* was not stated for
" the 30th March, and it appeared that there was, nevertheless, a
" service held upon that day, the number specified as the usual *average*
" was assumed to have been the number present on the 30th, and was
" inserted in the columns for that day. Where neither in the columns
" for the 30th March, nor yet in the columns for the average congrega-
" tion, was any number given, the deficiency was mentioned in the
" foot notes, as in the case just mentioned of omitted *sittings*. And
" so, where *neither sittings nor attendants* were supplied. It appears
" that the number of omissions which, in spite of the endeavours
" made to get the supplementary information, were obliged to be

" submitted to, are as follow : number of *sittings* not mentioned in
" 2,134 cases ; number of *attendants* unspecified in 1,004 cases ; and
" *neither sittings nor attendants* given in 390 cases. Estimates for these
" omissions have been made for certain of the Tables, on a principle
" explained in the Report. They have not, however, been interpolated
" in the regular Tables, but are given in separate Tables by them-
" selves. This course seemed most free from objections ; as the Tables
" now contain nothing beyond the original, authenticated figures—
" the omissions being stated in the notes, from which each reader can
" make his own computation, if desirous of so doing."

" It was also found that, frequently, an ambiguity prevailed in the
" answers given to the inquiries respecting 'free sittings.' Several
" of the returns from ancient parish churches, where, of course, no
" pew rents are received, describe the whole of the sittings as being
" therefore 'free.' But this was not the sense intended to be con-
" veyed by the question, which contemplated the case of sittings not
" only free from any money payment, but also free from any particular
" appropriation, whether by custom or by the allocation of church
" officers, or otherwise,—sittings, in fact, devoted especially to the
" poorer classses, and which they might in freedom occupy at their
" own option and selection. In all such cases, therefore, it was deemed
" advisable, in order to secure an uniformity of meaning throughout
" the returns, to mention merely the *total* number of sittings, making
" no apportionment of them into ' free ' and ' appropriated.' The
" effect of this was to ensure that all the sittings which are men-
" tioned in the Tables as ' free,' (3,947,371) are really free in the
" manner above described ; that the ' appropriated' sittings (4,443,093)
" are those which, either from a money payment or from customary
" occupancy, are not accessible to anybody indiscriminately ; and that
" the residue (1,077,274), not adequately described, may belong to
" either of these classes, but most likely in greater proportion to the
" latter."

" It will be perceived that one of the questions pointed to a distinc-
" tion desirable to be made between the ' general congregation ' and
" the ' Sunday scholars.' In many of the returns the distinction was
" not made, the *total* numbers only, including both these classes of
" attendants, being entered. As, therefore, no correct account could
" be obtained of the whole number of Sunday scholars usually mingling
" with our congregations, it is thought to be the better course in every
" instance to include them in one total. In several returns a service
" was returned as attended by Sunday scholars *only ;* in these instances
" the numbers have been disregarded, on the theory that such ser-
" vices partook more of the nature of school duties than of formal
" public worship. Sunday scholars have been reckoned as attending
" religious service only where, upon the same portion of the day, some
" numbers are inserted for a ' general congregation.' "

" Another point upon which an explanation of the course adopted
" may be useful is the following : it was wished to show, with respect
" to all the 30,240 places of worship, how many of them were open for
" service at each portion of the Sunday morning, afternoon, and

" evening, and how many were closed on each of those occasions.
" This, of course, was ascertained by the insertion of figures denoting
" a service, or of a cross (✕), denoting that no service was held. But
" in several cases, where the other particulars were given, the return
" was altogether blank upon the subject of *attendants*; and the question
" was, in what way to regard such cases. The course adopted has been,
" where the church or chapel is located in a *town*, to assume that a
" service was performed both *morning and evening*, and where the
" church or chapel is situate in the rural districts, to assume that
" services were celebrated in the *morning and afternoon*."

The limits necessary to the present "Abridgment" compel the
Editor to curtail the admirable "Introductory Sketch of the
Progress of Religious Opinions in England till the Period of the
Revolution of 1688." The thread of the narrative, however, has
been preserved, and the sketch, in its reduced proportions, will
serve to show how the country has grown into that state of
comparative religious freedom which so strikingly contrasts with
the ages which have passed away.

It is always found difficult to describe churches in terms
which are perfectly approved by their members; still it may be
hoped that the various notices given in the Report will be found
impartial, this having evidently been the object of its Author,
who has selected his information from the sources which appeared to possess the greatest authority. One of the most
interesting and valuable portions of the Report will be found
in the Author's remarks upon "Spiritual Provision and Destitution." So important, indeed, has it been deemed by the
Editor of the present Abridgment, that he has considered it best
to give it entire.

In selecting from the numerous Tables contained in the Report,
the object has been to extract those which were most likely to
be popularly useful for religious and statistical purposes, and to
render the possessor of the Abridgment as much as possible independent of the larger work,—to which, for more detailed information, it may be found necessary in some few cases to refer.

A successful commencement having been now made in the
important service of learning for ourselves, and showing to other
nations, the religious statistics of our own country, we may
anticipate at each succeeding decennial period that the returns
on "Religious Worship" will form a valuable part of the Census,
and serve as a powerful aid to the highest interests of the
community.

London,
January 5, 1854.

REPORT.

TO THE RIGHT HON. THE VISCOUNT PALMERSTON, M.P., G.C.B.
HER MAJESTY'S SECRETARY OF STATE FOR
THE HOME DEPARTMENT.

Census Office, 10th December 1853.

My Lord,

When the Census of Great Britain was taken, in 1851, I received instructions from Her Majesty's Government to endeavour to procure information as to the existing accommodation for Public Religious Worship.

Every exertion has been made to obtain accurate Returns upon which reliance may be placed ; and the duty of arranging these Returns in a tabular form, accompanied by explanatory remarks, has been confided by me chiefly to Mr. Horace Mann. He has devoted much time and labour to the subject ; and I trust that your Lordship will be of opinion that the task delegated to him has been well executed.

I have the honour to be,
My Lord,
Your faithful servant,
GEORGE GRAHAM,
Registrar-General.

REPORT.

TO

GEORGE GRAHAM, Esq.
&c.   *&c.*   *&c.*

REGISTRAR GENERAL OF BIRTHS, DEATHS, AND MARRIAGES.

SIR,

  IN fulfilment of the task with which you have entrusted me, I have now the honour to present, in a digested form, a Summary of the Returns collected at the recent Census, showing the amount of accommodation for worship provided by the various religious bodies in the country, and the extent to which the means thus shown to be available are used.

  Origin of the Inquiry as to Religious Worship; and Manner of its prosecution.

  It may, perhaps, be advantageous to preface the observations which, with your permission, I propose to offer on the state of religion in England, as disclosed in these returns, by a brief account of the origin of the Inquiry and the mode in which it has been prosecuted.

  It will, doubtless, be within your recollection that, when making preparation for the General Census, and determining what information was most worthy to be gathered by the aid of the complete machinery then specially to be provided, it appeared to you exceedingly desirable to seize upon so rare an opportunity in order to procure correct intelligence on two important subjects of much public interest and controversy, viz., the number and varieties and capabilities of the religious and the scholastic institutions of the country. In pursuance of this scheme, a set of Forms (reprinted in the Appendix to this volume*) was prepared and issued to the various enumerators, with instructions for their distribution and collection.

  These proceedings were adopted under the impression that the language of the Census Act—conferring on the Secretary of State the power to issue questions, not alone respecting the mere numbers, ages, and occupations of the people, but also as to such "further particulars" as might seem to him advisable—would amply warrant so important an investigation. When, however, in the House of Peers, objections were preferred against the contemplated Inquiry, and doubts expressed upon the applicability of the penal sections of the Act to parties who might choose withholding information on these subjects, it was deemed desirable to submit the question to the legal advisers of the Crown, and their opinion proved to be confirmatory of this view.

  As you, however, still retained a firm conviction of the great advantage to the public of the object for which preparations so extensive had already been matured, and for the satisfactory pursuit of which so great facilities existed, it was recommended by you to the Secretary of State that the investigation should be nevertheless continued; the various parties from whom information was to be requested being made aware that they were not by law *compellable* to furnish the particulars referred to in the Forms supplied to them. It seemed to you that a reliance on a general willingness to meet the wishes of the Government in so conspicuously valuable an object would be amply justified by nearly universal acquiescence; and that the necessary employment, for the

---

* It has not been deemed necessary to reprint, with this Abridgment, the "Forms" here referred to. [EDITOR].

ordinary purpose of the Census, of a staff of nearly 40,000 persons, visiting on two distinct occasions every house throughout Great Britain, offered an opportunity for procuring accurate statistics much too rare to be neglected—such indeed as could not possibly recur till, after another ten years' interval, the Census should again be taken in 1861.

The Secretary of State assenting to these views and your proposal, printed Forms were carefully distributed by the enumerators to the proper parties. In the case of returns for places of religious worship, the forms were left with the clergyman or minister, warden or deacon, or other officer connected with each place of worship.

The extent to which returns, in answer to this application, were received, affords abundant evidence of the hearty co-operation of the clergy and the ministers of all denominations in this voluntary labour. Such returns have been obtained from 14,077 churches belonging to the Church of England, and from 20,390 places of worship belonging to all other religious bodies. From this simple fact alone it will be manifest that these returns are nearly as complete as could be wished for; and that now, for the first time, there is given to the country a full picture of the state of its religion as exhibited by its religious institutions.

Number of Sects.   There are in England and Wales 35 different religious communities or sects,—27 native and indigenous, 9 foreign.* The following arrangement, shows them, under certain obvious considerable and minor classes, in the order of historical formation:

PROTESTANT CHURCHES:

> BRITISH:
>> Church of England and Ireland.
>> Scottish Presbyterians:
>>> Church of Scotland.
>>> United Presbyterian Synod.
>>> Presbyterian Church in England.
>> Independents, or Congregationalists.
>> Baptists:
>>> General.
>>> Particular.
>>> Seventh Day.
>>> Scotch.
>>> New Connexion General.
>> Society of Friends.
>> Unitarians.
>> Moravians, or United Brethren.
>> Wesleyan Methodists:
>>> Original Connexion.
>>> New Connexion.
>>> Primitive Methodists.
>>> Bible Christians.
>>> Wesleyan Association.
>>> Independent Methodists.
>>> Wesleyan Reformers.

PROTESTANT CHURCHES—continued.

> BRITISH:—continued.
>> Calvinistic Methodists:
>>> Welsh Calvinistic Methodists.
>>> Countess of Huntingdon's Connexion.
>> Sandemanians, or Glassites.
>> New Church.
>> Brethren.

> FOREIGN:
>> Lutherans.
>> German Protestant Reformers.
>> Reformed Church of the Netherlands.
>> French Protestants.

OTHER CHRISTIAN CHURCHES.
> Roman Catholics.
> Greek Church.
> German Catholics.
> Italian Reformers.
> Catholic and Apostolic Church.
> Latter-day Saints or Mormons.

JEWS.

* These include all the bodies which have assumed any formal organization. There are, in addition, many isolated congregations of religious worshippers, adopting various appellations, but it does not appear that any of them is sufficiently numerous and consolidated to be called a "sect."

The existence of so many separate sects will be considered an advantage or an evil, in proportion as the active exercise of private judgment, or the visible unity of the Church, if both be unattainable together, is esteemed the more important acquisition. Much too of the feeling, favorable or adverse, which the contemplation of such multiplied diversities must cause, will be dependent on the question whether, notwithstanding much apparent and external difference, substantial harmony with truth may not extensively prevail.

Of great importance evidently, therefore, is it to supply some sketch, however slight, of the prominent characteristics of each sect; partly for the sake of justice to the sects themselves, in order to reveal, in some of them, accordances, perhaps not generally hitherto suspected, with admitted truth—and partly for the sake of the community at large, in order to reveal the progress of erroneous doctrines, likewise, it may be, hitherto unnoticed.

Necessity of explanation

PROGRESS OF RELIGIOUS OPINIONS IN ENGLAND.

PROGRESS OF RELIGIOUS OPINIONS IN ENGLAND.

From A. D. 681 to the present time, an interval of more than eleven centuries, Christianity, in one form or another, has maintained itself as the predominant religion of the English people. Naturally, in the course of this protracted period, the ever-varying condition—social, intellectual, material—of the country, as successive generations made new acquisitions of enlightenment and liberty and wealth, effected corresponding variations in the aspect, both political and doctrinal, of the religious faith of the community. Thus we behold, in earliest times, particular articles of Christian faith and practice gathering the undivided homage of the people, and receiving sanction from the civil power, which also punishes diversity. In course of time these ancient tenets lose their hold upon the national affections; the civil sanction is transferred to other doctrines, and the civil penalties are now enforced against all opposition to the *new* belief. Gradually, however, these restraints upon opinion are withdrawn; existing creeds take form and practical embodiment; and further sects arise and organise and multiply, till, favoured by almost unbounded toleration, sects perpetually appear and disappear, as numerous and varied as the opinions or even as the fancies of men. Some slight review of these mutations in the national mind and in the fortunes of particular Churches seems almost essential to a satisfactory appreciation of the present state of England in regard to her religious institutions.

Definitive establishment of Christianity in England.

Christianity, when introduced among the Saxons, at once assumed an organized character. This was, of course, accordant with the episcopal model to which the missionaries were themselves attached. The conversion of the king of a Saxon State was immediately followed by the elevation of his benefactor to a bishopric, the territorial boundaries of which were generally conterminate with those of the kingdom itself. In course of time, as some of the dioceses were manifestly too extensive, divisions of the larger sees were made, and additional bishoprics created. The first partition of this kind was effected by Theodore, Archbishop of Canterbury, about A.D. 680; and the Council of Hertford, held in 693, enacted, or at least affirmed, that sees should become more numerous as the number of the faithful increased. In this manner the larger ecclesiastical divisions of the country were soon settled on a permanent basis; for, with the exception of some changes made in the reign of Henry VIII., and a few of very recent origin, the present bishoprics are the same as those established in the Anglo-Saxon times. The Bishops were ostensibly nominated by the clergy of the cathedral church, but the sovereigns generally influenced, if they did not

State of Christianity in Saxon times.

Bishops and Dioceses.

PROGRESS
OF RELIGIOUS
OPINIONS
IN ENGLAND.

altogether monopolize, the appointments. The authority of the prelates was very considerable. They ranked with the Earl, and each of their oaths was equivalent to those of 120 ceorls. Apart from their spiritual jurisdiction, they sustained an important position in the conduct of civil affairs,—possessing seats in the national Witena-gemot, and assisting the sheriffs in the local administration of justice.

Reveuues.

The funds for the support of Christianity were derived from various sources. At first they seem to have been exclusively supplied by voluntary offerings, of which the bishops had the sole disposal.* Afterwards, upon the erection of a church or the foundation of a religious establishment, it became the custom —probably in imitation of a practice which appears to have prevailed in nearly every age and every country of the world—for the founder to devote a *tenth* of all his property to purposes of religion and charity. *Tithes* thus appear to have had their origin in voluntary payments, and as such they were, doubtless, very generally rendered in the early periods of Anglo-Saxon rule, when the payment was considered applicable both to the provision for religious worship and to the relief of the poor. It was not till the middle of the sixth century that tithes were demanded by the clergy of Christendom as a *right;* nor were they declared to be such by any General Council prior to that of Lateran in 1215. In England, however, it was not long before a custom so generally adopted began to be regarded, first as a religious, and then as a legal, duty; and, accordingly, the legislature in the tenth century recognized the obligation, and provided for its due discharge, first, by declaring that defaulters should be liable to spiritual censures, and, ultimately, by enacting civil penalties for disobedience. Several minor customary payments, under the various names of *Church-shot*, *Light-shot*, and *Plough-alms*, seem also to have gradually acquired a legislative sanction. Monasteries, and similar religious institutions, were, in general, well provided for by the endowments settled on them by their founders, and by grants and gifts continually made to them by later benefactors.

Condition of the
Church subse-
quent to the
Norman Con-
quest.

For nearly 150 years immediately following the Conquest, the history of Christianity in England shows an almost continual advance of the power of the clergy and the Holy See. William the Conqueror, though personally little inclined to yield the smallest portion of his spiritual jurisdiction, nevertheless contributed materially, by steps adopted for political advantage, to augment the influence of Rome. While he himself maintained with spirit his supposed prerogatives,—not suffering any interference with the Church without his sanction, and requiring that no Pope should be received as such without his previous consent,—the various acts by which he introduced or strengthened precedents for papal intervention could not fail to be the efficacious means by which, in more perplexing times, or under less determined rulers, England would be brought to more complete dependence on the Court of Rome. Among these measures, not the least effectual was the separate ecclesiastical tribunal which he instituted for offences and disputes in which the clergy were concerned. This exclusive juris-diction, and the further advances made in enforcing clerical celibacy, tended much to erect the priesthood into an independent power in the state, asserting, first an equal, and at last a superior, position to the civil government.

1384—1509.

Nearly every Parliament from the time of Wycliffe to the reign of Henry VIII. (1384 to 1509) adopted measures to resist pontifical supremacy; and, not restricting their hostility to Rome, they even several times suggested to the sovereign the appropriation of Church property to secular objects. Two parties hence arose in the ranks of the Reformers.—one desiring both political and doctrinal reformation, the other limiting their aims to merely secular changes.

---

* Kemble, ii. p. 473. Lingard, vol. i. p. 180.

From 1534 this country may be said to have possessed a National Church; for ever since, with the brief exception which occurred in the reign of Mary, all the civil laws by which, in England, Christianity has been established and expounded, have derived their force entirely from the sanction of the native government of the state, apart from any, the slightest, interference of a foreign power.

PROGRESS OF RELIGIOUS OPINIONS IN ENGLAND.

Establishment of a National Church.

In 1536, the Convocation passed, and the King adopted, certain Articles, by which the faith of the Church of England was, for the time, authoritatively settled. In these, the Bible and the three creeds are set forth as the foundation of belief; baptism, penance, confession to a priest, belief in the corporal presence, are declared essential to salvation; justification is said to be obtained by the union of good works with faith. Images were to be used as examples, but not as idols; saints were to be honoured, but not worshipped; the use of holy water was allowed, but its efficacy was denied; indefinite prayer was permitted for the dead; and the existence of an unspecific purgatory was affirmed.* All the clergy were directed to explain these articles to their flocks. Latin and English Bibles were to be set up in the churches; and the children of the parish were to be taught, in the mother tongue, the Lord's Prayer, the Ten Commandments, and the Creed.† In the following year, 1537, the King put forth a fuller exposition of the orthodox belief in the shape of a book adopted by the Convocation and entitled "The Institution of a Christian Man," and in 1543 he published, of his own authority, a second edition of this work, with certain alterations favouring the ancient doctrines. These books were, each in turn, accepted as the standard of belief: but the test by which it was attempted to secure an uniformity of faith was the "Law of the Six Articles," passed in 1539. By this law were established, (1) the doctrine of the real presence,—(2) the communion in one kind only,—(3) the perpetual obligation of vows of chastity,—(4) the utility of private masses,—(5) the celibacy of the clergy,—and (6) the necessity of auricular confession. Death by fire, and forfeiture of all possessions, were the penalties of controverting the first article; imprisonment or death the penalty of opposition to the rest, according as the opposition was withdrawn or persevered in. In 1544, the Legislature somewhat mitigated the severity of this enactment; but the number of persons who were executed under its provisions was yet very great.

Changes effected by Henry VIII.

During the brief reign of Edward the Sixth the progress of the doctrinal Reformation was more rapid, and its character more definite. The law of the Six Articles was repealed; the celebration of private masses was prohibited; the laity were allowed the communion of the cup; marriage was permitted to the clergy; images were removed from all the churches; altars were converted to communion tables; and finally, in 1553, Forty-two Articles of Faith were issued by authority, establishing the doctrines of the Church of England nearly as they stand at present. A new Communion Service, differing but slightly from that now in use, was produced in 1547; and the English Liturgy, first introduced in 1549, and afterwards revised and somewhat altered, was confirmed by Parliament in 1552. To spread the new belief among the people, measures were adopted to promote and regulate the practice of preaching, which began to be a very powerful means of influencing popular opinion. Bishops were required to preach four times a year—to stimulate the parish clergy in this exercise—and to ordain for the ministry none who were unable to perform this necessary duty. As, however, the supply of preachers was, for some time,

Edward VI.

---

* Hume's History of England, vol. iv. p. 165.—Short's History of the Church of England, p. 109.
† This permission to read the Scriptures was restricted, in 1543, to gentlemen and merchants.

unavoidably deficient, a Book of Homilies, composed in chief by Cranmer, was appointed to be used in churches, together with the Paraphrase of Erasmus. The singing of psalms and hymns from Scripture was also now, for the first time, authorized.

Mary I.

Reaction to
Roman
Catholicism.

Mary, a sincere and zealous Romanist, succeeding to the sovereign authority at a time when the almost universal voice of the community affirmed it as the duty of the civil ruler to decide the nation's creed and to enforce compliance, naturally at once reversed her brother's policy—restored the former faith and practices—and put in energetic force against the Protestants the persecuting principles which they themselves so generally sanctioned. All the acts of Edward touching on religion were repealed; the doctrine of the corporal presence in the mass was re-affirmed; the Prayer Book and the Catechism were pronounced heretical; the celibacy of the clergy was prescribed, and every married clergyman ejected from his cure; severe enactments against heresy were passed; and a sort of inquisition to discover heretics was instituted. All the prominent reformers either fled across the sea or suffered in England at the stake. About 300 had already paid for their opinions with their lives when Mary's brief reign ended in 1558.

Elizabeth.

Elizabeth at once replaced the Church in the position it had occupied before the reign of Mary. Parliament again affirmed the sovereign's supremacy as head of the Church, and punished with extreme severity all those who questioned this prerogative.* In 1559 the Act of Uniformity† restored with little variance the Book of Common Prayer, and made it penal to be absent without reasonable cause from a church where it was used. In 1563 the second Book of Homilies was printed, and the Larger Catechism sanctioned. And the Articles of Religion—which, in 1563, had been subscribed (then numbering thirty-eight) by the Convocation—were, in 1571, adopted in their present shape and number, ratified by the Queen, and confirmed by Act of Parliament. ‡

Re-establish-
ment of Pro-
testanism.

Thus, Protestant Christianity was re-established as the national religion; and severe coercive measures were enacted to secure unanimous profession and obedience.

Progress of
Puritanism.

No sooner, however, had the victory been thus completed over one of the two great parties hostile to the settlement effected in the reign of Edward, than a vigorous and long protracted conflict with the other party was renewed. Both for their numbers and sincere activity these new antagonists were formidable foes. As, in deciding on the changes which should be admitted, Cranmer and the other founders of the Church displayed the cautious policy of statesmen rather than the pauseless ardour of religious partizans—more anxious to conciliate opponents and secure the utmost innovation practicable, than to contend uncompromisingly for all the progress they might think desirable—it followed, almost of necessity, that multitudes, deriving their opinions from the exercise of private judgment on the Scriptures recently unsealed to them, and urged, by natural reaction, to the utmost distance from the Church of Rome, would find their ardent expectations of the new establishment unrealized, and would lament as well the absence from its constitution and its ritual of much which they desired as the continued presence there of much which they disliked.

---

* The Queen preferred the title of " Supreme Governor " of the Church to " Supreme Head." All the bishops except one refused to take the oath and were in consequence deprived: 178 of the inferior clergy imitated their refusal with a similar result.
† 1 Eliz. cap. 2   ‡ 13 Eliz. cap. 12.

The Puritans, were not wholly presbyterian. The natural tendency of the religious movement in the public mind was to develop constantly new theories of ecclesiastical government, each fresh advance distinguished by a nearer approach to a democratic system. Although the Presbyterians, therefore, for a long time formed the vast majority of the opponents of the Church establishment, opinions much less favourable than theirs to clerical authority and State control in matters of religion soon began to gain adherents. Most conspicuous among the sects which entertained such notions were the *Independents*, who, rejecting equally the presbyterian and episcopal machinery, maintained that every individual congregation is a separate Church, complete and perfect in itself, and altogether independent of external oversight. They also held that the province of the civil magistrate did not extend to spiritual things, the State possessing no infallible means of distinguishing truth from error, and the true religion being best discovered and established by the unforced zeal of its disciples.—Similar opinions were maintained by the *Baptists*, who, about this period, began to grow into importance.

The reign of Charles the First beheld the crisis of the controversy. All the various severe repressive measures which were put in force proved ineffectual to check the spread of puritanic principles, and only served to render yet more bitter the hostility of their professors towards the ruling hierarchy. At last this long protracted opposition triumphed. Parliament, in 1641, abolished the Court of High Commission, and deprived the bishops of votes in the House of Peers. In 1643 episcopacy was itself abolished, and the chief direction of the Church intrusted to the "Westminster Assembly," a body chosen by the Parliament, and consisting of 120 clergymen and 30 laymen. This assembly, where the Presbyterians predominated, issued a Confession of Faith, a larger and a shorter Catechism, a form of Presbyterian Church government, and a "Directory" for public worship. Parliament, in 1645, suppressed the Prayer Book, and enjoined the use of the Directory—an outline service, which each minister was authorized to supplement at his discretion. Part only of the Confession (which was Calvinistic) was adopted by the legislature; and the form of government was not established, save in Lancashire and London, and not there without the safeguard of an ultimate appeal to Parliament. An ordinance was passed in 1644 by which the clergy were required to take the Covenant, and thus engage to uphold Presbyterianism; 3,000 of them refused, and were ejected from their benefices, being allowed one fifth part of their income for their future maintenance. In the absence of episcopacy, the discipline of the Church was administered by the Assembly, who ordained and appointed ministers. In this reign the *Quakers* first appeared, originated by George Fox.

By Cromwell's assumption of supreme authority in 1649 the influence of the Presbyterians was much diminished. The power of ordination was removed from the Assembly and intrusted to a committee of thirty-eight persons of different sects called *Triers* (nine of whom were laymen), who examined all the nominees for ministerial functions. In Wales, itinerant preachers were employed by a Commission out of revenues at its disposal. Tithes were continued to the clergy; but the proceeds of the bishop's lands, and tenths and first fruits, were made over to the Commissioners, with the design of aiding from the fund thus raised the stipends of the smaller livings.

The principle of toleration was first recognized in this administration; free exercise of their religion being guaranteed to all "who professed faith in God " in Christ Jesus;" and it was further added, "that none be compelled to " conform to the public religion by penalties or otherwise, but that endea-

PROGRESS
OF RELIGIOUS
OPINIONS
IN ENGLAND.

" yours be used to win them by sound doctrine and the example of a good " conversation."

The Restoration.

But the change in the national religion which was thus effected during the Interregnum, by the advance towards a Puritan establishment, was nearly as evanescent as was that which had been caused in the reign of Mary by the retrogression towards the ancient faith. With the lasting restoration of the monarchy, episcopacy also was enduringly restored. The ascent of Charles the Second to the vacant throne in 1660 seemed to have effaced from history the period of the Great Rebellion, and the Episcopal Church regained the dominant position, fenced by penal statutes, it had occupied in the days of Laud.

A previous professed endeavour to conciliate the Nonconformists failed. Like Mary, like Elizabeth, like James the First, so Charles the Second also, on the eve of his accession, promised tenderness to conscientious scruples; but the Savoy conference between the Nonconformists and Episcopalians, convened pursuant to this promise, ended in no tangible result. An Act of Uniformity, more stringent than the similar enactment of Elizabeth, was passed in 1662, by which all ministers refusing to assent to everything contained in the Book of Common Prayer, as recently amended, were to be ejected from their benefices on the next St. Bartholomew's Day; and accordingly 2,000 ministers were then deprived of their preferments. Several other statutes, varying in rigour, were enacted in this reign against the Nonconformists, for the purpose of protecting the Established Church. In 1661, the Corporation Act excluded all dissenters from municipal appointments. Two Conventicle Acts, in 1664 and 1670, made it penal for five persons, in addition to the occupiers of a house, to assemble for religious worship; and in 1665 the Five Mile Act imposed a penalty of 40l. on every Nonconformist minister who came within five miles of any corporate town, and also upon all, whether ministers or laymen, who, if not frequenting the Established Church, should teach in a public or private school. In 1673, the Test Act, aimed at Roman Catholics and Nonconformists equally, excluded them from civil offices and military commands. In 1678, in consequence of Oates's plot, the Roman Catholics were prohibited from sitting in Parliament. The King made several attempts to grant a toleration, but as these endeavours were supposed by Parliament to spring from a desire to favour Roman Catholics, they uniformly failed.* Still, towards the termination of this reign, a feeling of the impolicy of treating harshly nonconforming Protestants began to be displayed; and gradually the sentiment extended through the nation that a trivial diversity in modes of worship might be well allowed them without danger to the national establishment.

James II.

This feeling was much strengthened in the reign of James, when the Nonconformists declined to receive the toleration which the King, by an illegal stretch of his prerogative, held out to them. Several of the bishops, grateful for assistance rendered at a critical conjuncture, entertained a plan of comprehension, which, proceeding on an alteration of some portions of the liturgy, might bring again within the pale of the Established Church the mass of those who had abandoned her communion. In the troubles and excitement of the times, however, no advance was made in this direction; but a disposition to indulgence was excited in the ruling party, not unlikely to be fruitful when a favorable opportunity occurred. This opportunity was soon presented, when King

---

* It is stated that above 3,000 Protestant dissenters were imprisoned in the reign of Charles the Second; and that as many as 60,000 had in various ways, in the same period, suffered for religion. *See* Short's History of the Church of England, p. 559.

James the Second, partly for political and partly for religious causes, was, in 1688, expelled the throne. The claim of the Dissenters to a milder treatment could not well be disregarded, either by the monarch they had helped to elevate, or by the Church they had assisted to defend. Accordingly, the Toleration Act* bestowed, on all but Roman Catholics and such as denied the doctrine of the Trinity, full liberty of worship, upon paying tithes and other dues, taking the oaths of allegiance and supremacy, and certifying their places of worship to the bishops or the justices of the peace: Dissenting ministers being also required to sign thirty-five and a half of the Articles of the Established Church. The scheme for a comprehension was proceeded with, but proved abortive. A commission, appointed by the King, suggested sundry alterations in the liturgy; but these the Lower House of Convocation was unwilling to concede, and this, the last, endeavour to procure by comprehension greater uniformity was finally abandoned, and has never since that period been renewed.

The Revolution settled the Established Church upon its present basis. Several alterations, have indeed, been since effected in its relative position towards other sects; but not the slighest change has been effected in the Church itself, in its doctrines, polity, or worship. The principal effect of the Toleration Act was on the character of the Church as a national establishment. Before this statute, no discrepancy was deemed conceivable between the Church and the community: the one was looked upon as altogether co-extensive with the other. To dissent from the belief or mode of worship sanctioned by supreme ecclesiastical authority was much the same as to rebel against the civil power; and all who placed themselves in this predicament were either to be brought by fines and other punishments, to yield conformity, or, if intractable, were to be burnt or banished, and the absolute identity of Church and Nation thus restored. The Toleration Act in part destroyed this theory. The Episcopal Church was still considered "national," as being recognised as orthodox by national authority—endowed by law with the exclusive right to tithes and similar unvoluntary contributions—gifted with a special portion of the State's support—and subject generally to the State's control; but those who differed from her creeds and formularies were allowed, while aiding to support the legal faith, to worship in the way they deemed most scriptural and proper, subject for a time to some disqualifying statutes which have gradually been repealed or modified.†

* 1 W. & M. c.18.

† The principal of these were, the *Conventicle Act*, 22 Car. II. c. 1. (repealed in 1689), which made it penal to attend a Nonconformist meeting of more than five persons; the *Corporation Act*, 13 Car. II. c.1. (repealed in 1828), which disqualified for offices in corporations all who should decline to take the sacrament according to the rites of the Established Church, and to swear that it is in no case lawful to take arms against the king; the *Test Act*, 25 Car. II. c.2. (repealed in 1828), which disqualified from holding any place of trust or public office those who should refuse to take the oaths of allegiance and supremacy, subscribe a declaration against transubstantiation, and receive the Lord's Supper in accordance with the usage of the Church of England; the Act of 13 & 14 Car. II. c.4, by which dissenters were prohibited from keeping schools (modified in 1799, by allowing them to teach upon taking the usual oaths and subscribing the usual declaration); the provision (repealed in 1813) in the Toleration Act, excepting from its benefits all persons who denied the Trinity; the *Occasional Conformity Act*, 10 Anne. c. 2. (repealed in 1718), by which no person was eligible for public employment unless he *entirely* conformed; the *Schism Act*, 12 Anne, st. II. c. 7. (repealed in 1718), by which all schoolmasters were to be licensed by the bishops, and to be strict conformists.

The chief disabilities which, for the safeguard of the Established Church, are still imposed on other bodies, are the following:—all persons holding certain responsible civil and military offices, and all ecclesiastical and collegiate persons, preachers, teachers, and schoolmasters, high constables, and practitioners of the law, are required to promise, by oath or affirmation, allegiance to the Crown, and acknowledge its ecclesiastical supremacy, and also to abjure allegiance to the descendants of the Pretender, and to maintain the Act of Settlement.—No Dissenter can hold the mastership of a college or other endowed school, unless endowed since 1688, for the immediate benefit of Protestant Dissenters.—All meetings for religious worship of more than twenty persons besides the family, if held in a building not certified to the Registrar General, are subject to a penalty of 20*l*.—Every person appointed to any office, for admission to which it was necessary under the Test Act to receive the sacrament according to the custom of the Church of England, is to make a declaration "upon the true faith of a Christian," that he will never exercise any power, authority, or influence obtained by virtue of such office, to injure or disturb the English Church or its bishops and clergy. (Stephen's Commentaries, vol. iii. p. 108.)—Mayors or other

PROGRESS
OF RELIGIOUS
OPINIONS
IN ENGLAND.

Seceding
Churches.

The era of the Revolution, therefore, is the birthday of religious sects in England. For a long time previously they had been struggling into being; but from henceforth they obtained embodied life. The hasty glance bestowed upon the various phases of the land's religious history will not be deemed superfluous, if it serve to indicate with any clearness through what intellectual conflicts and political convulsions most of the extant varieties of creed have worked their way towards a separate embodiment and legal recognition. But from 1688 the history of our religion, ceasing to be identical with the history of the State, must not, as formerly, be looked for in the national annals or the pages of the statute book, but in the records of each individual church. A brief view, therefore, of the origin and course and principal peculiarities of these seceding bodies, will complete the sketch by which it seemed advisable to introduce the denominational statistics. In this view I purpose to bestow the chief attention upon Protestant seceding churches; as requiring, from the little that is popularly known concerning them, a fulness of explanation which the notoriety attaching to the leading features of the Church of England and the Church of Rome makes quite unnecessary in the case of those communities.

1688-1851.

Methodism.

Swedenborg.

Disruptions of
the Methodists.

Irving.

The Mormons.

From this proposed review it will be seen that four of the existing sects,—the Presbyterians, Independents, Baptists, and Society of Friends,—derive their origin directly from the conflict of opinions which produced and followed the Reformation.—The prolonged reaction which succeeded to the Puritan enthusiasm was not, as we shall see, disturbed till near the middle of the eighteenth century, when a marvellous revival of religious sentiment broke in upon the slumbers of the general Church, and in the form of Methodism, came to be condensed into the largest of the nonconforming bodies.—Next, as the author of a new belief, a Swedish noble and philosopher affirms himself to be divinely authorized to publish a fresh revelation both of truths communicated to himself by angels, and of truths before concealed beneath the hidden meaning of the Scriptures, but made manifest to him.—Towards the termination of the century, the patriarch of Methodism quits the world and leaves the vast community which hitherto had been consolidated by his influence and skill, a prey to discords, which, recurring at repeated intervals, detach considerable sections from the parent body,—this, however, scarcely pausing in its growth.—In recent days, the startling oratory of a Scottish minister convinces many that the prophesied millennial advent is at hand; and a church at once is founded claiming to possess the apostolic gifts which are to be exhibited upon the eve of such a consummation.—More recent still, and more remarkable, another claimant of celestial inspiration has appeared across the Atlantic; and the book of the prophet Mormon, like another Koran, is attracting its believers even from this country, whence continually little bands are voyaging to join, at the city of the Great Salt Lake, beneath the Rocky Mountains, the "Church of the Latter-day Saints."

principal magistrates, appearing at any Dissenting place of worship with the insignia of office, are disabled from holding any official situation.—Persons professing the Roman Catholic religion, must, in order to sit in parliament, or vote at parliamentary elections, or become members of lay corporations, take an oath abjuring any intention to subvert the Church establishment, and another, promising never to make use of any privilege to disturb the Protestant succession or the Protestant government. The latter oath must be taken to enable them to exercise any franchise or civil right, and to hold any office from which they were excluded by the Test Act. No Roman Catholic can present to any benefice, nor hold the office of Regent of the United Kingdom, Lord High Chancellor, Lord Lieutenant of Ireland, High Commissioner of the General Assembly of Scotland, nor any office in the Church or the ecclesiastical courts, or in the universities, colleges, or public schools.

THE CHURCH OF ENGLAND.

The doctrines of the Church of England are embodied in her Articles and Liturgy: the Book of Common Prayer prescribes her mode of worship; and the Canons of 1603 contain, so far as the clergy are concerned, her code of discipline.

Doctrines.

Bishops, Priests, and Deacons are the ministerial orders known to the episcopal establishment of England. In the Bishop lies the power of ordination of inferior ministers, who otherwise have no authority to dispense the sacraments or preach. Deacons, when ordained, may, licensed by the bishop, preach and administer the rite of baptism; Priests by this ceremony are further empowered to administer the Lord's Supper, and to hold a benefice with cure of souls.

Orders.

Besides these *orders*, there are also several *dignities* sustained by bishops and by priests; as (1) *Archbishops,* each of whom is chief of a certain number of bishops, who are usually ordained by him; (2) *Deans and Chapters,* who, attached to all cathedrals, are supposed to form the council of the bishop, and to aid him with advice; (3) *Archdeacons,* who perform a kind of episcopal functions in a certain portion of a diocese; (4) *Rural Deans,* who are assistants to the bishop in a smaller sphere.

Dignities.

These various orders and dignities of the Church have all (except cathedral deans) attached to them peculiar territorial jurisdictions. The theory of the Establishment demands that every clergyman should have his ministrations limited to a specific district or *Parish;* and, when England first became divided into parishes, the number of churches would exactly indicate the number of such parishes,—each parish being just that portion of the country, the inhabitants of which were meant to be accommodated in the newly-erected church. In course of years, however, either prompted by the growth of population or by their own capricious piety, proprietors erected and endowed, within the mother-parishes, fresh edifices which were either chapels of ease to the mother church or the centres of new districts, soon allowed by custom to become distinct ecclesiastical divisions known as "chapelries." In this way nearly all the soil of England became parcelled out in ecclesiastical divisions, varying greatly, both in size and population, as might be expected from the isolated and unsystematic efforts out of which they sprung. Of late years, as new churches have been built, some further subdivisions of the larger parishes have been effected by the bishops and commissioners empowered by acts of parliament. The number of ecclesiastical districts and new parishes thus formed was, at the time of the census, 1,255, containing a population of 4,832,491.

Territorial Divisions:

Parishes.

In the ancient Saxon period, ten such parishes constituted a *Rural Deanery.* The growth, however, of the population, and the increased number of churches, have now altered this proportion, and the rural deaneries are diverse in extent. At present there are 463 such divisions.

Rural Deaneries.

Archdeaconries, as territorial divisions, had their origin soon after the Norman Conquest, previous to which archdeacons were but members of cathedral chapters. Several new archdeaconries have been created within recent years, by the Ecclesiastical Commissioners, by virtue of the act of 6 & 7 Wm. IV. c. 77. The total number now is 71.

Archdeaconries.

Bishoprics or *Dioceses* are almost as ancient as the introduction here of Christianity. Of those now extant, all (excepting seven) were formed in Saxon or in

Dioceses.

THE CHURCH OF
ENGLAND.

British times. The Saxon bishoprics were generally co-extensive with the several kingdoms. Of the excepted seven, five were created by Henry the Eighth, out of a portion of the confiscated property of the suppressed religious houses, and the other two (viz. Manchester and Ripon), were created by the Act of 6 & 7 Wm. IV. c. 77. There are two *Archbishoprics* or *Provinces*: Canterbury, comprehending 21 dioceses, and York, comprising the remaining seven. The population of the former in 1851 was 12,785,048; that of the latter 5,285,687.

Patronage.

Incumbents of parishes are appointed, subject to the approval of the bishop, by *patrons*, who may be either corporate bodies or private persons. Of the 11,728 benefices in England and Wales, 1,144 are in the gift of the crown; 1,853 in that of the bishops; 938 in that of cathedral chapters and other dignitaries; 770 in that of the universities of Oxford and Cambridge, and the colleges of Eton, Winchester, &c.; 931 in that of the ministers of mother-churches; and the residue (6,092) in that of private persons. Incumbents are of three kinds; rectors, vicars, and perpetual curates. Rectors are recipients of *all* the parochial tithes; vicars and perpetual curates are the delegates of the tithe-impropriators, and receive a *portion* only. These appointments are for life. The ordinary curates 'are appointed each by the incumbent who desires their aid.

Revenues.

The income of the Church of England is derived from the following sources; lands, tithes, church-rates, pew-rents, Easter offerings, and surplice fees (i. e. fees for burials, baptisms, &c.) The distribution of these revenues may be inferred from the state of things in 1831, when it appeared to be as follows:—

	£
Bishops	181,631
Deans and chapters	360,095
Parochial clergy	3,251,159
Church-rates	500,000
	£4,292,885

In the course of the twenty years which have elapsed since 1831, no fewer than 2,029 new churches have been built, and the value of Church property has much increased; so that, after the considerable addition which must be made to the above amount, in order to obtain an accurate view of the total income of the Church in 1851, it is probable that it will be considerably upwards of 5,000,000*l.* per annum.

Stipends of the
Clergy.

The number of beneficed clergy in 1831 was 10,718: the average gross income, therefore, of each would be about 300*l.* per annum. At the same date there were 5,230 curates, the total amount of whose stipends was 424,695*l.*, yielding an average of 81*l.* per annum to each curate. But, as many incumbents possessed more than 300*l.* a year, and some curates more than 81*l.* a year, there must evidently have been some incumbents and curates whose remuneration was below those sums respectively.

Augmentations
of small livings.

For the purpose of raising the stipends of incumbents of the smaller livings, the Governors of Queen Anne's Bounty annually receive the sum of 14,000*l.*, the produce of First Fruits and Tenths; and the Ecclesiastical Commissioners apply to the same object a portion of the surplus proceeds of episcopal and capitular estates.

The progress of the Church of England has, in recent times, been very rapid; and conspicuously so within the twenty years just terminated. Latterly, a sentiment appears to have been strongly prevalent, that the relief of spiritual destitution must not be exclusively devolved upon the State; that Christians in their individual, no less than in their organized, capacity, have duties to discharge in ministering to the land's religious wants. Accordingly, a spirit of benevolence has been increasingly diffused; and private liberality is now displaying fruits, in daily rising churches, almost as abundant as in ancient times—distinguished, also, advantageously, from earlier charity, by being, it may fairly be assumed, the offspring of a more enlightened zeal, proceeding from a wider circle of contributors. The following statistics will exhibit this more clearly:—

In 1831, the number of churches and chapels of the Church of England amounted to 11,825. The number in 1851, as returned to the Census Office, was 13,854; exclusive of 223 described as being "not separate buildings," or as "used also for secular purposes;" thus showing an increase, in the course of 20 years, of more than *two thousand* churches. Probably the increase is still larger, really, as it can hardly be expected that the last returns were altogether perfect. The greater portion of this increase is attributable to the self-extending power of the Church,—the State not having, in the twenty years, contributed in aid of private benefactions, more than 511,385*l*. towards the erection of 386 churches. If we assume the average cost of each new edifice to be about 3,000*l*. the total sum expended in this interval (exclusive of considerable sums devoted to the *restoration* of old churches) will be 6,087,000*l*. The chief addition has occurred, as was to be expected and desired, in thickly-peopled districts, where the rapid increase of inhabitants has rendered such additional accommodation most essential. Thus, in Cheshire, Lancashire, Middlesex, Surrey, and the West Riding of Yorkshire, the increase of churches has been so much greater than the increase of the population, that the proportion between the accommodation and the number of inhabitants is now considerably more favourable than in 1831. (Table A.)

TABLE A.

County.	Population.		Number of Churches (separate Buildings).		Proportion of Churches to Population.	
	1831.	1851.	1831.	1851.	1831.	1851.
					One Church to	One Church to
CHESHIRE	334,391	455,725	142	244	2,355	1868
LANCASHIRE	1,336,854	2,031,236	292	521	4,578	3899
MIDDLESEX	1,358,330	1,886,576	246	405	5,522	4658
SURREY	486,434	683,082	159	249	3,059	2743
YORK (West Riding)	984,609	1,325,495	287	556	3,431	2384

It is true, indeed, that in the whole of England and Wales collectively the proportion shows no increase, but a decrease—being, in 1831, one church to every 1,175 inhabitants, while in 1851 it was one church to every 1,296; but the latter proportion is not inconsistent with the supposition that, in consequence of better distribution of the churches through the country, the accommodation in reality is greater now than was the case in 1831. But this must be more fully treated in a subsequent part of this Report.

The following view of the periods in which the existing structures were erected, will display, to some extent, the comparative increase in the several decennial intervals of the present century. Of the 14,077 existing churches, chapels, and other buildings belonging to the Church of England, there were built—

Before 1801	- - - - -	9,667
Between 1801 and 1811	- - -	55
„ 1811 and 1821	- - - -	97
„ 1821 and 1831	- - -	276
„ 1831 and 1841	- - -	667
„ 1841 and 1851	- - -	1,197
Dates not mentioned	- - -	2,118

This does not, indeed, with strict exactness, show the real number of churches built in each of these decennial intervals; for, possibly, some few, erected formerly, have been replaced by other and larger edifices, which would thus perhaps be mentioned with the later date. The tendency is, therefore, slightly, to augment unduly the numbers in the later, and unduly to diminish the numbers in the earlier periods; but this disturbing influence has probably been more than counteracted by the cases where the date has been left unmentioned. The statement, therefore, is perhaps a tolerably fair criterion of the progress of church-building in the nineteenth century. If the preceding estimate be accurate respecting the number of churches built *since* 1831, and if it be assumed, as is most likely, that the greater portion of the 2,118 churches, of which the dates of erection are not specified, were built before 1801, leaving perhaps 60 or 70 built in the period 1801–31; it will follow that, from 1801 to 1831, there must have been above 500 new erections, at a cost, upon the average, of probably 6,000*l.* apiece, being altogether 3,000,000*l.*, of which amount, 1,152,044*l.* was paid from parliamentary grants, originated in 1818. Subject to the above-mentioned qualification respecting the dates of churches renovated or enlarged, the whole result of the efforts made in the present century may be represented thus:—

Periods.	Number of Churches built.	Estimated Cost.		
		Total.	Contributed by	
			Public Funds.	Private Benefaction.
		£	£	£
1801 to 1831 - -	500	3,000,000	1,152,044	1,847,956
1831 to 1851 - -	2,029	6,087,000	511,385	5,575,615
1801 to 1851 - -	2,529	9,087,000	1,663,429	7,423,571

In the 13,051 returns which furnished information as to sittings, accommodation is stated for 4,922,412 persons. Making an estimate for 1,026 churches, for which no particulars respecting sittings were supplied, it seems that the total accommodation in 14,077 churches was for 5,317,915 persons. The number of *attendants* on the Census-Sunday (after an estimated addition on account of 939 churches, from which no returns of the attendants were received) was as follows:—*Morning*, 2,541,244; *Afternoon*, 1,890,764; *Evening*, 860,543.

UNENDOWED CHURCHES.

UNENDOWED PROTESTANT CHURCHES.

INTRODUCTION.

When the Reformation had successfully (at least in part) established the *Principal Diversities.*
important principle that the Bible, interpreted by individual judgment, is the
only rule of faith, it followed necessarily that of the many minds applied to
the investigation of the book thus opened for their study, some were found
to differ from each other and the rest respecting its essential meaning and
requirements. Naturally, also, those who held identical or closely similar
opinions upon any of the points of difference were gradually led to connect
themselves together in more or less intimate association. Thus were formed
the Lutheran, the Calvinian, and the Anglican Establishments; and thus, when
liberty of separate combination was obtained in England, various churches,
differing on various points of faith and order, were originated as distinct
ecclesiastical communities. The principal diversities which thus obtained (in
combination, more or less, with other differences,) a permanent embodiment,
may be included and arranged in three considerable classes :—

    I. Diversities respecting the essential DOCTRINES of the Gospel.

    II. Diversities respecting the RITES AND CEREMONIES enjoined by the
        Scriptures.

    III. Diversities respecting the scriptural ORGANIZATION OF THE CHURCH.

1. PRESBYTERIANS.

The origin of Presbyterianism is referable to the period just succeeding the *Origin.*
first triumphs of the principles of the Reformation. When those principles
had so far triumphed as to have detached considerable numbers from the
Romish faith, it then became essential, in order to provide for the spiritual
oversight of these new converts, to establish some ecclesiastical machinery in
lieu of that they had forsaken when forsaking the communion of the Church
of Rome; and it was therefore necessary to investigate the subject of Church
Government as indicated in the Scriptures. Accordingly, Calvin, when invited
to assume the post of ecclesiastical legislator for the city of Geneva, bent his
mind to the construction of a perfect system of church polity in harmony with
the supposed directions or suggestions of the Bible. The result of his
enquiries was the production of a code of laws which have since been universally recognized as the basis of the Presbyterian system. The fundamental
principles of this system are,—the existence in the church of but one order of
ministers, all equal (spoken of in Scripture under various appellations held to
be synonymous, as 'bishops,' 'presbyters,' and 'elders'), and the power of
these ministers—assembled, with a certain proportion of the laity, in local and
in general synods—to decide all questions of church government and discipline
arising in particular congregations.

The Scottish Kirk adopts the Confession, Catechism, and Directory prepared *In Scotland.*
by the Westminster Assembly as its standards of belief and worship. Its discipline is administered by a series of four courts or assemblies. (1) The *Kirk
Session* is the lowest court, and is composed of the minister of a parish and
a variable number of lay elders, appointed from time to time by the session
itself. (2) The *Presbytery* consists of representatives from a certain number of

contiguous parishes, associated together in one district. The representatives are the ministers of all such parishes and one lay elder from each. This assembly has the power of ordaining ministers and licensing probationers to preach before their ordination: it also investigates charges respecting the conduct of members, approves of new communicants, and pronounces excommunication against offenders. An appeal, however, lies to the next superior court; viz. (3) The *Provincial Synod*, which comprises several presbyteries, and is constituted by the ministers and elders by whom these presbyteries themselves were last composed. (4) The *General Assembly* is the highest court, and is composed of representatives (ministers and elders) from the presbyteries, royal burghs, and universities of Scotland, to the number (at present) of 363; of which number rather more than two fifths are laymen.

The National Church of Scotland has three presbyteries in England; that of *London*, containing five congregations,—that of *Liverpool and Manchester*, containing three congregations,—and that of the *North of England*, containing eight congregations.

Various considerable secessions have from time to time occurred in Scotland from the National Church, of bodies which, while holding Presbyterian sentiments, dissent from the particular mode in which they are developed by the Established Kirk, especially protesting against the mode in which church patronage is administered, and against the undue interference of the civil power. The principal of these seceding bodies are,—the "*United Presbyterian Church*," and the "*Free Church of Scotland*;" the former being an amalgamation (effected in 1847) of the "Secession Church" (which separated in 1732) with the "Relief Synod" (which seceded in 1752); and the latter having been constituted in 1843.

The "*United Presbyterian Church*" has five presbyteries in England, containing seventy-six congregations; of which, however, fourteen are locally in, Scotland, leaving the number locally in England 62.

The "*Free Church of Scotland*" has no ramifications, under that name, in England; but various Presbyterian congregations which accord in all respects with that community, and which, before the disruption of 1843, were in union with the Established Kirk, compose a separate Presbyterian body under the appellation of the "*Presbyterian Church in England*," having, in this portion of Great Britain, seven presbyteries and eighty-three congregations.

Any more extended notice of these three communities will more appropriately appear as an introduction to that portion of the Census publication which refers exclusively to Scotland.

The supremacy of the Independents in the army, in the time of the Commonwealth, prevented the enforcement of the system universally or stringently; and when the restoration of King Charles the Second was effected, the entire episcopal régime was re-established in its full integrity,—the Presbyterians not being able to obtain, as a compromise, even that modified synodical episcopacy, as designed by Archbishop Usher, to which they expressed themselves not indisposed to yield. The Act of Uniformity was passed, and 2,000 ministers were forced to quit the communion of the Church of England.

In 1691, a formal coalescence was accomplished between the Presbyterian and Congregational ministers of London, and at that time, and for nearly 30 years succeeding, it seems clear that the doctrinal tenets of the two bodies were the same, and thoroughly in harmony with the doctrinal portion of the Articles of the Church of England. But about a century ago, a most important alteration seems to have been silently effected in the doctrines held by English Presbyterian churches; and instead of the Calvinistic tenets held so firmly by the Puritans, the later Presbyterians began to cherish, most of them Arminian, many of them Unitarian, sentiments. Those who adhered to the standards of the Westminster Assembly are now either merged in Congregational churches, or connected with the Scottish Presbyterians. The rest, possessing neither presbytery, synod, nor assembly, and departing widely from the doctrines of the Westminster Confession, can be scarcely now denominated "Presbyterians" at all,—their only point of concord with that body being the simple manner, common to nearly all dissenters, of conducting public worship. Therefore, in the tabular returns which form part of this volume, the term "Presbyterian" will be restricted to its ancient meaning, and all churches formed of persons who do not receive the doctrine of the Trinity, (excepting General Baptists,) will be found included in the single class of "Unitarians."

2. INDEPENDENTS, OR CONGREGATIONALISTS.

The great distinctive principle on which is based the separate existence of that large and prosperous body called, indifferently, sometimes "Independents," sometimes "Congregationalists," has reference to the scriptural constitution of a Christian church. Rejecting equally the episcopal and presbyterian model, Congregational dissenters hold a "Church" to be synonymous with a "select congregation;" and a *Christian* church to be therefore a congregation of *true believers*. They assert that Scripture yields no evidence to justify the application of the term (ἐκκλησία) to any *aggregate* of individual assemblies, whether such aggregate consist of all that may be found within a definite locality, (as in the case of every *National* Church), or of all that manifest an uniformity of faith and discipline (as in every representative Free Church). In confirmation of this view, they quote the language of the Bible, where the plural—"churches"—is, they say, invariably employed when more than one particular association is referred to, saving only where the reference is to the invisible and universal church.

The *personal composition* of the congregation thus supposed to be the only proper "church" is, as already mentioned, that of a society of "true believers;" that is, persons who both openly profess their faith in the essential doctrines of the Gospel and evince the earnestness of their belief by a corresponding change of disposition and demeanour.

To express the total freedom of the body from exterior control, the term "*Independency*" is used; to convey the idea that every member of the church participates in its administration, "*Congregationalism*," a more modern appellation, is adopted.

Two descriptions only of church officers are viewed as warranted by scriptural authority; viz., bishops (or pastors) and deacons; the former instituted to promote the spiritual, and the latter to advance the temporal, welfare of the church. The various expressions, "bishop," "elder," "pastor," "presbyter," employed in Scripture, are employed, it is affirmed, indifferently and interchangeably, intending always a precisely similar office. Whether there should be in any congregation more than *one* such bishop, is conceived to be a matter undecided by the Scriptures, and left to the discretion of the church itself. The only valid "call" to the pastorate is held to be an invitation to that office by an individual church; and where a person is invited thus, no licence, as in Presbyterian, nor ordination, as in Episcopal churches, is considered to be requisite in order to confer authority to preach or to administer the sacraments. Still, after this election by an individual church, an ordination of the chosen minister by ministers of neighbouring churches is esteemed a fitting introduction to the pastoral office; and the custom always has been general, throughout the Independent body, of inaugurating newly chosen pastors at a special service, when they make profession of their orthodox belief and receive fraternal recognition from the other pastors present. But such ordination is not looked upon as imparting pastoral authority; this flows exclusively from the election by a church, without whose previous sanction ordination is regarded as of no avail. And, in the selection of its minister, a church is not restricted to a special class prepared by education for the office: any person who, by Christian character and aptitude for preaching, so commends himself as to receive an invitation to the ministry, is recognized as being lawfully a pastor. Yet is an educated ministry considered very desirable; and, practically, the majority of Congregational ministers in modern times receive preparatory training at the various Theological Academies and Colleges belonging to the general body. But while scriptural authority is thus asserted for the existence of a ministerial order, no restriction to this order of the exclusive privilege of preaching is contended for; religious exhortation is permitted and encouraged in all those who, having gifts appropriate, feel prompted so to use them.

The theory which Independents cherish of the scriptural model of a Christian church induces them, of course, to look with disapproval on all State Establishments of religion. Hostile, as already intimated, to the slightest interference from external bodies—even where, as in the Presbyterian communities, the partly popular assembly may be not unfairly taken to reflect with faithfulness the best ideas and abilities of all the individual churches—Independents are inevitably still more hostile to the interference of a secular and miscellaneous body like the national parliament, to whose decision they assert all questions of dispute in national establishments must actually or virtually be referred. And not alone upon the ground of interference with self-government do Independents disapprove of national churches: even if the State were to allow the fullest freedom and confine its operations to the mere provision of the necessary funds for public worship, there would still remain insuperable conscientious scruples springing from their notions of the impropriety of all endowments for religious purposes. Religion, they contend, should be committed, for its maintenance and propagation, to the natural affection of its votaries.

Although the Congregational body thus consists of many wholly independent churches, unamenable to any higher court or jurisdiction than themselves, and disavowing all subscription to confessions, creeds, or articles of merely human composition, it is nevertheless (according to its eulogists), distinguished in a singular degree by uniformity of faith and practice. From the period of its origin to the present time, no memorable separation of a part of this community from the remainder has occurred; and the doctrines preached when Independency was first announced in England were the same as those now heard from nearly every Congregational pulpit.

A convocation of this nature met, in 1658, at the Savoy, and published an epitome of faith and order as obtaining then among the Independent churches; and in 1831 was founded the "Congregational Union of England and Wales," a delegated conference of ministers and laymen, meeting twice a year for consultation on the state and prospects of the body, and for such co-operative action as can be adopted for its welfare without violation of the principle of Independency. The constitution of the Union, therefore, provides that it "shall not in any case assume a legislative authority, or become a court of appeal." The Independents think that by these voluntary councils they obtain the benefits without the disadvantages of legal combination: unity, fraternity, and common action are, they say, abundantly secured, while no church feels the irritating fetters of a forced conformity.

The doctrines of the Congregational churches are almost identical with those embodied in the Articles of the Established Church, interpreted according to their Calvinistic meaning. As Independents do not recognise the advantage of subscription to a formal creed, this inference is drawn from general reputation rather than from any collocation of authentic written standards. Reference, however, to the "Declaration of Faith, Order and Discipline," issued by the Congregational Union in 1838,—which, though not binding upon any of the churches, is believed to be dissented from by none,—will furnish ample evidence of this substantial harmony.

The origin of Independency is referable to the latter portion of the sixteenth century. It is probable that some conventicles were secretly established soon after the accession of Elizabeth, but the first prominent advocate of congregational principles appeared in 1580 in the person of Robert Brown, a man of ancient family, related to Lord Treasurer Burleigh. Zealous and impetuous of spirit, he diffused his sentiments by preaching from place to place, principally in the county of Norfolk. After residing for three years in Zealand, where he formed an Independent church, he returned to England in 1585, and again itinerated through the country with considerable success. At length, having suffered thirty-two incarcerations in as many different prisons, he conformed to the Established Church, and obtained the rectory of Oundle. But his followers rapidly increased, so much so, that an act of parliament was passed in 1593, directed specially against them. Sir Walter Raleigh, in the course of the discussion on this measure, estimated the number of the Brownists (as they then were called) at upwards of 20,000, exclusive of women and children. They were treated with great rigour, and several martyrs to these opinions were executed in the reign of Elizabeth. A church had been formed in London, in 1592, in Nicholas Lane; but this persecution drove many to the continent, where several churches were established in Amsterdam, Rotterdam, and Leyden; that at Leyden being under the pastoral charge of Mr. Robinson, who is often spoken of as the real founder of Independency. Mr. Jacob, another of the exiles, returned to England in 1616, and then established an Independent church in London. During the Long Parliament, the Independents gained a season of comparative freedom; meeting openly, and gathering strength, especially in the *character* of their converts,—for the Independent leaders were amongst the foremost of the age for talents and sagacity. When Cromwell, therefore, (himself an Independent,) had assumed supreme authority, their principles obtained a potent recognition; and a general toleration, one of their distinguishing ideas, was in great degree effected, notwithstanding strenuous resistance by the Presbyterians, whose system was thus prevented from obtaining wide and stringent application. From the Restoration to the Revolution, Independents suffered much, in common with the other bodies of dissenters; but since the latter period they have gained considerable and constantly increasing liberty, and now present the aspect of a large and united community, second to none amongst seceding churches for position and political importance.

The earliest account of the number of Independent congregations refers to 1812; before that period, Independent and Presbyterian congregations were returned together. In 1812, there seem to have been 1,024 Independent churches in England and Wales (799 in England, and 225 in Wales). In 1838, an estimate gives 1,840 churches in England and Wales. The present Census makes the number 3,244 (2,604 in England and 640 in Wales); with accommodation (after making an allowance for 185 incomplete returns) for 1,063,136 persons. The *attendance* on the Census-Sunday was as follows— after making an addition for 59 chapels for which the numbers are not given— *Morning,* 524,612; *Afternoon,* 232,285; *Evening,* 457,162.

The following Table shows the various institutions for religious objects supported wholly or chiefly by the Congregational body; others with which the Independents are intimately connected will be found in the List of General Societies at page cxvii of the Report. The *Educational* Institutions of the Congregationalists are referred to in the Census Report on that subject.

NAME OF INSTITUTION.	Date of Foundation.	Ordinary Annual Income. [From the latest Returns.]	NAME OF INSTITUTION.	Date of Foundation.	Ordinary Annual Income. [From the latest Returns.]
	A.D.	£		A.D.	£
Congregational Union of England and Wales	1830	438	THEOLOGICAL COLLEGES. Western College, Plymouth -	1752	600
London Congregational Chapel Building Society -	1848	3,366	Rotherham Independent College	1756	527
Congregational Fund Board -	1695	2,000	Airedale College, Bradford, Yorkshire -	1784	1,501
Ministers' Friend or Associate Fund	1823	805	Hackney Theological Seminary	1803	805
BRITISH MISSIONS. Home Missionary Society -	1819	5,143	Lancashire Independent College	1816	2,683
Irish Evangelical Society -	1814	2,464	Brecon Independent College	1813	500
Colonial Missionary Society -	1836	5,144	Spring Hill College, Birmingham -	1838	1,581
FOREIGN MISSIONS. London Missionary Society -	1795	65,317	New College, St. John's Wood -	1850	3,760

3. BAPTISTS.

The distinguishing tenets of the Baptists relate to two points, upon which they differ from nearly every other Christian denomination; viz. (1), the proper *subjects*, and (2), the proper *mode*, of baptism. Holding that the rite itself was instituted for perpetual celebration, Baptists consider, (1), that it was meant to be imparted only on profession of belief by the recipient, and that this profession cannot properly be made by proxy, as the custom is by sponsors in the Established Church, but must be the genuine and rational avowal of the baptized person himself. To illustrate and fortify this main position, they refer to many passages of Scripture which describe the ceremony as performed on persons of undoubtedly mature intelligence and age, and assert the absence from the sacred writings of all statement or inevitable implication that by any *other* persons was the ceremony ever shared. *Adults* being therefore held to be the only proper *subjects* of the ordinance, it is also held that (2), the only proper *mode* is, not, as generally practised, by a sprinkling or affusion of the water on the person, but, by a total immersion of the party *in* the water. The arguments by which this proposition is supposed to be successfully maintained, are gathered from a critical examination of the meaning of the word βαπτίζω—from the circumstances said to have accompanied the rite whenever its administration is described in Scripture—and from general accordance of the advocated mode with the practice of the ancient Church.

These views are entertained in common by all Baptists. Upon other points, however, differences prevail, and separate Baptist bodies have in consequence

been formed. In England the following comprise the whole of the various
sections which unitedly compose the Baptist denomination :　　　　　　　　　s. BAPTISTS

General (Unitarian) Baptists.
General (New Connexion) Baptists.
Particular Baptists.
Seventh Day Baptists.
Scotch Baptists.

The "Seventh Day Baptists" differ from the other General Baptist churches
simply on the ground that the seventh, not the first, day of the week should
be the one still celebrated as the sabbath. They established congregations
very soon after the first introduction of Baptists into England, but at present
they have only two places of worship in England and Wales.
　　　　　　　　　　　　　　　　　　　　　　　　　　　　　Seventh Day
　　　　　　　　　　　　　　　　　　　　　　　　　　　　　Baptists.

The "Scotch Baptists" derive their origin from the Rev. Mr. M'Lean,　Scotch Baptists
who, in 1765, established the first Baptist Church in Scotland. Their doctrinal
sentiments are Calvinistic, and they differ from the English Particular Baptists
chiefly by a more rigid imitation of what they suppose to be the apostolic
usages, such as love feasts, weekly communion, plurality of pastors or elders,
washing each other's feet, &c. In England and Wales there are but 15 congregations of this body.

The Baptists, as an organized community in England, date their origin from　History.
1608, when the first Baptist church was formed in London ; but their tenets have
been held, to greater or to less extent, from very early times. The Baptists
claim Tertullian (A.D. 150-220), and Gregory of Nazianzen (A.D. 328-389), as
supporters of their views, and contend, on their authority, that the immersion of
adults was the practice in the apostolic age. Their sentiments have ever since,
it is affirmed, been more or less received by nearly all the various bodies of
seceders which from time to time have parted from the Church of Rome ; as the
Albigenses and Waldenses, and the other innovating continental sects which
existed prior to the Reformation. From the agitation which accompanied that
great event, the opinions of the Baptists gained considerable notice, and the
holders of them underwent considerable persecution.

In 1832 the Calvinistic Baptist Churches are reported at 926, which number,
by the addition (say of 200) for the *General* Baptists and the New Connexion,
would be raised to 1,126. In 1839 the Calvinistic Baptist congregations
were computed at 1,276, and allowing 250 for the other Baptist Churches,
the total number would be 1,526. These several estimates relate exclusively
to *England*. *Wales*, for the periods for which accounts are extant, shows that
in 1772 there were 59 congregations (of all kinds of Baptists); that in 1808
there were 165 congregations (also of all kinds) ; while in 1839 there were
244 congregations of *Calvinistic* Baptists. At the recent Census the numbers
were :—

BAPTIST CONGREGATIONS.

	England.	Wales.	TOTAL.
General Baptist (Unitarian) - · · ·	90	8	98
General Baptist (New Connexion) · -	179	8	183
Particular Baptists (Calvinistic) · · ·	1574	373	1,947
Seventh Day Baptists - · · ·	2	.	2
Scotch Baptists - · · · · ·	12	3	15
Baptists Undefined - · · · · ·	492	58	550

4. BAPTISTS.

The following are the principal societies and institutions supported by the Baptists; others to which they in part contribute are included in the List of General Societies on page cxvii of the Report.

NAME OF SOCIETY OR INSTITUTION.	Date of Foundation.	Income for the Year 1851.	NAME OF SOCIETY OR INSTITUTION.	Date of Foundation.	Income for the Year 1851.
	A.D.	£	FOREIGN MISSIONS.	A.D.	£
Baptist Union - - - -	1813	126	*Baptist Missionary Society -	1792	19,065
*Particular Baptist Fund -	1717	2,495	†General Baptist Missionary Society - - - -	1816	2,017
Bath Society for aged Ministers	1816	472			
*Baptist Tract Society -	1841	150	THEOLOGICAL COLLEGES:		
Bible Translation Society -	1840	1,777	*Bristol - - - -	1770	1,120
*Baptist Building Fund - -	1824	795	*Stepney - - - -	1810	1,812
BRITISH MISSIONS.			*Bradford - - - -	1804	1,004
Baptist Home Missionary Society - - -	1797	3,895	*Pontypool - - - -	1807	618
			*Haverfordwest - - -	1839	295
Baptist Irish Society - -	1814	2,298	†Leicester - - - -	1843	501

Societies to which the asterisk (*) is prefixed belong to the *Particular* or Calvinistic Baptists; those marked thus (†) belong to the New Connexion of *General* or Arminian Baptists; where no distinctive mark occurs, the society is supported by both of these bodies jointly.

---

4. THE SOCIETY OF FRIENDS, or QUAKERS.

4. THE SOCIETY OF FRIENDS, or QUAKERS.

Origin of the Society.

The "Society of Friends" is the youngest of the four surviving sects which trace their origin to that prolific period which closed the era of the Reformation, and presents an embodiment of perhaps the extremest protest made against the ceremonial religion sanctioned by the Church of Rome. Its founder (whose *George Fox.* opinions are, with those of others his contemporaries, still received as the standard of orthodoxy) was George Fox, the son of a Leicestershire weaver, who, in 1646, at the age of 22, commenced the public proclamation of his sentiments. *His opinions.* Conceiving that, in spite of the advance which had been made towards more spiritual worship, far too much reliance was still placed in forms and ceremonies and mere human agency in the work of man's redemption, he put forward, as the prominent topic of his preaching, the necessity of the immediate influence of the Spirit of God upon the souls of men; without which influence, he taught, neither could the truths of Scripture be correctly understood nor effectual faith excited.

Divine guidance.

Fox and the early Friends believed that the direct divine suggestions could unfailingly be recognized as such by those receiving them, and thus distinguished from the usual promptings which result from ordinary motives. It was, doubtless, owing much to this conviction that they shewed such extraordinary courage in the propagation of their views, and such unshaken fortitude in suffering the consequent persecution. Believing that the course of conduct which seemed right to them was actually instigated and commanded by express divine authority, no threatenings nor dangers could divert them from pursuing it. The magistrates in vain precluded them from preaching in a certain neighbourhood: they were sure to be found, the next day, labouring in that precise locality. In vain their meetings were dispersed by the civil force, and the persons present carried off to prison: on their next appointed day of worship another congregation was invariably found to occupy the vacant edifice, and follow unresistingly their predecessors to the gaol. Obedience to the same conviction of imperious duty led them often into churches, to proclaim, when opportunity was offered, their distinctive principles; and sometimes it induced them to address epistles of advice to sovereigns or judges, urging them to govern justly and administer the laws with righteousness. The Journal of George Fox abounds in passages implying that both he and his associates believed themselves to be directed in their movements by divine inspiration, and even that they sometimes thus obtained the power to prophesy.

As most of the names bestowed by custom on the days and months derive their origin from Pagan superstition, Friends object to use them; substituting "first day," "second day," "first month," "second month," for "Sunday," "Monday," "January," and "February," respectively; and so on of the rest.

The whole community of Friends is modelled somewhat on the Presbyterian system. Three gradations of meetings or synods,—monthly, quarterly, and yearly,—administer the affairs of the Society, including in their supervision matters both of spiritual discipline and secular polity. The MONTHLY MEETINGS, composed of all the congregations within a definite circuit, judge of the fitness of new candidates for membership, supply certificates to such as move to other districts, choose fit persons to be *Elders* to watch over the ministry, attempt the reformation or pronounce the expulsion of all such as walk disorderly, and generally seek to stimulate their members to religious duty. They also make provision for the poor of the society, (none of whom are, consequently, ever known to require parochial relief,) and secure the education of their children. *Overseers* also are appointed to assist in the promotion of these objects. At monthly meetings, also, marriages are sanctioned previous to their solemnisation at a meeting for worship.—Several monthly meetings compose a QUARTERLY MEETING, to which they forward general reports of their condition, and at which appeals are heard from their decisions.—The YEARLY MEETING holds the same relative position to the quarterly meetings as the latter do to the monthly meetings, and has the general superintendence of the society in a particular country: that held in London comprehends the quarterly meetings of Great Britain, by all of which representatives are appointed and reports addressed to the yearly meeting. Representatives also attend from a yearly meeting for Ireland held in Dublin. It likewise issues annual epistles of advice and caution, appoints committees, and acts as a court of ultimate appeal from quarterly and monthly meetings.

A similar series of meetings, under regulations framed by the men's yearly meeting, and contained in the Book of Discipline, is held by the female members, whose proceedings are, however, mainly limited to mutual edification.

Connected with the yearly meeting is a MEETING FOR SUFFERINGS, composed of ministers, elders, and members chosen by the quarterly meetings. Its original object was to prevail upon the government to grant relief from the many injuries to which the early Friends were constantly exposed. It has gradually had the sphere of its operations extended, and is now a standing committee representing the yearly meeting during its recess, and attending generally to all such matters as affect the welfare of the body.

There are also meetings of preachers and elders for the purpose of mutual consultation and advice, and the preservation of a pure and orthodox ministry.

In case of disputes among Friends, they are not to appeal to the ordinary courts of law, but to submit the matter to the arbitration of two or more of their fellow-members. If either party refuses to obey the award, the Monthly Meeting to which he belongs may proceed to expel him from the society.

From the period of the Revolution of 1688 the Friends have received the benefits of the Toleration Act. By the statutes of 7 & 8 Wm. III, c. 34, and

4. THE SOCIETY OF FRIENDS, OR QUAKERS. 3 & 4 Wm. IV., c. 49., their solemn affirmations are accepted in lieu of oaths; and the abrogation of the Test Act renders them eligible for public offices.

Progress of the Society. The first assemblies of the Friends for separate public worship were held in Leicestershire in 1644 In 1652 the Society had extended itself throughout most of the northern counties, and before the Restoration, meetings were established in nearly all the English and Welsh counties, as well as in Ireland, Scotland, the West Indies, and the British provinces of North America. The Society in the United Kingdom is not now increasing its numbers: The Friends themselves account for this, in part, by the constant emigration of members to America, where the body is much more numerous than in England. But they do not hesitate to admit that much is attributable to the feebler endeavours now than formerly to gain proselytes. Since 1800 their number, if computed by the number of their meeting-houses, has diminished. In 1800 they possessed 413 meeting-houses, while the number returned to the Census in 1851 was only 371. They say, however, that this does not inevitably indicate a smaller number of professors; since, of late, there has been a considerable tendency amongst them to migrate from the rural districts, and to settle in the larger towns. Small communities are to be found in parts of France, Germany, Norway, and Australia.

5. UNITARIANS.

5. UNITARIANS. Differences of opinion respecting the person of Christ are very ancient. Arius, a presbyter of Alexandria, whose name is most familiar in connexion with the anti-Trinitarian dispute, existed early in the fourth century, but Sabellius had preceded him in the third, in propagation of very similar sentiments. The " Arian heresy " provoked extensive discord in the general church ; and we read of states and princes choosing sides in this mysterious controversy, and undertaking sanguinary wars for its decision. The "heresy" prevailed to some considerable extent in Britain in the earliest period of Christianity, before the arrival of the Saxons.

In the sixteenth century, another form of anti-Trinitarian doctrine was originated by Lælius and Faustus Socinus, and obtained a wide success in Poland. From these two prominent maintainers of their sentiments, the modern Unitarians are often called " Socinians ;" but they themselves repudiate the name,—in part because of a diversity of creed on some particular points, and partly from repugnance to be held as followers of any human teacher. In Switzerland, Servetus, by the instigation or consent of Calvin, was burnt, in 1553, for entertaining these opinions.

In England, also, similar sentiments prevailed about the middle of the sixteenth century, and subsequently two Arians were burnt to death in the reign of James the First. John Biddle was imprisoned for the offence in the time of the Commonwealth, and died in prison in 1662. Milton was a semi-Arian. But little progress was effected till the opening of the eighteenth century, when many of the old Presbyterian ministers embraced opinions adverse to the Trinitarian doctrine. A noticeable controversy on the subject was begun in 1719, in the west of England, and two Presbyterian ministers, in consequence of their participation in these sentiments, were removed from their pastoral charges. Nevertheless, the Presbyterian clergy gradually became impregnated, although for some time they gave no particular expression from their pulpits to their views in this respect. In course of little time, however, their congregations either came to be entirely assimilated with themselves in doctrine, or in part seceded to the Independent body. Thus, the ancient Presbyterian chapels and

endowments have, in great degree, become the property of Unitarians, whose   5. UNITARIANS.
origin, as a distinct community in England, may be dated from the first
occurrence of such virtual transfers, viz., from about the period just subsequent
to 1730.

The modern Unitarians differ from the ancient Anti-Trinitarians, chiefly by   Tenets.
attributing to the Saviour less of divine and more of human nature. Indeed, He is described by several of their most conspicuous writers as a man
" constituted in all respects like other men." His mission was, they say, to
introduce, by God's appointment, a new moral dispensation; and His death they
look upon not as a sacrifice or an atonement for sin, but as a martyrdom in
defence of truth.*   Not admitting the essential sinfulness of human nature, they
do not admit the necessity of an atonement: they consider that a conscientious
diligent discharge of moral duties will be adequate to secure for men their future
happiness. In consequence of their disbelief in the divinity of Christ, they avoid
all personal addresses to Him, whether of prayer or praise. The Scriptures they
believe to contain authentic statements; but they do not allow the universal
inspiration of the writers. Many of the modern Unitarians believe that all
mankind will ultimately be restored to happiness. This creed is very prevalent
amongst the Unitarians of America, where upwards of 1,000 churches are reported to profess it. It is there called " Universalism."

Persons denying the doctrine of the Trinity were excepted from the benefits of   Civil position.
the Toleration Act. and remained so until 1813, when the section in that statute
which affected them was abrogated. Since that period they have been exactly
in the same position as all other Protestant Dissenters with respect to their political immunities.

The form of ecclesiastical government adopted by the Unitarians is substan-   Church govern-
tially " congregational;" each individual congregation ruling itself without   ment.
regard to any courts or synods.

Returns have been received at the Census Office from 229 congregations   Numbers.
connected with this body.

6. UNITED BRETHREN, or MORAVIANS.

6. UNITED
BRETHREN, or
MORAVIANS.

Origin.

Christianity was introduced into Bohemia in the ninth century, from Greece;
but it was not long before the Papal system, aided by the Emperor, became
established firmly in that country. Still, the inhabitants were not disposed to
yield their cherished sentiments; and, stimulated by the writings of Wycliffe and
the preaching and martyrdom of Huss and Jerome, they afterwards distinguished
themselves, though unsuccessfully, as firm adherents to the doctrines of the
Reformation. In the persecution which resulted from the triumph of the Emperor in the war with the Elector Palatine, the Protestant clergy were banished
from the kingdom. They retired to Poland; where, in 1632, Commenius was
appointed " Bishop of the dispersed brethren from Bohemia and Moravia." In
Moravia, ostensible conformity with Romish worship was enforced; but many of
the brethren, cherishing the Protestant faith, met secretly together for devotion,
and, as opportunity occurred, fled thence into the Protestant states of Germany.
Ten of these, in 1722, obtained permission from Count Zinzendorf to settle on
a portion of his lands. The little settlement thus formed was called " Hernhutt," the watch of the Lord. Count Zinzendorf himself soon came to be the

* Belsham's Calm Inquiry, pp. 447-455.

S. UNITED BRETHREN, or MORAVIANS.

head of the new church, which, in 1727, had grown to 500 persons. They debated then about a combination with the Lutheran church; but the decision of the lot, to which they appealed upon the matter, was in favour of their continuance as a distinct society. They, therefore, formed themselves into a regular community, with the designation of "Unitas Fratrum," and began to establish congregations in various parts of Europe, and to send forth missionaries to remotest settlements. Their first establishment in England seems to have occurred in 1742.*

Doctrines.

The doctrines of the United Brethren are in harmony with those propounded in the "Confession of Augsburgh." At a general synod held at Barby, in 1775, the following declaration was adopted: "The chief doctrine to which the "Church of the Brethren adheres, and which we must preserve as an invaluable "treasure committed unto us, is this—that *by the sacrifice for sin made by Jesus* "*Christ, and by that alone,* grace and deliverance from sin are to be obtained "for all mankind. We will, therefore, without lessening the importance of any "other article of the Christian faith, steadfastly maintain the following five "points:—

"1. The doctrine of the universal depravity of man; that there is no health "in man, and that, since the fall, he has no power whatever left to help himself.

"2. The doctrine of the divinity of Christ: that God, the creator of all "things, was manifest in the flesh, and reconciled us to himself; that he is "before all things, and that by him all things consist.

"3. The doctrine of the atonement and satisfaction made for us by Jesus "Christ: that he was delivered for our offences, and raised again for our justi-"fication: and that, by his merits *alone,* we receive freely the forgiveness of sin "and sanctification in soul and body.

"4. The doctrine of the Holy Spirit, and the operations of His grace: that "it is He who worketh in us conviction of sin, faith in Jesus, and pureness in "heart.

"5. The doctrine of the fruits of faith: that faith must evidence itself by "willing obedience to the commandments of God, from love and gratitude."†

Orders.

The Moravian church is formed according to the episcopal model. The bishops have been ordained in regular descent from those of the ancient Bohemian church. To bishops alone belongs the power of ordaining ministers. The other orders are presbyters and deacons.

Discipline.

The discipline of the church is regulated by certain written "Congregational Orders or Statutes," with which every one admitted as a member of the church expresses his concurrence. It consists of a series of reproofs and admonitions; the ultimate and highest punishment being that of excision from the community.

Government.

The chief direction of the affairs of the church is committed to a board of elders, appointed by the general synods, which assemble at irregular intervals varying from seven to twelve years. Of these boards, one is universal, and the others local: the former being resident at Hernhutt, and maintaining a general supervision over every part of the society — the latter being specially connected with particular congregations. Bishops, beyond their power of ordination, have no authority except what they derive from these boards. There are *female* elders, who attend at the boards; but they do not vote.

---

* See Southey's Life of Wesley, chapter 5.
† See Conder's View of all Religions, page 252.

The number of persons actually members of the "Unity" does not exceed 12,000 in the whole of Europe, nor 6,000 in America; but at least 100,000 more, it is considered, are in virtual connexion with the society and under the spiritual guidance of its preachers. The number of their chapels in England and Wales, reported by the Census officers, was 32, with 9,305 sittings.

6. UNITED BRETHREN, or MORAVIANS.

Numbers.

The United Brethren have always been distinguished by their efforts to establish missionary stations in the most remote and neglected portions of the globe. In 1851 they had 70 settlements distributed amongst the Hottentots, the Greenlanders, the Esquimaux, the Indians, the Australian aborigines, and the Negroes of the West Indies and America. The number of missionaries was 294; and the converts (not mere nominal professors) then belonging to the missionary congregations amounted to 69,149. The expense of the mission is about 13,000l. annually; three fourths of which are raised by other Christian bodies (principally by the Church of England) who appreciate the eminent value of these labours.

Missions.

7. WESLEYAN METHODISTS.*

7. WESLEYAN METHODISTS.

Different kinds.

Under the general term of "Methodists" are comprehended two principal and several subordinate sections, having totally distinct ecclesiastical organizations. The two grand sections differ from each other upon points of *doctrine*; one professing Arminian, and the other Calvinistic, sentiments. The former are the followers of John Wesley, and from him are called "Wesleyan Methodists"— the latter were originated by the labours of George Whitfield, but their founder's name is not perpetuated in their title, which is, generally, that of "Calvinistic Methodists." Each of the two grand sections is divided into several smaller sections, differing from each other upon points of *church government* and discipline: the *Wesleyan Methodists* comprise the "Original Connexion," the "New Connexion," the "Primitive Methodists," and the "Wesleyan Association"— the *Calvinistic Methodists* comprise the body bearing that specific name, and also the churches belonging to what is known as "The Countess of Huntingdon's Connexion."

THE ORIGINAL CONNEXION.

As at present settled, the form of church government somewhat resembles that of the Scottish Presbyterian churches in the order of the courts, in the relation they bear to each other, and in their respective constitutions and functions. The difference is in the greater degree of authority in spiritual matters exercised by the Wesleyan ministers, who preside in their courts not as mere chairmen or moderators, but as pastors. This is said by them to secure an equitable balance of power between the two parties, lay and clerical, in these courts, and thus to provide against abuse on either side. How far this is the case will be more clearly seen by a description of these various courts, tracing them upwards from the lowest to the highest,—from the Class to the Conference.

Church Government.

The CLASSES were the very first of the arrangements introduced by Mr. Wesley. They consist, in general, of about 12 persons; each class having its appointed "leader," (an experienced Christian layman, nominated by the superintendent

Classes.

---

* See Watson's "Life of Wesley;" Southey's "Life of Wesley;" Rigg's "Principles of Wesleyan Methodism;" Rigg's "Congregational Independency and Wesleyan Connexionalism contrasted;" Article in "Cyclopædia of Religious Denominations," by Rev. W. L. Thornton, M.A.; Minutes of the Conference, 1850-51-52-3; Grindrod's Compendium.

7. WESLEYAN
METHODISTS.

of a circuit, and appointed by a leaders' meeting,) whose duty is to meet his class once every week—converse with each class member, hear from him a statement of his spiritual condition, and give appropriate counsel. Every member of a class, except in cases of extreme poverty, is expected to contribute at least a penny per week towards the funds of the society. Out of the proceeds of this contribution, assisted by other funds, the stipends of the ministers are paid. The system of class meetings is justly considered the very life of Methodism.

Ministers.

The public worship of these societies is conducted in each circuit by two descriptions of preachers, one clerical the other lay. The clerics are separated entirely to the work of the ministry—are members of, or in connexion with, or received as probationers by, the Conference—and are supported by funds raised for that purpose in the classes and congregations. From one to four of these, called "itinerant preachers," are appointed annually for not exceeding three years in immediate succession to the same circuit. Their ministry is not confined to any particular chapel in the circuit, but they act interchangeably from place to place, seldom preaching in the same place more than one Sunday without a change, which is effected according to a plan generally re-made every quarter. Of itinerant preachers there are at present about 915 in Great Britain. The lay, or "local" preachers as they are denominated, follow secular callings, like other of their fellow subjects, and preach on the sabbaths at the places appointed for them in the above-mentioned plan; as great an interval being observed between their appointments to the same place as can be conveniently arranged.

Mode of worship.

The public services of Methodists present a combination of the forms of the Church of England with the usual practice of Dissenting Churches. In the larger chapels, the Church Liturgy is used; and, in all, the Sacrament is administered according to the Church of England rubric. Independently of Sabbath worship, Love Feasts are occasionally celebrated; and a midnight meeting, on the last day of each year, is held as a solemn "Watch Night," for the purpose of impressing on the mind a sense of the brevity and rapid flight of time.

At present there are 428 circuits in Great Britain. Besides preaching in the various chapels in their respective circuits, the itinerant preachers administer the sacraments of Baptism and the Lord's Supper. One or other of them, according to an arrangement amongst themselves, meets every class in his circuit once in every quarter, personally converses with every member, and distributes to all such as have throughout the past three months walked orderly a *ticket*, which authenticates their membership. One of the ministers in every circuit is called the "superintendent," whose duties, in addition to his ordinary labours as a travelling preacher, are, to see that the Methodist discipline is properly maintained,—to admit candidates into membership (subject to a veto by a Leaders' meeting),—and to expel from the society any member whom a Leaders' meeting shall pronounce guilty of any particular offence. Appeal, however, lies from his decision to a District meeting, and ultimately to the Conference. There is also a "circuit steward," whose duty is to receive from the society stewards the contributions of class members, and to superintend their application for the purposes of the circuit.

The Conference.

The CONFERENCE, the highest Wesleyan court, is composed exclusively of ministers. It derives its authority from a deed of declaration, executed by Mr. Wesley in 1784, by which it was provided that, after the decease of himself and his brother Charles, 100 persons, named in the deed, " being preachers and

" expounders of God's holy word, under the care and in connexion with the
" said John Wesley," should exercise the authority which Wesley himself
possessed, to appoint preachers to the various chapels. Vacancies in the
" hundred" were to be filled up by the remainder at an annual Conference. In
pursuance of this deed, a Conference of 100 ministers meets yearly in July, with
the addition of the representatives selected by the district meetings, and such
other ministers as are appointed or permitted to attend by the district committees. The custom is, for all these ministers to share in the proceedings
and to vote; though all the decisions thus arrived at must be sanctioned by
the legal " hundred," ere they can have binding force. The Conference must
sit for at least five days, but not beyond three weeks. Its principal transactions
are, to examine the moral and ministerial character of every preacher—to
receive candidates on trial—to admit ministers into the connexion—and to
appoint ministers to particular circuits or stations. Independently of its functions under this deed poll, the Conference exercises a general superintendence
over the various institutions of the body; including the appointment of
various committees, as, (1) The Committee of Privileges for guarding the
interests of the Wesleyan Connexion; (2) The Committee for the management
of Missions; (3) The Committee for the management of Schools for educating
the children of Wesleyan ministers; (4) The General Book Committee (for
superintending the publication and sale of Wesleyan works); (5) The Chapel
Building Committee (without whose previous consent in writing no chapel,
whether large or small, is to be erected, purchased, or enlarged); (6) The Chapel
Relief Committee; (7) The Contingent Fund Committee; (8) The Committee
of the Auxiliary Fund for worn-out ministers and ministers' widows; and the
committees for the various schools, theological institutions, &c.

The Conference has also assumed to itself the power of making new laws
for the government of the Connexion; provided that, if any circuit meeting
disapprove such law, it is not to be enforced in that circuit for the space of
one year. Any circuit has the power of memorializing Conference on behalf of
any change considered desirable, provided the June quarterly meeting should so
determine.

The doctrines held by the Wesleyans are substantially accordant with the
Articles of the Established Church, interpreted in their Arminian sense. In this
they follow Mr. Wesley rather than Arminius; for although the writings of
the latter are received with high respect, the first four volumes of Wesley's
Sermons, and his Notes on the New Testament (which they hold to be " neither
Calvinistic on the one hand nor Pelagian on the other ") are referred to as the
standard of their orthodoxy. The continued influence of their founder is
manifested by the general adherence of the body to his opinions on the subject
of attainment to Christian perfection in the present life—on the possibility of
final ruin after the reception of divine grace—and on the experience by every
convert of a clear *assurance* of his acceptance with God through faith in Jesus
Christ.

Doctrines.

The Census Accounts show 6,579 chapels in England and Wales, belonging
to this Connexion in March 1851; containing (allowance being made for defective
returns) accommodation for 1,447,580 persons. The number of *attendants* on
the Census Sunday was: Morning, 492,714; Afternoon, 383,964; Evening,
667,850: including an estimate for 133 chapels, for which the number of attendants was not stated.

7. WESLEYAN METHODISTS.

Religious Societies.

The following Table shows the principal societies and institutions for religious objects supported by the Wesleyan Original Connexion. Others, in part supported by Wesleyans, are mentioned in the General List at page cxvii of the Report.

NAME OF SOCIETY OR INSTITUTION.	Date of Foundation.	Annual Income.	NAME OF SOCIETY OR INSTITUTION.	Date of Foundation.	Annual Income.
	A.D.	£		A.D.	£
Contingent Fund - - -	1756	10,065	Wesleyan Seamen's Mission - - -	1848	160
Auxiliary Fund - - -	1813	7,163	Wesleyan Missionary Society - - -	1817	105,570
The Children's Fund - -	1818	3,230			
Wesleyan Theological Institution - - - - -	1834	4,668	Kingswood and Woodhouse Grove School - - -	1748 1811	8,048
General Chapel Fund - -	1818	3,984	Education Fund - - -	1837	2,800

Centenary.

In 1839 was celebrated the Centenary of the existence of Wesleyan Methodism; and the gratitude of the people towards the system under which they had derived so much advantage was displayed by contributions to the large amount of 216,000*l.*, which sum was appropriated to the establishment of theological institutions in Yorkshire and at Richmond—the purchase of the "Centenary Hall and Mission House" in Bishopsgate Street—the provision of a missionary ship—the discharge of chapel debts—and the augmentation of the incomes of the Methodist religious societies.

Of late years a considerable agitation (to be more particularly mentioned when describing "Wesleyan Reformers") has diminished to a great extent the number of the members in connexion. It is stated that by this division the Original Connexion has sustained a loss of 100,000 members.

THE METHODIST NEW CONNEXION.

Origin.

For some time after Mr. Wesley's death in 1791, considerable agitation was observable throughout the numerous societies which, under his control, had rapidly sprung up in every part of England. The more immediate subjects of dispute had reference to (1), "the right of the people to hold their public "religious worship at such hours as were most convenient, without being "restricted to the mere intervals of the hours appointed for service in the "Established Church," and (2), "the right of the people to receive the "ordinances of Baptism and the Lord's Supper from the hands of their own "ministers, and in their own places of worship;" but the principal and funda- mental question in dispute concerned the right of the laity to participate in the spiritual and secular government of the body. Wesley himself had, in his life- time, always exercised an absolute authority; and after his decease the travelling preachers claimed the same extent of power. A vigorous opposition was, how- ever, soon originated, which continued during several years; the Conference attempting various unsuccessful measures for restoring harmony. A "Plan of Pacification" was adopted by the Conference in 1795, and was received with general satisfaction so far as the ordinances were concerned; but the question of lay influence remained untouched till 1797, when the Conference conceded that the Leaders' meetings should have the right to exercise an absolute *veto* upon the *admission* of new members to the Society, and that no member should be *expelled* for immorality, "until such immorality had been proved at a Leaders' meeting." Certain lesser rights were at the same time conceded to the quarterly meetings, in which the laity were represented by the presence of their stewards and class leaders. But this was the extent of the concessions made by the preachers; and all propositions for lay-delegation to the Conference and the district meetings were conclusively rejected.

Foremost amongst many who remained unsatisfied by these concessions was the Rev. Alexander Kilham, who, singularly enough, was born at Epworth in Lincolnshire, the birthplace of the Wesleys. Mr. Kilham, first acquiring prominence as an assertor of the right of Methodists to meet for worship in church hours and to receive the sacraments from their own ministers, was gradually led to take an active part in advocacy of the principle of lay participation in the government of the Connexion.

Originated by a movement for a certain and specific alteration in the *constitution* of Wesleyan Methodism, the New Connexion differs from the parent body only with respect to those ecclesiastical arrangements which were then the subjects of dispute. In doctrines, and in all the essential and distinctive features of Wesleyan Methodism, there is no divergence: the Arminian tenets are as firmly held by the New as by the Old Connexion; and the outline of ecclesiastical machinery—comprising classes, circuits, districts, and the Conference—is in both the same. The grand distinction rests upon the different degrees of power allowed in each communion to the laity. It has been shown that, in the "Original Connexion," all authority is virtually vested in the preachers: they alone compose the Conference—their influence is paramount in the inferior courts—and even when, as in financial matters, laymen are appointed to committees, such appointments are entirely in the hands of Conference. The "New Connexion," on the contrary, admits, in all its courts, the principle of lay participation in church government: candidates for membership must be admitted by the voice of the existing members, not by the minister alone; offending members cannot be expelled but with the concurrence of a Leaders' meeting; officers of the body, whether leaders, ministers, or stewards, are elected by the church and ministers conjointly; and in District Meetings and the annual Conference lay delegates (as many in number as the ministers) are present, freely chosen by the members of the churches.

The progress of the New Connexion since its origin has been as follows, in the aggregate, comprising England, Ireland, and the colonies:*

Year.	Members.	Year.	Members.
1797	5,000	1833	14,784
1803	5,280	1840	21,836
1813	8,067	1846	20,002†
1823	10,794	1853	21,384‡

At present (1853) the state of the Connexion, *in England and Wales*, is reported to be as follows:§

Chapels	301	Members	16,070
Societies	298	Sabbath schools	273
Circuit preachers	95	Sabbath-school teachers	7,335
Local preachers	814	Sabbath-school scholars	44,337

Returns have been received at the Census Office from 297 chapels and stations (mostly in the northern counties) belonging to this Connexion, containing accommodation, after an estimate for 16 defective returns, for 96,964 persons. The number of *attendants* on the Census Sunday was: Morning 36,801; Afternoon,

---

* Jubilee of the New Connexion, pp. 804, 812, 325, 345, 305.
† The diminution of numbers in this year, as compared with 1840, was owing to the fact that 4,703 members were lost between the years 1841 and 1842, as the result of expelling a popular preacher on account of unsound doctrine. See Minutes of Conference, 1841.
‡ Minutes of Conference, 1853, p. 11; and Missionary Report for 1853.
§ Minutes of Conference, p. 10.

7. WESLEYAN METHODISTS.

22,620; Evening, 39,624: including an estimate for three chapels, the attendance in which was not stated.

Funds.

In 1847 the Jubilee of the connexion was celebrated, and it was resolved to raise a fund of 20,000*l.*, to be appropriated to the relief of distressed chapels, to the erection of a theological institution, the extension of home and foreign missions, and the provision for aged and retired ministers.

PRIMITIVE METHODISTS.

Origin.

About the commencement of the present century, certain among the Wesleyans (and conspicuously Hugh Bourne and William Clowes) began to put in practice a revival of these modes of operation, which had by that time been abandoned by the then consolidated body. The Conference of 1807 affirmed a resolution adverse to such unprescribed expedients; and the consequence of this disapprobation was the birth of the Primitive Methodist Connexion,—the first class being formed at Standley in Staffordshire in 1810. The following table, furnished by the Conference itself, will show the progress made by the connexion since that period.

Progress.

Periods.	Chapels.		Preachers.		Class Leaders.	Members.	Sabbath Schools.		
	Connexional.	Rented Rooms, &c.	Travelling.	Local.			Schools.	Teachers.	Scholars.
1810	..	..	..	..	..	10	..	..	..
1811	..	..	2	..	..	200	..	..	..
1820	..	..	202	1,435	..	7,842	..	..	..
1830	421	..	240	2,719	.	35,733	..	..	..
1840	1,149	..	487	6,550	..	73,990	..	11,968	60,508
1850	1,555	3,515	519	8,524	6,162	104,762	1,278	20,114	108,510
1853	1,789	3,565	568	9,594	6,767	108,926	1,535	22,798	121,394

These statistics refer as well to the foreign stations of the Connexion as to England and Wales; but the deduction to be made upon this account will not exceed two or three per cent. of the above figures. The number of chapels, &c. returned by the Census officers was only 2871 so that many of the above must probably be small rooms, which thus escaped the notice of the enumerators. The number of connexional circuits and missions is, altogether, 313, of which, 13 are in Canada, 2 in South Australia, 1 in New South Wales, 1 in Victoria, and 3 in New Zealand. The "Missions," whether abroad or at home, are localities in which the labours of the preachers are remunerated not from local sources, but from the circuit contributions or from the general funds of the connexion appropriated to missions.

Doctrines and Polity.

The doctrines held by the Primitive Methodists are precisely similar to those maintained by the Original Connexion, and the outline of their ecclesiastical polity is also similar, the chief distinction being the admission, by the former body, of lay representatives to the Conference, and the generally greater influence allowed, in all the various courts, to laymen.

Camp meetings, though occasionally held, are much less frequent now than formerly: the people, it is thought, are more accessible than 50 years ago to other agencies.

BIBLE CHRISTIANS.

The "Bible Christians" (sometimes called Bryanites) are included here among the Methodist communities, more from a reference to their sentiments and polity than to their origin. The body, indeed, was not the result of a secession from the Methodist Connexion, but was rather the origination of a new community, which, as it grew, adopted the essential principles of Methodism.

The founder of the body was Mr. William O'Bryan, a Wesleyan local preacher in Cornwall, who, in 1815, separated from the Wesleyans, and began himself to form societies upon the Methodist plan. In a very few years considerable advance was made, and throughout Devonshire and Cornwall many societies were established; so that, in 1819, there were nearly 30 itinerant preachers. In that year, the first Conference was held, when the Connexion was divided into 12 circuits. Mr. O'Bryan withdrew from the body in 1829.

In doctrinal profession there is no distinction between "Bible Christians" and the various bodies of Arminian Methodists.

The forms of public worship, too, are of the same simple character; but, in the administration of the Sacrament of the Lord's Supper, "it is usual to receive " the elements in a sitting posture, as it is believed that that practice is more " conformable to the posture of body in which it was at first received by Christ's " Apostles, than kneeling; but persons are at liberty to kneel, if it be more " suitable to their views and feelings to do so."*

According to the Census returns, the number of chapels belonging to the body Statistics. in England and Wales in 1851 was 482; by far the greater number being situated in the south-western counties of England. The number of sittings, (after adding an estimate for 42 imperfect returns,) was 66,834. The attendance on the Census-Sunday was: *Morning*, 14,902; *Afternoon*, 24,345; *Evening*, 34,612; an estimate being made for eight chapels the number of attendants at which was not stated in the returns. The Minutes of Conference for 1852† present the following view :—

	In Circuits.	In Home Missionary Stations.	Total.
Chapels · · · · · · ·	293	110	403
Itinerant Ministers · · · ·	61	52	113
Local Preachers · · · · ·	714	345	1,059
Members · · · · · · ·	10,146	3,716	13,862

THE WESLEYAN METHODIST ASSOCIATION.

In 1834 a controversy was originated as to the propriety of the proposed Origin. establishment of a Wesleyan Theological Institution; and a minister who disapproved of such a measure, and prepared and published some remarks against it, was expelled from the Connexion. Sympathizers with him were in similar manner expelled.

The "Association" differs from the "Old Connexion" only with regard to the specific subjects of dispute which caused the rupture. The only variations,

---

* "A Digest of the Rules and Regulations of the people denominated Bible Christians, Compiled by order of the Annual Conference," 1838.
† "Extracts from the Minutes of the 34th Annual Conference of the ministers and representatives of the people denominated Bible Christians," 1852.

7. WESLEYAN
METHODISTS.

therefore, are in constitutional arrangements, and the principal of these are as follows :—

Annual
Assembly.

The Annual Assembly (answering to the Old Wesleyan Conference) is distinguished by the introduction of the laity as representatives. It consists of such of the itinerant and local preachers, and other official or private members, as the circuits, societies, or churches in union with the Association (and contributing 50*l.* to the support of the ministry) elect.* The number of representatives is regulated by the number of constituents. Circuits with less than 500 members send one; those with more than 500 and less than 1,000 send two; and such as have more than 1,000 send three. The Annual Assembly admits persons on trial as preachers, examines them, receives them into full connexion, appoints them to their circuits, and excludes or censures them when necessary. It also directs the application of all General or Connexional Funds, and appoints a committee to represent it till the next Assembly. But it does not interfere with strictly local matters, for "each circuit has the right and "power to govern itself by its local courts, without any interference as to "the management of its internal affairs."†

Discipline.

As was to be expected from the reason of its origin, the Association gives more influence to the laity in matters of church discipline than is permitted by the Old Connexion. Therefore it is provided, that "no member shall be "expelled from the Association except by the direction of a majority of a "leaders' society or circuit quarterly meeting."‡

Statistics.

According to the Minutes of the 17th Annual Assembly, the following was the state of the Association in England and Wales in 1852, no allowance having, however, been made for several incomplete returns :—

Itinerant preachers and missionaries	90
Local preachers	1,016
Class leaders	1,353
Members in society	19,411
Chapels	329
Preaching places, rooms, &c.	171
Sunday schools	322
Sunday-school teachers	6,842
Sunday-school scholars	43,389

The Census Returns make mention of 419 chapels and preaching rooms containing (after an estimate for the sittings in 34 cases of deficient information) accommodation for 98,813 persons. The attendance on the Census-Sunday (making an allowance for five chapels the returns from which are silent on this point) was: *Morning*, 32,308; *Afternoon*, 21,140; *Evening,* 40,655.

WESLEYAN METHODIST REFORMERS.

In 1849, another of the constantly recurring agitations with respect to ministerial authority in matters of church discipline arose, and still continues. Some parties having circulated through the Connexion certain anonymous pamphlets called "Fly Sheets," in which some points of Methodist procedure were attacked in a manner offensive to the Conference, that body, with a view to ascertain the secret authors (suspected to be ministers), adopted the expedient of tendering to every minister in the Connexion a "Declaration," reprobating

---

* "Connexional Regulations of the Wesleyan Methodist Association;" 3d edition, p. 3.
† "Connexional Regulations of the Wesleyan Methodist Association;" 3d edition.
‡ Ibid. p. 10.

the obnoxious circulars, and repudiating all connexion with the authorship. Several ministers refused submission to this test, as being an unfair attempt to make the offending parties criminate themselves, and partaking of the nature of an Inquisition. The Conference, however, held that such a method of examination was both scripturally proper, and accordant with the usages of Methodism; and the ministers persisting in their opposition were expelled. This stringent measure caused a great sensation through the various societies, and meetings were convened to sympathize with the excluded ministers. The Conference, however, steadily pursued its policy—considered all such meetings violations of Wesleyan order—and, acting through the superintendent ministers in all the circuits, punished by expulsion every member who attended them. In consequence of this proceeding, the important question was again, and with increased anxiety, debated,—whether the admission and excision of church members is exclusively the duty of the minister, or whether, in the exercise of such momentous discipline, the other members of the church have not a right to share.

The agitation on these questions (and on some collateral ones suggested naturally by these) is still prevailing, and has grown extremely formidable. It is calculated that the loss of the Old Connexion, by expulsions and withdrawals, now amounts to 100,000 members. The Reformers have not yet ostensibly seceded, and can therefore not be said to form a separate Connexion. They regard themselves as still Wesleyan Methodists, illegally expelled, and they demand the restoration of all preachers, officers, and members who have been excluded. In the meantime, they have set in operation a distinct machinery of Methodism, framed according to the plan which they consider ought to be adopted by the parent body. In their own returns it is represented that they had in 1852, 2,000 chapels or preaching places, and 2,800 preachers.

At the time of the Census, in March 1851, the movement was but in its infancy; so that the returns received, though possibly an accurate account of the then condition of the body, will fail to give an adequate idea of its present state. From these returns it seems there were at that time 339 chapels in connexion with the movement; having accommodation (after estimates for 51 defective schedules) for 67,814 persons. The attendance on the Census-Sunday (making an allowance for five cases where the numbers were not given) was as follows: *Morning*, 30,470; *Afternoon*, 16,080; *Evening*, 44,953.

8. CALVINISTIC METHODISTS.

George Whitfield, born in 1714, the son of an innkeeper at Gloucester, where he acted as a common drawer, was admitted as a servitor in Pembroke College Oxford, in 1732. Being then the subject of religious impressions, to which the evil character of his early youth lent force and poignancy, he naturally was attracted to those meetings for religious exercises which the brothers Wesley had a year or two before originated. After a long period of mental anguish, and the practice, for some time, of physical austerities, he ultimately found relief and comfort; and, resolving to devote himself to the labours of the ministry, was admitted into holy orders by the Bishop of Gloucester. Preaching in various churches previous to his embarkation for Georgia, whither he had determined to follow Mr. Wesley, his uncommon force of oratory was at once discerned, and scenes of extraordinary popular commotion were displayed wherever he appeared. In 1737 he left for Georgia, just as Wesley had returned. He ministered with much success among the settlers for three months, and then came back to England, for the purpose of procuring aid towards the foundation of an orphan house for the colony. The same astonishing sensation was created

8.
*CALVINISTIC
METHODISTS.

by his preaching as before; the churches overflowed with eager auditors, and crowds would sometimes stand outside. Perceiving that no edifice was large enough to hold the numbers who desired and pressed to hear him, he began to entertain the thought of preaching in the open air; and when, on visiting Bristol shortly after, all the pulpits were denied to him, he carried his idea into practice, and commenced his great experiment by preaching to the colliers at Kingswood. His first audience numbered about 200; the second 2,000; the third 4,000, and so from ten to fourteen and to twenty thousand.* Such success encouraged similar attempts in London; and accordingly, when the churchwardens of Islington forbade his entrance into the pulpit, which the vicar had offered him, he preached in the churchyard; and, deriving more and more encouragement from his success, he made Moorfields and Kennington Common the scenes of his impassioned eloquence, and there controlled, persuaded, and subdued assemblages of thirty and forty thousand of the rudest auditors. He again departed for Georgia in 1748, founded there the orphan house, and, requiring funds for its support, again returned to England in 1751.

Separation of
Whitfield and
Wesley.

Up to this period, Wesley and Whitfield had harmoniously laboured in conjunction; but there now arose a difference of sentiment between them on the doctrine of election, which resulted in their separation. Whitfield held the Calvinistic tenets, Wesley the Arminian; and their difference proving, after some discussion, to be quite irreconcileable, they thenceforth each pursued a different path. Mr. Wesley steadily and skilfully constructing the elaborate machinery of Wesleyan Methodism; and Whitfield following his plan of field itinerancy, with a constant and amazing popularity, but making no endeavour to originate a sect. He died in New England in 1769, at the age of 55.†

Present position
of Whitfield's
followers.

His followers, however, and those of other eminent evangelists who sympathized with his proceedings, gradually settled into separate religious bodies, principally under two distinctive appellations; one, the "Countess of Huntingdon's Connexion," and the other, the "Welsh Calvinistic Methodists." These, in fact, are now the only sections which survive as individual communities; for most of Whitfield's congregations, not adopting any connexional bond, but existing as independent churches, gradually became absorbed into the Congregational body.

THE COUNTESS OF HUNTINGDON'S CONNEXION.

Origin.

Selina, daughter of the Earl of Ferrers, and widow of the Earl of Huntingdon, was one of those on whom the preaching of Whitfield made considerable impression. In 1748 he became her chaplain; and by his advice she assumed a kind of leadership over his followers, erected chapels, engaged ministers or laymen to officiate in them, and founded a college at Trevecca in South Wales, for the education of Calvinistic preachers. After her death, this college was, in 1792, transferred to Cheshunt (Herts), and there it still exists.

The doctrines of the Connexion are almost identical with those of the Church of England, and the form of worship does not materially vary; for the Liturgy is generally employed, though extemporary prayer is frequent.

Although the name "Connexion" is still used, there is no combined or federal ecclesiastical government prevailing. The congregational polity is practically adopted; and of late years, several of the congregations have become, in name as well as virtually, Congregational churches.

---

* Southey's Life of Wesley, vol. i. p. 201.
† Whitfield during his thirty-four years' ministry is said to have preached no fewer than 18,000 sermons, being more than ten per week.

The number of chapels mentioned in the Census as belonging to this Connexion, or described as "English Calvinistic Methodists," was 109, containing (after an allowance for the sittings in five chapels, the returns for which are defective,) accommodation for 38,727 persons. The attendants on the Census-Sunday (making an estimated addition for seven chapels the returns from which were silent on the point) were: *Morning*, 21,103; *Afternoon*, 4,380; *Evening*, 19,159.

WELSH CALVINISTIC METHODISTS.

The great revival of religion commenced in England by Wesley and Whitfield had been preceded by a similar event in Wales. The principal agent of its introduction there was Howel Harris, a gentleman of Trevecca, in Brecknockshire, who, with a view to holy orders, had begun to study at Oxford, but, offended at the immorality there prevalent, had quitted college, and returned to Wales. He shortly afterwards began a missionary labour in that country, going from house to house, and preaching in the open air. A great excitement was produced; and multitudes attended his discourses. To sustain the religious feeling thus awakened, Mr. Harris, about the year 1736, instituted "Private Societies," similar to those which Wesley was, about the same time, though without communication, forming in England. By 1739 he had established about 300 such societies in South Wales. At first, he encountered much hostility from magistrates and mobs; but after a time his work was taken up by several ministers of the Church of England; one of whom, the Reverend Daniel Rowlands, of Llangeitho, Cardigan, had such a reputation, that "persons " have been known to come 100 miles to hear him preach on the Sabbaths of " his administering the Lord's Supper;" and he had no less than 2,000 communicants in his church. In 1742, 10 clergymen were assisting in the movement, and 40 or 50 lay preachers. The first chapel was erected in 1747, at Builth in Brecknockshire.

In the meantime, North Wales began to be in similar manner roused; and, in spite of considerable persecution, many members were enrolled, and several chapels built. The Rev. Thomas Charles, of Bala, one of the founders of the British and Foreign Bible Society, was, towards the termination of the century, a prominent instrument in effecting this result.

The growth of the movement, both in North and South Wales, was extremely rapid; but the process of formation into a separate body was more gradual and slow. At first, as several of the most conspicuous labourers were clergymen of the Established Church, the sacraments were administered exclusively by them; but, as converts multiplied, the number of Evangelical clergymen was found inadequate to the occasion: many members were obliged to seek communion with the various dissenting bodies; till, at last, in 1811, 21 among the Methodist preachers were ordained, at a considerable Conference, and from that time forth the sacraments were regularly administered by them in their own chapels, and the body assumed distinctly the appearance of a separate Connexion.

A *county* in Wales corresponds with a Wesleyan "Circuit," or to a Scottish Presbytery. All the church officers within a county, whether preachers or leaders of private societies, are members of the "Monthly Meeting" of the county. The province of this meeting is, to superintend both the spiritual and secular condition of the societies within the county.

Monthly Meetings.

The "Quarterly Association" performs all the functions of the Wesleyan "Conference," or of the "Synod" amongst Presbyterians. There are two

Quarterly Associations.

meetings held every quarter; one in North Wales, and the other in South Wales. The Association consists of all the preachers and leaders of private societies in the Connexion. "At every Association, the whole Connexion is " supposed to be present through its representatives, and the decisions of this " meeting are deemed sufficient authority on every subject relating to the body " through all its branches. It has the prerogative to superintend the cause of " Christ among the Welsh Calvinistic Methodists through Wales and England, " to inquire into the affairs of all the private and monthly societies, and to " direct any changes or alterations which it may think requisite." It is at this meeting that the ministers are selected who are to administer the sacraments.

Ministers.

The ministers, among the Welsh Calvinistic Methodists, are itinerant. They are selected by the private societies, and reported to the monthly meetings, which examine into their qualifications, and permit them to commence on trial. A certain number only, who must previously have been preachers for at least five years, are ordained to administer the sacraments, and this ordination takes place at the Quarterly Associations. The preachers are appointed each to a particular county; but generally once in the course of a year they undertake a missionary tour to distant parts of Wales, when they preach twice every day, on each occasion at a different chapel. Their remuneration is derived from the monthly pence contributed by the members of each congregation; out of which fund a trifling sum is given to them after every sermon. In 1837, a college for the education of ministers was established at Bala, and in 1842 another was established at Trevecca.

Doctrines.

The doctrines of the Welsh Calvinistic Methodists may be inferred from the appellation of the body, and be said to be substantially accordant with the Articles of the Established Church, interpreted according to their Calvinistic sense.

Statistics.

The number of chapels returned at the Census as pertaining to the body was 828; containing (after an estimate for 53 chapels which made no return of sittings) accommodation for 211,951 persons. The *attendance* on the Census-Sunday was: *Morning*, 79,728; *Afternoon*, 59,140; *Evening*, 125,244. It is computed that the body have expended in the erection and repairs of their chapels, between the year 1747 and the present time, a sum amounting to nearly a million sterling. From the "*Dyddiadur Methodistaidd*" for 1853 we learn that the number of ministers was 207, and of preachers 234. The number of communicants was stated on the same authority at 58,577.

The principal societies supported by the Connexion are those connected with Home and Foreign Missions; the contributions to which amount to about 3,000*l.* a year. The operations of the Home Mission are carried on among the English population inhabiting the borders between England and Wales. The Foreign Mission has a station in Brittany (south of France)—the language of that country being a sister dialect of the Welsh—and stations at Cassay and Sylhet in India, the presidency of Bengal.

9. SANDEMANIANS or GLASSITES.

The Sandemanians—sometimes called Glassites, both appellations being derived from the names of the founders of the sect—first came into notice in Scotland about 1728 or 1729; when Mr. Glass, a minister of the Scottish National Church, avowed opinions on Church Government approaching very nearly those maintained by Congregationalists. Robert Sandeman appeared in advocacy of the same opinions about 1757, and formed a congregation in London in 1762.

The prominent doctrine of the Sandemanians, on which they differ from most other churches, relates to the nature of justifying faith, which Sandeman maintained to be " no more than a simple *assent* to the divine testimony, passively " received by the understanding."

Sandemanians, also, observe certain peculiar practices, supposed by them to have been prevalent amongst the primitive Christians, such as weekly sacraments, love feasts, mutual exhortation, washing each others feet, plurality of elders, the use of the lot, &c.

The number of Sandemanian congregations in England, reported by the Census officers, was six; the number of sittings (after an estimate for two chapels where the information was not given) was 956; and the number of attendants on the Census-Sunday was : *Morning*, 439 ; *Afternoon*. 256; *Evening*, 61.

10. THE NEW CHURCH.

This body of Christians claims to possess an entirely new dispensation of doctrinal truth derived from the theological writings of Emanuel Swedenborg ; and, as the name imports, they refuse to be numbered with the sects of which the general body of Christendom is at present composed.

· Emanuel Baron Swedenborg was born at Stockholm in 1688, and died in London in 1772. He was a person of great intellectual attainments, a member of several of the learned societies of Europe, and the author of very voluminous philosophical treatises. In 1745 he separated himself from all secular pursuits, relinquished his official labours in the Swedish State, and commenced the career which led to a religious movement. In that year, and thenceforth, he was favoured, he reports, with continual communications from the spiritual world, being oftentimes admitted into heaven itself and there indulged with splendid visions of angelic glory and felicity. The power was given him to converse with these celestial residents ; and from their revelations, sometimes made directly to himself and sometimes gathered by him from the course of their deliberations, he obtained the most important of his doctrines. His own account of the matter is thus stated in a letter to a friend :—" I have been called to a holy " office by the Lord Himself, who most graciously manifested Himself before " me, His servant, in the year 1745, and then opened my sight into the " spiritual world, and gave me to speak with spirits and angels, as I do even to " this day. From that time I began to publish the many arcana which I " have either seen, or which have been revealed to me, concerning heaven and " hell, concerning the state of man after death, concerning true divine worship, " and concerning the spiritual sense of the Word, besides other things of the " highest importance, conducive to salvation and wisdom."

Origin.
Baron Swedenborg.

The general result of these communications was to convince the Baron that the sacred writings have two senses—one their natural, the other their spiritual, sense; the latter of which it was his high commission to unfold. The natural sense is that which is alone received by other Christian Churches—the words of Scripture being understood to have the same signification (and no other) which they bear in ordinary human intercourse; the spiritual sense is that which, in the judgment of the New Church, is concealed within the natural sense of these same words,—each word or phrase possessing, in addition to its ordinary meaning, an interior significance corresponding with some spiritual truth.

Doctrine of Correspondences.

10. THE NEW CHURCH.

The principal tenets he deduced from this interior meaning of the Holy Word, and which his followers still maintain, are these :—That the Last Judgment has already been accomplished (viz. in 1757);—that the former "Heaven and Earth" are passed away; that the "New Jerusalem," mentioned in the Apocalypse, has already descended, in the form of the "New Church;" and that, consequently, the second Advent of the Lord has even now been realized, in a spiritual sense, by the exhibition of His power and glory in the New Church thus established.

The usual doctrine of the Trinity is not received; the belief of the New Church being, "that the Father, Son, and Holy Spirit are one in the person of " our Lord Jesus Christ, comparatively as soul, body, and proceeding operation " are one in every individual man."

The New Church also rejects the doctrine of justification by faith alone, and the imputed righteousness of Christ: salvation, it inculcates, cannot be obtained except by the combination of good works with faith. "To fear God, " and to work righteousness, is to have charity; and whoever has charity, " whatever his religious sentiments may be, will be saved."

The resurrection, it is believed, will not be that of the material body, but of a spiritual body; and this will not immediately pass into a final state of being, but be subject to a kind of purgatory* where those who are interiorly good will receive truth corresponding with their state of goodness, and thus be fitted for heaven; while those who are interiorly evil will reject all truth, and thus be among the lost.

Rites.

The Sacraments of Baptism and the Lord's Supper are administered in the New Church. The former is believed to be "a sign and a medium, attended " with a divine influence, of introduction into the Lord's Church; and it " means that the Lord will purify our minds from wicked desires and bad " thoughts, if we are obedient to His holy word." The latter is believed to be " a sign and a medium, attended with a divine influence, for introducing the " Lord's true children, as to their spirits, into heaven; and it means that the " Lord feeds their souls with His divine goodness and truth."

Mode of worship.

The mode of worship adopted by the followers of Swedenborg resembles in its general form that of most other Christian bodies: the distribution of subjects in their Liturgy, and the composition of their hymns and prayers, being, of course, special; but no particular form is considered to be binding on each society.

Polity.

The general affairs of the New Church are managed by a Conference, which meets yearly, composed of ministers and laymen in conjunction; the proportion of the latter being determined by the size of the respective congregations which they represent: a society of from 12 to 50 members sending one representative, and societies of from 50 to 100 members and those of upwards of 100 members sending each two and three representatives respectively. There is nothing, however, in Swedenborg's writings to sanction any particular form of Church-government.

Religious Societies.

The principal societies for disseminating the doctrines of the New Church are, the "Swedenborg Printing Society," established in 1810, and the "Missionary and Tract Society," established in 1821. The income of the former, for 1852-3, from subscriptions and donations, was 33*l.*; and that of

---

* This word scarcely expresses the exact belief of the New Church on the point. An " intermediate state" would perhaps have been a more correct expression.—[EDITOR].

the latter, for 1851-2 was 235*l.* The number of tracts issued was 23,942. Missionaries are employed in different parts of England.

Among the first disciples of the new faith were two clergymen of the Church of England, the Rev. Thomas Hartley, (who translated the work on "Heaven and Hell,") and the Rev. John Clowes (who translated the "Arcana Cœlestia," &c.). In December 1783, eleven years after Swedenborg's decease, an advertisement brought 5 persons to meet together for reading and conversation; which number had increased to thirty in 1787. About this time the formation of a definite religious society was commenced; provision was made for public worship; and a system of ministerial ordination was adopted. At the 15th conference, held in Manchester in August 1822, there were 8 ministers and 37 delegates, representing 24 congregations. At the Census of 1851 the number of congregations was ascertained to be 50; of which the greater number were in Lancashire and Yorkshire. It is considered, however, by members of the body, that the mere number of their chapels gives a very inadequate idea of the prevalence of their opinions: many, they say, ostensibly connected with other churches, entertain the prominent doctrines of the New Church.

11. THE BRETHREN.*

Those to whom this appellation is applied receive it only as descriptive of their individual state as Christians—not as a name by which they might be known collectively as a distinct religious *sect*. It is not from any common doctrinal peculiarity or definite ecclesiastical organization that they have the appearance of a separate community; but rather from the fact that, while all other Christians are identified with some particular *section* of the Church of God, the persons known as "Brethren" utterly refuse to be identified with any. Their existence is, in fact, a protest against all sectarianism; and the primary ground of their secession from the different bodies to which most of them have once belonged, is, that the various tests by which, in all these bodies, the communion of true Christians with each other is prevented or impeded, are unsanctioned by the Word of God. They see no valid reason why the Church (consisting of all true believers) which is *really* one, should not be also *visibly* united, having as its only bond of fellowship and barrier of exclusion, the reception or rejection of those vital truths by which the Christian is distinguished from the unbeliever. Looking at existing churches, it appears to them that *all* are faulty in this matter; *national* churches by adopting a too lax—*dissenting* churches by adopting a too limited—criterion of membership. The former, it appears to Brethren, by considering as members all within a certain territory, mingle in one body the believers and the unbelievers; while the latter, by their various tests of doctrine or of discipline, exclude from their communion many who are clearly and undoubtedly true members of the universal Church. The Brethren, therefore, may be represented as consisting of all such as, practically holding all the truths essential to salvation, recognize each other as, on that account alone, true members of the only Church. A difference of opinion upon aught besides is not regarded as sufficient ground for separation; and the Brethren, therefore, have withdrawn themselves from all those bodies in which tests, express or virtual, on minor points, are made the means of separating Christians from each other.

In the judgment of the Brethren, the disunion now existing in the general Church is the result of a neglect to recognize the Holy Spirit as its all-sufficient

---

* Commonly called the "Plymouth Brethren."—[EDITOR].

guide. Instead, they say, of a reliance on His promised presence and sovereignty as Christ's vicar on earth, ever abiding to assert and maintain His Lordship in the Church according to the written Word, men, by their creeds and articles, have questioned the sufficiency of Scripture as interpreted to all by Him, and, by their ministerial and ritual appointments, have assumed to specify the channels through which only can His blessings be communicated. All these various human forms and systems are believed by Brethren to be destitute of scriptural authority, and practically restrictive of the Holy Spirit's operations.

Chiefly with regard to *ministry* are these opinions urged; the usual method of ordaining special persons to the office, being held to be unscriptural and prejudicial. They conceive that Christians in general confound *ministry* (i. e. the exercise of a spiritual gift) with *local charges*, as eldership, &c. Such charges, they infer from Scripture, required the sanction of Apostles or their delegates, to validate the appointment (Acts xiv. 23., Titus i. 5.); whereas the " gifts " never needed any human authorization (Acts xviii. 24-28, Rom. xii., 1 Cor. xii-xvi., Phil. i. 14., 1 Peter iv. 9, 10.) Further they urge that while *Scripture warrants the Church to expect a perpetuity of " gifts "*—as evangelists, pastors, teachers, exhorters, rulers, &c.—because they are requisite for the work of the ministry (Ephes. iv. 7-13)—*it nowhere guarantees a permanent ordaining power*, without which the nomination or ordaining of elders is valueless. *All* believers are, it is affirmed, true spiritual priests capacitated for worship (Heb. x. 19-25), and any who possess the qualifications from the Lord are authorized to evangelise the world or instruct the Church; and such have not alone the *liberty*, but also an *obligation* to employ whatever gift may be entrusted to their keeping. Hence, in their assemblies, Brethren have no pre-appointed person to conduct or share in the proceedings; all is open to the guidance of the Holy Ghost at the time, so that he who believes himself to be so led of the Spirit, may address the meeting, &c. This arrangement is considered to be indicated as the proper order in 1 Cor. xiv.—to flow from the principle laid down in 1 Cor. xii.,—and to be traceable historically in the acts of the Apostles. By adopting it the Brethren think that they avoid two evils by which all existing sects are more or less distinguished; the first, the evil of not employing talents given to believers for the Church's benefit—the second, the evil of appointing as the Church's teachers men in whom the gifts essential for the work have not yet been discovered. The Brethren, therefore, recognize no separate orders of "clergy" and "laity"—all are looked upon as equal in position (Matt. xxiii. 8., 1 Cor. x. 17, xii. 12-20, &c.), differing only as to " gifts " of ruling, teaching, preaching, and the like (Rom. xii. 4-8., 1 Cor. xii. 18, 28, &c.). The ordinances, consequently, of baptism, when administered, and the Lord's Supper, which is celebrated weekly, need no special person to administer or preside (Acts ix. 10-18, x. 48, xx. 7, 1 Cor. xi.) Another feature of some importance is, that wherever gifted men are found among the Brethren, they, in general, are actively engaged in preaching and expounding, &c. *on their own individual responsibility to the Lord and quite distinct from the Assembly.* So that though they may occasionally use the buildings where the Brethren meet, it is in no way as ministers of the Brethren but of Christ.

The number of places of worship which the Census officers in England and Wales returned as frequented by the Brethren was 132; but probably this number is below the truth, in consequence of the objection which they entertain to acknowledge any sectarian appellation. Several congregations may be included with the number (96) described as " Christians " only.

UNENDOWED CHURCHES, NOT PROTESTANT.

1. ROMAN CATHOLICS.

The Toleration Act of 1688, by which the Protestant Dissenters were relieved from many of the disabilities that previously attached to them, procured no change in the position of the Roman Catholics. They still remained subjected to the penalties inflicted by the various statutes which, since Elizabeth's accession, had been passed for their discouragement. These were exceedingly severe. Apart from the punishments awarded for the semi-political offence of denying, or refusing to admit the Sovereign's supremacy, the Acts of Recusancy (1 Eliz. c. 2., and 23 Eliz. c. 1.) exposed them to considerable fines for non-attendance at the service of the Established Church; and by other statutes they were not permitted to establish schools in England, nor to send their children to be taught abroad—they were excluded from all civil and military offices, from seats in either House of Parliament, and from the practice of the law,—they were not allowed to vote at Parliamentary Elections—proselytes to popery, and those who were the means of their conversion, were subjected to the penalties of treason—and, by various oaths and tests as well as by express provision, they were hindered in the exercise of their religious worship, and prevented from promulgating their doctrines. Their condition was, in fact, deteriorated in the reign of William III.—some enactments of especial rigor being sanctioned.*

Whether from the effect of these enactments, or from the natural progress of the principles of Protestantism, it is certain that at this time the number of professing Roman Catholics in England, who, in the reign of Elizabeth, were, according to Mr. Butler, a majority, or, according to Mr. Hallam, a third of the population, had considerably declined. A Report presented to William, divides the *freeholders* of England and Wales, as follows—

Conformists	-	-	-	2,477,254
Nonconformists	-	-	-	108,676
Papists	-	-	-	13,856
				2,599,786

And the number of *persons* of the Roman Catholic faith is said to be only 27,696. This statement, allowing for all probable deficiencies, sufficiently exhibits the great diminution which, from various causes, had occurred since the period of the Reformation.

Not much alteration in the position of the Roman Catholics took place for nearly a century after the Revolution. As the temper of the times grew milder, many of the penal laws were not enforced; though, while the throne remained exposed to the pretensions of the Stuart family, the laws themselves continued on the Statute Book: indeed, some further measures were enacted during the agitations consequent upon the Catholic Rebellion of 1715. When, however,

---

* "In 1699, the 11th of William, an Act passed, for *Further preventing the growth of Popery*, of peculiar severity. A reward of one hundred pounds is offered for apprehending any priest or Jesuit. Papists not taking the oaths in six months, after eighteen years of age, are declared incapable of inheriting lands, &c.; and the next of kin, a Protestant, is to enjoy the same: also, Papists are made incapable of purchasing lands. Ambassadors are not to protect priests that are subjects of England. Sending a child to be educated abroad in the Romish religion is punishable by a forfeit of one hundred pounds. Popish parents are obliged to allow a maintenance to their children, becoming protestant, at the Chancellor's determination."—Charles Butler's Historical Memoirs of the English Catholics, vol. ii. p. 54.

in the person of George III., the Brunswick dynasty was firmly settled on the throne, a course of mitigating legislation was commenced, which gradually relieved the Roman Catholics from all restraints upon their worship, and from nearly all the incapacities attached to their religion. In 1778, the first remedial Act was passed, repealing the provision in the 10th and 12th of William III., by which the Catholics were disabled from taking lands by descent. The Gordon Riots of 1780, rather aided than retarded the advance of public sentiment towards additional relief; and, in 1791, Mr. Pitt, (having obtained from the chief continental universities, unanimous opinions that the Pope possessed no civil authority in England, that he cannot absolve the subjects of a sovereign from their allegiance, and that the principles of the Roman Catholic faith do not excuse or justify a breach of faith with heretics), procured the passing of another bill, by which, upon taking a form of oath prescribed, the Catholics were secured against most of the penalties pronounced by former Acts.* They were left, however, still subjected to the Test and Corporation Acts, by which they were excluded from all civil and military offices; were prohibited from sitting in either House of Parliament, and were disabled from presenting to advowsons. The removal of the chief of these remaining disabilities was zealously urged upon the Parliament for many years successively. In 1813 an important measure, framed with this intention, was defeated in the Commons by a majority of only *four;* while, in 1821, a bill to the same effect passed through the lower House but was rejected by the Peers. At length, in 1828, the Test and Corporation Acts were abrogated, and in 1829 the Catholic Emancipation Act bestowed on Roman Catholics substantially the same amount of toleration which was granted to the Protestant Dissenters.

Concurrently with the alleviation of their civil state, the number of the Catholics appears to have been gradually augmenting. In 1767 a return reports their number to be 67,916; and another return in 1780 enumerates 69,376. About this time, the number of *chapels* was about 200. The following is extracted from a Roman Catholic work :† it shows the progressive increase in the number of such chapels in England and Wales since 1824 :

Year.	Number of Chapels.	Year.	Number of Chapels.	Year.	Number of Chapels.
1824 - -	346	1834 - -	417	1844 - -	506
1825 - -	370	1835 - -	417	1845 - -	512
1826 - -	384	1836 - -	423	1846 - -	520
1827 - -	382	1837 - -	431	1847 - -	536
1828 - -	387	1838 - -	429	1848 - -	543
1829 - -	394	1839 - -	444	1849 - -	552
1830 - -	392	1840 - -	463	1850 - -	574
1831 - -	397	1841 - -	466	1851 - -	583
1832 - -	403	1842 - -	479	1852 - -	603
1833 - -	411	1843 - -	497	1853 - -	616

Upon the same authority, the number of colleges belonging to the church is now (1853) eleven, and of religious houses 88, (of which 15 are for men, and

---

* Persons taking the oath were exempted from the operation of the Acts of Recusancy; were allowed, under certain regulations, to meet for worship and to establish schools; were relieved from the oath of supremacy and the declaration against transubstantiation; were not compelled to register their deeds and wills; and were delivered from the double land tax thitherto imposed upon them.

† Catholic Statistics 1823 to 1853.

73 for women); while the number of the priests is 875. The following Table (B.) displays the increase, as to priests and religious houses, since 1841.

TABLE B.

Year.			Number of Religious Houses.	Number of Priests.	Year.			Number of Religious Houses.	Number of Priests.
1841	-	-	17	557	1848	-	-	47	719
1842	-	-	21	606	1849	-	-	53	774
1843	-	-	28	648	1850	-	-	64	788
1844	-	-	28	659	1851	-	-	68	826
1845	-	-	33	666	1852	-	-	78	856
1846	-	-	39	685	1853	-	-	88	875
1847	-	-	42	699					

The number of chapels from which returns have been received at the Census Office is 570; with sittings (after an allowance for 48 chapels making no return upon this point) for 186,111. The number of *attendants* on the Census-Sunday (making an estimated addition for 27 chapels the returns from which were silent on this point) was: *Morning*, 252,783; *Afternoon*, 53,967; *Evening*, 76,880. It will be observed, that in the morning the number of attendants was more than the number of sittings: this is explained by the fact that in many Roman Catholic chapels there is more than one morning service, attended by different individuals.

2. THE CATHOLIC AND APOSTOLIC CHURCH.*

The following sketch, supplied by a member of this body, will perhaps convey, with certain qualifications, a correct idea of its sentiments and position :—

" The body to which this name is applied make no exclusive claim to it:
" they simply object to be called by any other. They acknowledge it to be
" the common title of the one Church baptised into Christ, which has existed
" in all ages, and of which they claim to be members. They have always protested
" against the application to them of the term 'Irvingites;' which appellation
" they consider to be untrue and offensive, though derived from one whom,
" when living, they held in high regard as a devoted minister of Christ.

" They do not profess to be, and refuse to acknowledge that they are,
" separatists from the Church established or dominant in the land of their
" habitation, or from the general body of Christians therein. They recognize
" the continuance of the Church from the days of the first apostles, and of the
" three orders of bishops, priests, and deacons, by succession from the apostles.
" They justify their meeting in separate congregations from the charge of
" schism, on the ground of the same being permitted and authorized by an
" ordinance of paramount authority, which they believe God has restored for the
" benefit of the whole Church. And so far from professing to be another sect in
" addition to the numerous sects already dividing the Church, or to be 'the One
" Church,' to the exclusion of all other bodies, they believe that their special
" mission is to re-unite the scattered members of the one body of Christ.

"The only standards of faith which they recognize are the three creeds of
" the Catholic Church—the Apostles' creed, the Nicene or Constantinopolitan
" creed, and that called the creed of St. Athanasius. The speciality of their
" religious belief, whereby they are distinguished from other Christian com-
" munities, stands in this: that they hold apostles, prophets, evangelists, and
" pastors to be abiding ministries in the Church, and that these ministries,

* Commonly known as " Irvingites."—[EDITOR.]

" together with the power and gifts of the Holy Ghost, dispensed and distributed
" among her members, are necessary for preparing and perfecting the Church
" for the second advent of the Lord; and that supreme rule in the Church
" ought to be exercised, as at the first, by twelve apostles, not elected or
" ordained by men, but called and sent forth immediately by God.

" The congregations which have been authorized as above stated are placed
" under the pastoral rule of angels or bishops, with whom are associated, in the
" work of the ministry, priests and deacons. The deacons are a distinct and
" separate order of ministers taken from the midst of, and chosen by, the
" respective congregations in which they are to serve, and are ordained either
" by apostles or by angels receiving commission thereunto. The priests are
" first called to their office by the word through the prophets, ("no man taking
" this honour to himself,") and then ordained by apostles; and from among
" the priests, by a like call and ordination, are the angels set in their places.

" With respect to the times of worship, the Holy Eucharist is celebrated, and
" the communion administered, every Lord's day, and more or less frequently
" during the week, according to the number of priests in each particular
" congregation; and, where the congregations are large, the first and last hours
" of every day, reckoning from 6 A.M. to 6 P.M., are appointed for divine
" worship; and, if there be a sufficient number of ministers, there are, in
" addition, prayers daily at 9 A.M. and 3 P.M., with other services for the more
" special object of teaching and preaching.

" In the forms of worship observed, the prayers and other devotions to be
" found in the principal liturgies of the Christian Church are introduced by
" preference, wherever appropriate; and in all their services the bishops and
" clergy of the Catholic Church, and all Christian kings, princes, and governors,
" are remembered before God. It may also be observed, that in their ritual
" observances and offices of worship external and material things have their
" place. They contend that, as through the washing of water men are admitted
" into the Christian covenant, and as bread and wine duly consecrated are
" ordained to be used not merely for spiritual food but for purposes of sacra-
" mental and symbolic agency, so also that the use of other material things,
" such as oil, lights, incense, &c., as symbols and exponents of spiritual
" realities, belongs to the dispensation of the Gospel.

" Besides free-will offerings, the tenth of their increase, including income of
" every description, is brought up to the Lord (it being regarded as a sacred
" duty that tithe should be dedicated to His service alone), and is apportioned
" among those who are separated to the ministry.

" In England there are about 30 congregations, comprising nearly 6,000
" communicants; and the number is gradually on the increase. There are also
" congregations in Scotland and Ireland, a considerable number in Germany,
" and several in France, Switzerland, and America."

Of late years, it is said, the church has made considerable progress, so that
from 1846 to 1851 the number of communicants in England has increased by a
third, while great success has been achieved on the continent and in America.
Returns from 32 chapels (chiefly in the southern counties of England) have
been furnished to the Census Office. These contained (allowing for one
chapel for which the sittings are not mentioned) accommodation for 7,437
persons. The *attendance*, on the Census-Sunday, was (making an estimated
addition for two chapels with regard to which no information was received)
Morning, 3,176; *Afternoon*, 1,659; *Evening*, 2,707.

3. THE LATTER DAY SAINTS, or MORMONS. *

Although, in origin, the Mormon movement is not English, but American, yet, as the new creed, by the missionary zeal of its disciples, has extended into England, and is making some not inconsiderable progress with the poorer classes of our countrymen, it seems desirable to give, as far as the inadequate materials permit, some brief description of a sect, the history of whose opinions, sufferings, and achievements, shows, perhaps, the most remarkable religious movement that has happened since the days of Mahomet.

Joseph Smith, the prophet of the new belief, was born in humble life in 1805, at Sharon in the state of Vermont, from whence in 1815 he removed with his parents to Palmyra, New York. When about 15 years old, being troubled by convictions of his spiritual danger, and perplexed by the multitude of mutually hostile sects, he saw, he says, while praying in a grove, a vision of "two personages," who informed him that his sins were pardoned, and that all existing sects were almost equally erroneous. This vision was repeated three years afterwards, in 1823, when an angel, he reports, informed him that the American Indians were a remnant of the Israelites, and that certain records, written by the Jewish prophets and containing history and prophecy, had, when the Indians fell into depravity, been buried in the earth at a spot which the angel indicated. Smith was further told, that *he* had been selected as the instrument by which these valuable records should be brought to light; the revelations they contained being necessary for the restoration of that purity of creed and worship from which all the modern churches had alike departed.

Accordingly, upon the 22d of September 1823, Smith, the story runs, discovered in the side of a hill, about four miles from Palmyra in Ontario County, a stone box, just covered by the earth, in which was deposited the "Record,"— a collection of thin plates of gold, held together by three golden rings. Part of this golden book was sealed, but the portion open to inspection was engraven thickly with "Reformed Egyptian" characters. Together with the book he found two crystal lenses "set in the two rims of a bow," apparently resembling an enormous pair of spectacles; this instrument he said was the Urim and Thummim used by ancient seers.

The simple inspection of these treasures was the whole extent of Smith's achievements on his first discovery of them; he was not permitted by the angel to remove them until four years afterwards, on the 22d of September 1827. During the interval he received occasional instruction from his supernatural visitant.

The news of his discovery attracted such attention, and procured him so much obloquy, that, according to the narrative of his biographers, he was exposed to personal violence, and was obliged to fly to Pennsylvania, carrying his golden plates concealed in a barrel of beans.† When thus in some security, he, by the aid of the Urim and Thummim, set to work upon the translation of the unsealed portion, which, when complete, composed a bulky volume, which he called the "Book of Mormon"—"Mormon," meaning, he explained, *more good*, from "*mor*," a contraction for *more*, and "*mon*," Egyptian for *good*. "Mormon," too, was the name of a supposed prophet living in the fourth or fifth century,

---

* See "The Mormons, a contemporary History;" "Remarkable Vision, by Orson Pratt, one of the twelve apostles of the Church of Jesus Christ of Latter Day Saints;" "The Voice of Joseph, a brief account of the Rise, Progress, and Persecutions of the Church of Jesus Christ of Latter Day Saints, with their present position and property in Utah Territory, by Lorenzo Snow, one of the twelve apostles;" "A Voice of Warning, by Parley P. Pratt;" "The only Way to be Saved, by Lorenzo Snow;" "The Seer;" "Book of Doctrine and Covenants of the Church of Jesus Christ of Latter Day Saints, selected from the Revelations of God, by Joseph Smith, President;" third European edition. 1852.

† A Voice of Warning, p. 87.

who, after the principal portion of the American Israelites had fallen in battle, and the whole of them become degenerate, engraved on plates a summary of their history and prophecies. These plates, his son, Moroni, in the troublous times which followed, hid for safety in a hill then called Cumora, about the year A.D. 420.

Mormons defend the authenticity of this recital, by asserting the improbability that Smith, an illiterate person, could invent it, and, unaided, write so large and peculiar a volume. To the objection that the golden plates are not produced, they give Smith's own reply to the applications made to him by his disciples for a view—that such an exhibition of them is prohibited by special revelation. Nevertheless, in further proof of Smith's veracity, three "witnesses" were found to testify that they had actually seen the plates, an angel having shewn them; and a similar testimony was borne by eight other "witnesses,' —four of these belonging to a family named Whitmer, and three being the two brothers and the father of Smith. The utmost that Smith did towards allowing access by indifferent parties to the plates, was to give to one of his inquiring followers a copy upon paper of a portion of the plates in the original hiero- glyphics, viz., the "Reformed Egyptian." This was submitted by the yet unsatisfied disciple to Professor Anthon of New York, who, however, did not recognise the characters as those of any ancient language known to him The Mormon advocates appear to think these evidences irresistible.†—Upon the other hand, it is asserted, by opponents of the Saints, that about the years 1809—12, a person of the name of Solomon Spaulding, who had been a clergyman, conceived and executed the design of writing a religious tale, the scenes and narrative of which should be constructed on the theory that the American Indians were the lost ten tribes of Israel. This work, when finished, he entitled " *The Manuscript found*;" and the purport of the fiction was, to trace the progress of the tribes from Jerusalem to America, and then describe their subsequent adventures in the latter country,—"Mormon" and his son " Moroni" being prominent characters, and Nephi, Lehi, and the Lamanites (names frequently occurring in the Book of Mormon) being also mentioned. The MS. of this production, it is further stated, found its way into the hands of one Sidney Rigdon, who was intimately connected with Smith from the commencement of his career.

The "*Book of Mormon*" was succeeded by a "*Book of Doctrine and Covenants*," being a collection of the special revelations made to Smith and his associates upon all points connected with the course and welfare of the church. This was continually enlarged as further revelations, consequent upon the varying fortunes and requirements of the body, were received. Amongst these was one by which the "Aaronic Priesthood" was revived— another by which baptism by immersion was commanded—a third for the institution of "Apostles"—and others for the temporal regulation of the church from time to time.* In these productions the peculiar phraseology of the sacred scriptures was profusely imitated.

It appears that at the end of about three years after Smith's announcement of himself as a prophet, about 30 persons were convinced of the reality of his pretensions, and from this time forward converts rapidly increased. Smith removed to Kirtland, in Ohio, and set up a mill, a store, and a bank.

It was not without opposition that this progress was effected. As appears to be usual upon the rise of new religious sects, the Mormons were accused of

---

* The "doctrine" of this book is contained in seven lectures on Faith, originally delivered before a class of elders in Kirtland, Ohio. Some of the "revelations" are very minute: as, for instance, one authorizing Newel R. Whitney to retain his store for a little season; others directing Titus Billings to dispose of his land—Martin Harris to lay his monies before the Bishop of the Church—Sidney Rigdon to write a description of the land of Zion—Joseph Smith to receive support from the Church, and to have a house built in which to live and translate—&c.

holding many outrageous and immoral doctrines, and, amongst them, that of a community of wives. The popular hostility was often violently manifested, and the saints were subjected to much ill-treatment. Smith himself, in 1832, was tarred and feathered by a midnight mob; and, in the following year, the whole of the Mormons in Missouri (amounting to above a thousand persons) were expelled from Independence, Jackson County, which had been described by Smith as the Zion appointed by revelation for the resting-place of the saints. They removed to Clay County, where, in 1837, they were joined by the prophet himself, whose bank in Kirtland had failed. Meantime, the prejudice against the Mormons followed them to their new habitation, and, in 1838, after several sanguinary outbreaks, Joseph Smith and his brother Hyrum were imprisoned, and the whole community of Mormons were expelled from their possessions in Missouri. They took refuge in the neighbouring state of Illinois. Here, in 1839, their prophet, who had managed to escape from prison, joined them. They now numbered 15,000 souls.

In Illinois, they chose the village of Commerce as their residence, which soon became converted into a considerable town, of which the prophet was appointed mayor. This town they called Nauvoo, or "Beautiful," according to the language of the Book of Mormon. A body of militia, called the Nauvoo Legion, was established—Smith being "General." In 1841, a "revelation" ordered the construction of a splendid temple, towards which object all the saints were to contribute a full tithe of their possessions. It is said that they expended on this structure nearly a million of dollars.

In Nauvoo, the Mormons seem to have increased and prospered greatly: the town extended fast; the temple gradually rose; and the prophet was the absolute head of a comparatively powerful community, which hardly recognised the ordinary laws of the state. In 1843 he became a candidate for the Presidency, and put forth a statement of his views. In 1844, however, occurred the final catastrophe of his life. A Nauvoo paper, having printed certain scandal of him, was, by order of the council of the town, suppressed, and its office rased; on which, the editors retired to Carthage, and obtained a warrant against Smith and his brother. This warrant Smith refused to recognise: the county force prepared to execute it; and the Saints prepared their city for defence. To save the town, however, Smith surrendered on the promise of protection from the governor. This promise proved of little value; for, on the 27th of June 1844, a mob broke into Carthage prison, and Joseph and Hyrum Smith were shot.

Upon the prophet's death there were two competitors for the vacant supremacy—Sidney Rigdon and Brigham Young. The former was the earliest associate of Smith, and professed to be acquainted with "all his secrets;" but, as the prominent advocate of the "Spiritual Wife" doctrine, he was looked upon with disfavour as the virtual author of much of the suspicion and hostility with which the Mormons were regarded. Brigham Young succeeded therefore to the post of "Prophet" (which he still retains), and Rigdon was expelled from the community. An interval of scarcely interrupted progress followed, during which the temple was completed; but in 1845 the troubles were renewed: perpetual conflicts, in which blood was shed, occurred, and the city of Nauvoo itself was regularly besieged. At length the Mormons, conscious of their inability alone to cope with their antagonists, and seeing that no confidence could be reposed upon the law for their protection, undertook (since nothing less would satisfy their enemies) that they would altogether quit the State—commencing their departure in the spring of 1846.

This time it was no mere temporary, neighbouring refuge which the Mormons sought. The elders of the church, aware of the hostility to which it would be

constantly exposed in any portion of the populated States, resolved, with equal
policy and daring, to escape entirely from the settled territory, and to seek far
off, beyond the Rocky Mountains, some secluded and unoccupied retreat in
which they could, secure from molestation, build their earthly "Zion," and, by
gathering thither from all quarters of the world the converts to their faith, become
a thriving and a powerful community, too potent to be further interfered with.
This remarkable pilgrimage, involving the removal of some thousands of men,
women, children, cattle, and stores, over thousands of untrodden miles—across
wide unbridged rivers—by the difficult passes of snow-capped mountains—and
through deserts, prairies, and tribes of predatory Indians—was at once commenced.
A party of pioneers set out from Nauvoo in February 1846, when it was still
winter—the waggons crossing the Mississippi on the ice. These were to prepare
the way for the main body of the citizens, who, according to stipulation, might
remain in Nauvoo till these preparations were completed. Their departure was,
however, hastened by the fresh hostility of their opponents, who—concluding
from the progress still continued in the decorations of the temple that the
Mormons secretly intended to elude their promise and return—attacked the
town in September 1846, and expelled the whole of its remaining population.
These then followed and overtook the pioneering party, which, after dreadful
sufferings from cold and heat, from hunger and disease, had, finding it impossible to reach their destination till the following year, encamped upon the
banks of the Missouri, on the lands of the Omahas and Pottawatamies. Here
they had sown the land to some extent with grain, the crops of which were to be
reaped by their successors. After a dreary winter, spent in this location, they
began their march towards their final settlement. In April 1847 the first
detachment of 143, with 70 waggons, crossed the Rocky Mountains ; arriving
at the basin of the Great Salt Lake, in the latter portion of July, in time to sow
the land for an autumn crop. The second party started in the summer with
566 waggons and a great supply of grain. The others followed in the course of
1848—their passage much alleviated by the tracks prepared by their predecessors
and the harvests left for them to gather.

The valley of the Great Salt Lake is a territory of considerable extent, enclosed
on all sides by high rocky mountains. The Lake itself is nearly 300 miles in
circumference, with islands rising from its surface to an elevation of some
thousand feet : its shores are covered in some places with the finest salt, and its
water is as buoyant as the waves of the Dead Sea. Portions of the land are
desert ; but a vast expanse is wonderfully fertile and abounds in all facilities for
pasturage and cultivation. Here, the Mormons have now firmly fixed themselves, and made, since 1848, continual progress. Further settlements have
been established, and several cities founded : that of the Great Salt Lake itself
has a plot of several acres destined to support a temple whose magnificence
shall far exceed the splendour of the former Nauvoo edifice. Relying on the
inexhaustible resources of the region to sustain innumerable inhabitants, the
principal endeavour of the rulers is to gather there as many immigrants as
possible professing the same faith. They calculate that thus, established in an
almost inaccessible retreat, with numbers continually augmenting, they will
soon be able to defy external enmity and rear upon a lasting basis their ecclesiastical republic. Missionary agents are despatched to almost every portion of
the world to make fresh converts and facilitate their transit to America. In
England these endeavours have been followed by no slight success : it is
computed that at least as many as 30,000 persons here belong to the community, and nearly 20,000 have already, it is said, departed for the Great
Salt Lake. This settlement itself, has now, by the name of " Utah " been
admitted to the United States Confederacy ; but it seems, from a report of the

judges sent there by the recent President, that the authority of the federal government is virtually set at nought; the laws and their administration being always found accordant with the pleasure of the Mormon rulers.

A printed " Creed " presents the following summary of their opinions, but omits some rather material points :—

" We believe in God the eternal Father, and his Son Jesus Christ, and in the " Holy Ghost.

" We believe that men will be punished for their own sins, and not for " Adam's transgressions.

" We believe that through the atonement of Christ all mankind may be " saved, by obedience to the laws and ordinances of the Gospel.

" We believe that these ordinances are : 1st. Faith in the Lord Jesus Christ. " 2d. Repentance.   3d. Baptism by immersion for the remission of sins. " 4th. Laying on of hands for the gift of the Holy Spirit.   5th. The Lord's " Supper.

" We believe that men must be called of God by inspiration, and by laying " on of hands by those who are duly commissioned to preach the Gospel and " administer in the ordinances thereof.

" We believe in the same organization that existed in the primitive church, " viz., apostles, prophets, pastors, teachers, evangelists, &c.

" We believe in the powers and gifts of the everlasting Gospel, viz., the gift " of faith, discerning of spirits, prophecy, revelation, visions, healing, tongues " and the interpretation of tongues, wisdom, charity, brotherly love, &c.

" We believe in the Word of God recorded in the Bible.   We also believe " the Word of God recorded in the Book of Mormon and in all other good " books.

" We believe all that God has revealed, all that he does now reveal; and " we believe that he will yet reveal many more great and important things " pertaining to the Kingdom of God, and Messiah's second coming.

" We believe in the literal gathering of Israel, and in the restoration of the " ten tribes; that Zion will be established upon the Western continent; that " Christ will reign personally upon the earth a thousand years; and that the " earth will be renewed and receive its paradisaical glory.

" We believe in the literal resurrection of the body, and that the dead in " Christ will rise first, and that the rest of the dead live not again until the " thousand years are expired.

" We claim the privilege of worshipping Almighty God according to the " dictates of our conscience, unmolested, and allow all men the same privilege, " let them worship how or where they may.

" We believe in being subject to kings, queens, presidents, rulers, and " magistrates, in obeying, honouring, and sustaining the law.

" We believe in being honest, true, chaste, temperate, benevolent, virtuous, " and upright, and in doing good to all men; indeed, we may say that we " follow the admonition of Paul,—we ' believe all things,' we ' hope all things,' " we have endured very many things, and hope to be able to ' endure all things.' " Every thing virtuous, lovely, praiseworthy, and of good report we seek after, " looking forward to the ' recompense of reward.' "

A rather more specific outline of some points of their belief is given by one of their apostles.   According to him, the Saints believe that all mankind, in consequence of Adam's sin, are in a state of ruin : from this, however, they are all delivered by the sacrifice of Christ, and are made secure of everlasting happiness, unless they commit any *actual* sin.   Infants, therefore, being irresponsible, will be eternally redeemed; and such among the people of the earth as have not had the benefit of revelation will receive a mitigated punishment.   The rest, in order

3. THE LATTER DAY SAINTS, or MORMONS.

to be saved from endless ruin, must comply with four conditions:—(1) they must *believe* in Christ's atonement; (2) they must *repent* of their transgressions; (3) they must receive *baptism* by immersion for the remission of sins, administered only by one authorized of Christ; and (4) they must receive the *laying on of hands* for the gift of the Holy Ghost—*this* ordinance also being, like that of baptism, only to be administered by duly authorized apostles or elders. All who comply with these conditions obtain forgiveness of their sins and are made partakers of the Holy Ghost—enjoying, too, the gifts of prophecy and healing, visions and revelations, and the power of working miracles.*

Among the prominent opinions, not included in these statements, are their doctrines of the materiality of the Deity,† and of the twofold order of the priesthood, viz., the Melchisedek and the Aaronic. They are also charged by their opponents with the practice and the sanction of polygamy; and evidence is not unplentiful of their allowance of something closely similar; and in their various publications very peculiar doctrines on the subject of marriage are propounded.‡ Their standard books, however, specially denounce the crime.§

Numbers in England.

In England and Wales there were, in 1851, reported by the Census officers as many as 222 places of worship belonging to this body—most of them however being merely rooms. The number of sittings in these places (making an allowance for 53, the accommodation in which was not returned) was 30,783. The *attendance* on the Census-Sunday (making an estimated addition for 9 chapels from which no intelligence on this point was received) was: *Morning*, 7,517; *Afternoon*, 11,481; *Evening*, 16,628. The preachers, it appears, are far from unsuccessful in their efforts to obtain disciples: the surprising confidence and zeal with which they promulgate their creed—the prominence they give to the exciting topics of the speedy coming of the Saviour and his personal millennial reign—and the attractiveness to many minds of the idea of an infallible church, relying for its evidences and its guidance upon revelations made perpetually to its rulers,— these, with other influences, have combined to give the Mormon movement a position and importance with the working classes, which, perhaps, should draw to it much more than it has yet received of the attention of our public teachers.

---

* Remarkable Visions, by Orson Pratt, pp. 12-16.

† The Materialism of the Mormons examined and exposed, by T. W. P. Taylder. Absurdities of Immaterialism, or a Reply to T. W. P. Taylder's Pamphlet, by Orson Pratt.

‡ Report of Judges of the State of Utah, 1851; Captain Stansbury's Description of the Mormon Settlement, &c. In the pages of "The Seer," a periodical conducted by Orson Pratt, the doctrine of plurality of wives is openly advocated. Marriage, however, is there said to be the exclusive privilege of the righteous—the wicked who marry doing so at their own peril. Whether a man is righteous or wicked is a point to be determined by the prophets of the Mormon Church: and as this can only be ascertained by the aid of inspiration, it is argued that no marriage can be safely contracted in communities which do not believe in a continuance of revelations.

§ Book of Doctrine and Covenants, sections LXV. and CIX.

ISOLATED CONGREGATIONS
(not connected with any particular sect).

IN addition to the congregations which belong to the preceding regularly organized bodies, there are individual congregations, mostly altogether independent of each other, or at all events without the formal coalescence which is requisite to constitute a "sect." Five classes may be noticed of these congregations:

1. Those in which the members of some two or more of the preceding sects *unite* in worship—probably from inability alone and severally each to support a place of worship and a minister. Of these amalgamated congregations the most numerous are those (to the number of 61) in which the *Independents* join with *Baptists.* The whole of these combinations, and their frequency, are shewn as follows:—

> 1. Combinations of sects.

Independents and Baptists, 61 congregations; Independents, Baptists, and Wesleyans, 2 congregations; Independents and Wesleyans, 3 congregations; Independents and Calvinistic Methodists, 1 congregation; Independents and Primitive Methodists, 1 congregation; Baptists and Wesleyans, 2 congregations; Baptists, Wesleyans, and Moravians, 1 congregation; Presbyterians and Particular Baptists, 1 congregation; Mixed (constituent sects not stated), 54 congregations; Wesleyan Christian Union, 1 congregation; Neutral, 1 congregation.

It must not, indeed, be thought that these are the only instances in which the members of, or sympathizers with, particular communities, are found together, worshipping in common: few congregations are without a certain number who, while strictly claimable by other bodies, find their difference of sentiment on ritual observances no obstacle to union when the fundamental doctrines preached are similar. But the congregations named above, it is assumed, are not, as in the cases just supposed, ostensibly connected either with the one or with the other of the bodies to which, in theory, the various attendants are attached; but, on the contrary, exist apart and independently, by special understanding and arrangement of the two or more uniting parties.

2. Another class of miscellaneous congregations is composed of such as are formed by the adherents to some *doctrine* to which special value is attached, and which is thus maintained with greater prominence than by the regular churches. To this class the following may be referred:—

> 2. Congregations based upon the profession of peculiar doctrines.

Calvinists, 81 congregations; Calvinists (supralapsarians), 1 congregation; Huntingtonians, 1 congregation; Universalists, 2 congregations; Millenarians, 5 congregations; Predestinarians, 1 congregation; Trinitarian Predestinarians, 1 congregation.

3. A third group may be made of congregations, which, disliking to be identified with anything appearing to be sectarian, refuse to call themselves by any but a very general or a merely negative appellation; as,

> 3. Unsectarian congregations.

Christians, 96 congregations; Christian Association, 8 congregations; Orthodox Christians, 1 congregation; New Christians, 1 congregation; Christ's Disciples, 3 congregations; Primitive Christians, 1 congregation; New Testament Christians, 2 congregations; Original Christians, 1 congregation; United Christians, 1 congregation; Gospel Pilgrims, 2 congregations; Free Gospel Christians, 14 congregations; Believers, 1 congregation; Non Sectarian, 7 congregations; No particular Denomination, 7 congregations; Evangelists, 4 congregations ; Gospel Refugees, 1 congregation; Freethinking Christians, 2 congregations.

4. Others, while admitting a connexion with some one of the more extensive sections into which the Christian Church is now divisible, have either forgotten or declined to specify a more minute association; such are,

Protestant Christians, 3 congregations ; Evangelical Protestants, 1 congrega-. tion; Protestant Free Church, 1 congregation; Trinitarians, 1 congregation; Protestant Dissenters, 24 congregations ; Dissenters, 6 congregations; Evangelical Dissenters, 3 congregations ; Episcopalian Seceders, 1 congregation.

5. A fifth class of separate congregations may be formed of those which are the offspring of the *Missionary* operations of the other bodies, acting either individually or in combination; such are the congregations raised and supported by the

London City Mission, 7 congregations ; Railway Mission, 1 congregation ; Town Mission, 17 congregations; Home Mission, 1 congregation; Mission Society, 8 congregations ; Seamen's Bethel, 11 congregations ; Christian Mission, 3 congregations.

Doubtless, these will not include the *whole* of the congregations gathered and sustained by the agency of these societies and others having kindred objects : many, it is likely, are returned with some particular denomination.

6. A residue will still be left of congregations difficult to classify. Such are the following: —

Free Church, 8 congregations; Teetotalers, 1 congregation; Doubtful, 43 congregations; Benevolent Methodists, 1 congregation; General, 2 congrega-. tions; Israelites, 1 congregation; Christian Israelites, 3 congregations; Stephenites, 1 congregation; Inghamites, 9 congregations; Temperance Wesleyans, 1 congregation; Temperance Christians, 1 congregation; Freethinkers, 2 congregations; Rational Progressionists, 1 congregation; Southcottians, 4 congregations.

The last of these, perhaps, deserves some notice. It derives its name from Johanna Southcott, who was born in 1750 in humble circumstances in Devonshire. In 1792 she commenced a career as a prophetess, making various announcements of events which were, she said, about to happen, and of revelations made to her respecting the millenial advent of the Saviour. Several thousand persons, it is said, believed her mission, amongst whom she distributed sealed packets which were thought by their possessors to contain the virtue of "charms." Being afflicted with a malady which gave to her the aspect of pregnancy, she prophesied that she was destined to become the mother of a *Second Shiloh;* and accordingly a splendid cradle and some other considerable preparations for the birth were made by her disciples; but her death, which happened shortly afterwards, displayed the baselessness of their anticipations. Nevertheless her followers would not resign their confidence that her prognostications would be certainly fulfilled ; asserting that, for the accomplishment of her predictions, she would shortly re-appear, restored to life. It seems that there are still in England four congregations of persons entertaining this belief.

FOREIGN CHURCHES.

The previous notices comprise the whole of the Religious Bodies which are native to this country, or which act upon the native population. Of the *Foreign Churches*, it is only necessary to enumerate the congregations which belong to each. Foreign *Protestants* have *eleven* congregations; thus distributed— LUTHERANS, 6; FRENCH PROTESTANTS, 3; REFORMED CHURCH OF THE NETHERLANDS, 1; GERMAN PROTESTANT REFORMERS, 1. Other Foreign Christian Churches have 5 congregations, namely—GERMAN CATHOLICS, 1; ITALIAN REFORMERS, 1; and GREEK CHURCH, 3.

The JEWS (a nation and a Church at once) have 53 synagogues, with accommodation (after an estimate for three defective returns) for 8,438 worshippers.

IF the preceding sketch has given any adequate idea of the faith and order of the various churches which possess in common the religious area of England, it will probably be seen to what a great extent, amidst so much ostensible confusion and diversity, essential harmony prevails. Especially is this apparent if we limit our regard to Protestant communions; which, indeed, comprise together nineteen-twentieths of our religious population. With respect to these, the differences which outwardly divide are not to be compared with the concordances which secretly, perhaps unconsciously, unite. The former, with but few exceptions, have relation almost wholly to the mere formalities of worship—not to the essential articles of faith. The fundamental doctrines of the Reformation, as embodied in the standards of the Church of England, are professed and preached by Presbyterians, Independents, Baptists, Methodists, and many minor sects, comprising more than nineteen-twentieths of the Nonconforming Protestant community; and though the different organization of these several bodies seems to present externally an aspect of disunion, probably a closer scrutiny will show that they are separated only as to matters whose importance, even if considerable, is not vital, and that thus they may, without excess of charity, be recognized as truly, though invisibly, united to the general Church of Christ. Perhaps in a people like the English—trained to the exercise of private judgment, and inured to self-reliance—absolute agreement on religious subjects never can be realized; and certainly if, at the trifling cost of a merely superficial difference, the ever various sympathies or prejudices of the people can obtain congenial resting place, we scarcely can behold with discontent a state of things by which, at worst, external rivalry is substituted for internal disaffection; while this very rivalry itself—perhaps in part, and growingly, a generous emulation—tends to diffuse the Gospel more extensively, since thus religious zeal and agency are roused and vastly multiplied. Rather, perhaps, we shall be led to recognize with some degree of satisfaction the inevitable existence of such co-operative diversity; and shall perceive, with Milton, that "while the Temple " of the Lord is building, some cutting, some squaring the marble, some " hewing the cedars, there must needs be many schisms and many dissections " made in the quarry and in the timber ere the House of God can be built: " and when every stone is laid artfully together, it cannot be united into a " continuity, it can but be contiguous in this world; neither can every piece of " the building be of one form; nay, rather the perfection consists in this, that " out of many moderate varieties and brotherly dissimilitudes, that are not

" vastly disproportional, arises the goodly and graceful symmetry that commends
" the whole pile and structure."* Nor has this *virtual* union been, in recent
times, unfruitful of much *manifested* concord. Common objects are increasingly
pursued by common efforts; not a few of our existing and perpetually rising
institutions for promoting moral and religious progress being founded on the
ample basis which permits the members of the different churches to commingle
in associated labour.

Amongst the constituencies, in the committees, and upon the platforms, of
the various religious societies, are found, conjoining in harmonious action,
ministers and members of perhaps a dozen different sects; while one considerable
organization† has for its *exclusive* object the promotion of fraternal sentiment
and intercourse between the various Evangelical Communions. Other indications
likewise are not wanting, which, combined with these, may reasonably raise
the hope that many of the Protestant communities are gradually tending to
a closer union and a more combined activity, proceeding from a heartier appreciation of the vital doctrines all alike profess and a diminished ardor on behalf
of those subordinate arrangements of church discipline and order with regard
to which they find themselves obliged to differ.

Much, no doubt, of this substantial concord is attributable to our system of
religious freedom, which, allowing the unchecked development of all ecclesiastical
peculiarities, has thus conferred on none the artificial value which results from
prohibition; and perhaps the expectation may be reasonably entertained that,
under this same influence, the spirit of uncompromising peace will gain yet
further potency—that liberty to separate on minor, will beget still more the disposition to unite on greater, questions—and that thus the Toleration Act will
prove, in its results, to have been the most effective Act of Uniformity.

If these remarks have in them any considerable share of truth, it will be
evident how necessary was the task of showing, in connexion with a statement
of existing means of spiritual instruction, how many of the various bodies are
pursuing, though by different paths, the same grand objects; so that, when
endeavouring to estimate our actual deficiency, we may not prematurely and
despondingly exaggerate our all-too-formidable need, but recollect that though,
in certain districts, there may be an absence of machinery belonging to particular
communities, the same essential truths may be both faithfully and effectively
imparted through the agency of other churches. Many spots there are,
unhappily, in England, where the whole provision made by all the churches put
together is inadequate to the occasion: such a deficiency as *this* it is which
properly betokens " spiritual destitution "; and the actual extent of this deficiency we now may, aided by the previous explanations, safely pass to indicate.

---

* Areopagitica ; or Speech for the Liberty of Unlicensed Printing.
† The " Evangelical Alliance," founded in 1846. The basis of this association is an agreement
in holding and maintaining what are generally understood to be evangelical views in regard to
the most important matters of doctrine; and its great object is "to aid in manifesting the
unity which exists among the true disciples of Christ." This object is sought to be attained
principally by annual conferences of members and by continual correspondence with Christian
brethren in different parts of the world.

SPIRITUAL PROVISION AND DESTITUTION.

THERE are two methods of pursuing a statistical inquiry with respect to the religion of a people. You may either ask each individual, directly, what particular form of religion he professes; or, you may collect such information as to the religious *acts* of individuals as will equally, though indirectly, lead to the same result. The former method was adopted, some few years ago, in Ireland, and is generally followed in the continental states when such investigations as the present are pursued. At the recent Census, it was thought advisable to take the latter course; partly because it had a less inquisitorial aspect,—but especially because it was considered that the outward *conduct* of persons furnishes a better guide to their religious state than can be gained by merely vague professions. In proportion, it was thought, as people truly are connected with particular sects or churches, will be their activity in raising buildings in which to worship and their diligence in afterwards frequenting them; but where there is an absence of such practical regard for a religious creed, but little weight can be attached to any purely formal acquiescence. This inquiry, therefore, was confined to obvious *facts* relating to two subjects.— 1. The amount of ACCOMMODATION which the people have provided for religious worship; and, 2. The number of persons, as ATTENDANTS, by whom this provision is made use of.

1.—ACCOMMODATION.

IF, by a happy miracle, on Sunday, March the 30th 1851, an universal feeling of devotion had impressed our population, and impelled towards the public sanctuaries all whom no impediment, of physical inability or needful occupation, hindered; if the morning or the evening invitation of the service-bell had called, no less from the crowded courts of populous towns and the cottages of scattered villages than from the city mansions and the rural halls, a perfect complement of worshippers; for what proportion of the 17,927,609 inhabitants of England would accommodation in religious buildings have been necessary? *Maximum of required accommodation in places of worship.*

The reply to this inquiry will determine mainly the extent by which our actual supply of spiritual ministration is inadequate to the demand.

Various computations have been made respecting the number of sittings proper to be furnished for a given population. With respect to *towns*, it has been thought by some that accommodation for 50 per cent. would be sufficient; while others have considered that provision for not less than 75 per cent. should be afforded. Dr. Chalmers took the mean of these two estimates, and concluded that five eighths, or 62½ per cent., of the people of a town might attend religious services, and ought to have facilities for doing so.* *Various estimates.*

The maximum for rural districts is put lower than that for towns; the distance of the church from people's residences operating as an unavoidable check upon attendance. But, as, for the purpose of this estimate, the *rural* population will consist of only those who live remote as well from villages containing churches as from towns,—in fact, of only those who are remote from any place of worship, —the proportion deemed to be sufficient for a *town* may be applied, with very slight reduction, to the whole of England—town and country both together; and, according to the best authorities, this proportion seems to lie between 50 and 60 per cent. of the entire community.

---

* Christian and Economic Polity of a Nation, vol. i. p.123. Mr. E. Baines (an excellent authority on subjects of this nature) assumes that accommodation for 50 per cent. of the gross population would be ample.—Letters on the Manufacturing Districts.

Considerable deduction to be made from the total population.
1. Young children.

From many valid causes, there will always be a considerable number of persons absent from public worship. First, a large deduction from the total population must be made on account of *infants and young children;* of whom there were in England and Wales, in 1851, as many as 4,440,466 under ten years of age—2,348,107 of this number being under five. Of course, opinions vary as to the earliest age at which a child, in order to acquire a habit of devotion, should be aken to a place of worship : some begin occasional attendance before they reacn five years of age, while others are retained at home much later. Many parents too, no doubt, conceive that the attendance of their children at a Sunday-school is a sufficient tax upon their tender strength. Perhaps it will not, therefore, be unreasonable to assume that, either on account of immaturity or Sunday-school engagements, about 3,000,000 children will be always justifiably away from public worship.

2. Invalids and aged persons.

There will also always be in any large community a certain number kept at home by *sickness.* It is estimated that the proportion of persons constantly sick, or incapacited by infirmities of age for active duties, is about five per cent. of the population; and, as the *degree* of indisposition which in general detains a prudent person from church or chapel is much slighter than that contemplated in this calculation, we shall probably not err in taking nearly seven per cent. of the 15,000,000 (which remain after deducting the 3,000,000 children who have already been supposed to be absent), and putting down 1,000,000 persons as the number usually and lawfully away from public worship on the ground of *sickness or debility.**

3 Persons in charge of houses &c.

Another large deduction must be made for those who are necessarily left in charge of houses and in attendance upon the two preceding classes. There were, in 1851, in England and Wales, 3,278,039 inhabited houses. If some of these in country parishes were left untenanted, locked up, while the inmates were at service, others doubtless were in charge of more than one domestic; so that we may safely take the whole 3,278,039 houses as representing so many individuals legitimately absent from religious edifices on account of *household duties.* Many of these, no doubt, would discharge a double occupation, as guardians of the house and attendants upon children or invalids; but some addition must unquestionably be made for a distinct array of nurses, or of parents unavoidably detained at home, and also for the medical practitioners, whose Sunday services can scarcely be dispensed with.

4. Persons employed on public conveyances.

A fourth considerable class, of which a certain number will be always absent from religious worship, is the class employed in connexion with the various *public conveyances;* as railways, steamboats, omnibuses, coaches, barges on canals, &c.† It is impossible to form an estimate of the precise *extent* to which employment in this way may be admitted as an adequate excuse for non-attendance on religious ordinances; since opinions are extremely various as to the extent to which the use of conveyances upon the Sunday is to be considered a work of " necessity or mercy." It cannot, however, be doubted that, practically, whatever views are likely to prevail upon the subject of Sabbath labour, very many persons will be constantly engaged in ministering to the public need of locomotion.

Result of these deductions.

Not attempting any numerical estimate of various minor classes, and designedly not making any deduction on account of Sunday traders, or the

---

* The number of persons in England and Wales in 1851, aged 70 years and upwards, was 508,305: aged 75 and upwards, there were 253,143: aged 80 and upwards, there were 107,041: aged 85 and upwards, there were 33,201: upwards of 90, there were 7,796: above 95 there were 1,545: and 215 were upwards of 100.
† It is estimated that the number of men engaged, in London alone, upon omnibuses, on the Sunday, is as many as 6,000.

criminal population—since the object is to show the amount of accommodation needed for those who are *able*, not merely for those who are *willing*, to attend—it seems to follow from the previous computations that about 7,500,000 persons will, of necessity, be absent whenever divine service is celebrated; and, consequently, that sittings in religious buildings cannot be required for *more* than 10,427,609, being rather more than 58 per cent. of the entire community. It will be convenient for the subsequent calculations to deal with 58 per cent. exactly, and assume that the number always able to attend is 10,398,013.

It by no means results, from this, that the adult portion of the remaining 42 per cent. of the population (7,500,000 in round numbers) is entirely without opportunities of frequenting public worship; for, as there is generally more than one service on the Sunday, it is practicable, and in fact customary, to carry on a system of *relief*—some who attend service at one period of the day occupying at the other period the place of those who were before prevented; thus enabling these to attend a later service in their turn. This system is especially adopted in the case of domestic servants; consequently, though there is probably always about the *same number* (viz. 7,500,000) detained at home by lawful causes, this number will not always be composed of the *same persons*.

The custom of double, and sometimes treble, services each Sunday introduces an important element into the question of the number of sittings needful for a given population. It has been shown above, that sittings cannot be wanted for more than 10,398,013 persons (being the full number able to attend at one time). But does it therefore follow that there should be *as many* sittings as this number of persons? It is obvious that if attendance upon public worship *once a day* be thought sufficient for each individual, it is possible to conceive a case where, all the churches and chapels being open *twice* a day, the whole population could attend, though sittings should exist for only half their number. For instance; if in a district, with ten thousand persons able to attend, the places of worship (open twice upon the Sunday) should contain 5,000 sittings, it is possible for the whole ten thousand to attend them, simply by the one half going in the morning and the other in the evening: and if *three* services are held, a further diminution of the number of sittings might be made without depriving any person of the opportunity of attending *once*. This, though of course an extreme illustration, cannot fail to show the necessity of settling, ere a trusty calculation can be made of the accommodation needful for the country, whether it is to be assumed that a single sitting may be occupied by more than one person on one Sunday, or whether we must aim at a provision so extensive that every person may be able (if inclined) to attend each Sunday *twice* or oftener—in fact, at *every* service. Practically, I believe it will be found that very many persons think their duties as to Sabbath worship adequately discharged by *one* attendance; and most likely we may safely count upon the permanent continuance of a large class thus persuaded. Still, as no definite conception can be formed of the extent to which this practice is adopted—and as it might reasonably be contended that neglect of any opportunities for worship should not be *presumed*, but that such an extent of accommodation should be furnished as would utterly exclude excuse for non-attendance—it will be the better plan if, merely indicating the existence of the practice as an element in the question, I assume that the provision needful for the population should consist of at least as many sittings as there are individuals not incapacitated by the causes previously mentioned, viz., 10,398,013, or 58 per cent. Indeed, whatever diminution in the estimate may be supposed to be allowable on account of double services will probably be more than counterbalanced by the absolute necessity there is that nearly every building should possess some *surplus* of accommodation; for as, practically, it is impossible that

Effect of double services.

each religious body can compute so nicely its position and attractiveness as to provide exactly as many sittings as are wanted from it, and no more,—as some will naturally leave a margin for anticipated progress, which perhaps may not be realized, while others will miscalculate the other way, and grow beyond their utmost expectations,—there must needs be a certain excess of supply beyond demand, continuing as long as there exists a variety of churches, and the liberty for people to prefer one church before another. I am therefore inclined to consider that accommodation for 58 per cent. of the population is no more than would be absolutely needful if all persons able to attend were also willing.

The maximum of accommodation is affected by its distribution over the country. But, of course, in order to be adequate to the wants of the community, the buildings which should contain these 10,398,013 sittings must be so located on the surface of the country as to bring the accommodation they afford within the reach of all by whom it is required. If many churches and chapels be clustered in a narrow compass, or if several thinly peopled parishes have each a church with more accommodation than is wanted, it will follow that in other portions of the country there must necessarily be some deficiency, unless the aggregate of sittings be raised *above* 10,398,013. So that what is wanted is, not merely such a number of sittings as shall equal the total number of persons capable of using them, but also such a *distribution* of these sittings as will render them *available* by all requiring them. A provision of 10,398,013 sittings for the whole of England would only be sufficient if *in every part* of England there should prove to be accommodation for as many as 58 per cent. It will presently be shown how far the actual distribution of religious buildings in this country affects the question of the adequacy or inadequacy of existing accommodation.

By what religious bodies should the necessary accommodation be provided? Having advanced thus far, we meet a question much more difficult and delicate than any which has hitherto encountered us ; this is, assuming that 10,398,013 sittings ought to be provided, would the provision be satisfactory supposing that that number could be furnished by the aid of *all the various churches and congregations in the aggregate?* or is it essential that they should belong to one particular church exclusively? or to a certain number of churches which agree upon particular fundamental doctrines? These are questions which are obviously beyond the range of this Report, and which must be discussed and settled for themselves by the different readers of the Tables. In the meantime, while endeavouring to estimate in some degree the actual extent of "spiritual destitution," it may fairly be allowed, perhaps, to take the whole accommodation in the gross ; since it is probable that yet for many years to come each church will continue to retain a hold upon the sympathies of a portion of our population, which then, of course, as now, will not require, as they would not accept, accommodation in the buildings of other denominations. The course of argument, however, will be of general applicability, and can easily be adapted to the Church of England or to any other body.

Actual provision according to the Census. What, then, is the number of sittings actually furnished, by the agency of all the various churches, towards the accommodation of the 10,398,013 persons who, if only willing, would be able constantly to occupy them? The returns from 31,943 places of religious worship, many of them of course being simply rooms in houses, give an aggregate of sittings to the number of 9,467,738. But as 2524 other places have omitted to return the number of their sittings, an estimate for these, computed from the average of complete returns*, will raise the total

---

* In this calculation a separate average has been taken for each denomination; but it has not been thought essential to proceed so minutely as to distinguish whether the places of worship supplying defective returns are situate in town or country localities, nor how many of them are separate and entire buildings. It is not probable that any closer scrutiny would materially alter the estimate. Where, however any reliable indication of the number of sittings has been furnished by a statement of the number of *attendants*, this has been adopted rather than the *average*.

number of sittings reported to the Census Office to 10,212,563. This, when compared with the number calculated as desirable (10,398,013), shows a deficiency in the whole of England and Wales of 185,450.

The point, then, to which we have arrived is this : assuming that the joint provision made by all the sects together may be reckoned in the computation, the deficiency, upon the whole of England and Wales, will be only to the extent of 185,450 sittings (or for only 1·03 per cent. of the population), *if the entire provision now existing is found to be so well distributed over the country as that no part has too little and no part too much.* We must, therefore, now inquire how far this necessary distribution has been realized.

Adequacy of existing accommodation if equally distributed.

Every portion of the country, I assume, should have accommodation for 58 per cent. of the inhabitants.* It would clearly be of no avail that one part should have more than this per-centage if another part had less; for since, according to the estimate, *no more* than 58 per cent. of the population could be present at one time at a religious service, it is evident that if in any place the number of sittings would accommodate a much *greater* proportion than 58 per cent., there would be in that locality a surplus of unused and useless sittings, generally inaccessible to residents in other neighbourhoods, and quite as unavailable as if they had never been provided. What is required is, not alone an *aggregate* per-centage of 58 per cent. in an extensive area (such as the whole of England, or the whole of an English county); for this would not be any proof of adequate provision, since the rural portions might possess an unavailable abundance, while the urban portions suffered under an extreme deficiency; but that same per-centage in localities of size so circumscribed that inequalities of distribution could but slightly operate. Then, what localities, of definite character, of this appropriate size, can be selected for comparison, by which to estimate more accurately our requirements? Of course, with regard to the Church of England, there should be accommodation for the 58 per cent. *in every parish*, since the very theory of a parochial arrangement is that the people of a parish should attend the parish church and none besides; but probably it is not needful to investigate so carefully as this. The Registration Districts, or Poor Law Unions, (of which there are in England and Wales 624,) will afford convenient limits for comparison; and if in any of these we find a total amount of accommodation adequate for 58 per cent. of the inhabitants, we shall probably not err to any great extent, (although, no doubt, we shall to *some* extent,) if we conclude that there is room for 58 per cent. within the reach of all the dwellers in the District. The selection too of Districts as the standards of comparison will obviate the difficulty which, if *parishes* were taken, would arise with reference to the members of Dissenting Bodies, who, ignoring altogether the parochial system, often cross the limits of the parish where they dwell in order to attend a chapel situate beyond its boundaries. By taking the somewhat wider area of *Districts*, the disturbance to the calculations from this cause will be reduced to unimportance.

Effect of unequal distribution.

While the total number of sittings in England and Wales is as many as 10,212,563, leaving at first sight a deficiency of only 185,450 as compared with the number requisite to provide for 58 per cent. of the population, yet by the unequal distribution of these 10,212,563 there is really not accommodation *within reach of those who want it,* for a greater number than 8,753,279, leaving an actual deficiency of 1,644,734 sittings. Probably, indeed, the deficiency is even larger.

---

* This may be taken as sufficiently near. In some parts, however, from peculiar circumstances, it is evident that this proportion will in some degree be varied. There may be a greater number of children or a greater number of servants, &c.—circumstances adequate to alter to a trifling extent the proportion of persons able to attend a place of worship.

The objection, which prevails against a comparison of the total accommodation of *England* with the total population of England, also applies in some degree against a comparison of the total accommodation with the total population of a *district*. Unequal distribution may exist in the latter case as well as in the former, though, no doubt, to a much less extent. The means of course exist by which a computation could be made for each particular *parish;* but as this would be a formidable task, and as the calculation, for the reason mentioned, would be strictly applicable only to the Church of England, it will probably be well to base the estimate on *districts;* thus assuming that the whole provision of a district is diffused throughout the district in an equal proportion to the population, and merely introducing the preceding observations to show that the above computed deficiency of sittings in the country, quite sufficiently alarming, is an *under* statement.

Particular illustrations of unequal distribution. By a reference to the District Table (pp. cclxxvi–ccxcv of the Report), we obtain some curious illustrations of the widely varying condition of particular localities: some fortunately basking in excess of spiritual privileges, others absolutely "perishing for lack of knowledge." Probably a more instructive collocation cannot be produced than that presented by two neighbouring districts of the metropolis —the City of London, and Shoreditch. These stand respectively Nos. 19 and 20 in the topographical arrangement of the London districts; the former has accommodation for 81 per cent. of its inhabitants, the latter for 18; the former has a superfluity of 13,338 sittings*, the latter a deficiency of 43,755. Table (I.) in the SUMMARY TABLES gives a limited selection of the most conspicuous cases of abundance and of poverty: from which it will be seen how widely the proportions vary; Shoreditch having only 18 sittings to every 100 persons, while Machynlleth, in North Wales, has as many as 123 to every 100. It will be noticed, indeed, how favourably Wales in general is circumstanced—nearly all the districts having a considerable surplus of provision.

Comparative accommodation in Town and Country Districts. As was to be expected, it is chiefly in the large and densely-peopled *towns* that a deficiency is felt; the rural districts are supplied in general with adequate, sometimes with superabundant, provision. It appears from Table 3. that the *urban* parts of England, containing an aggregate population of 8,294,240 persons, have accommodation for 3,814,215 or 46 per cent. of this number; while the rural parts, containing a population of 9,633,369 have provision for 6,398,348 or 66·5 per cent.

TABLE 3.

COMPARATIVE ACCOMMODATION in URBAN and RURAL PARISHES.

	Population, 1851.	Number of Sittings provided by all Religious Bodies.	Proportion per Cent. of Sittings to Population.
URBAN PARISHES - -	8,294,240	3,814,215	46·0
RURAL PARISHES - -	9,633,369	6,398,348	66·5
ENGLAND AND WALES -	17,927,609	10,212,563	57·0

* An ingenious proposal has been made, with reference to the city churches, by the Rev. Charles Hume, Rector of St. Michael's, Wood Street. He suggests that, as the city has too many churches while the suburbs have too few, the very buildings themselves might be removed from the one place to the other. His scheme embraces a provision for the endowment of new districts for these churches in their new localities; the patronage remaining as at present.

These "urban districts" here, however, include small country towns, which seem to be as well supplied as any other portion of the country. If we take the *large* towns only (*See* Table 4.), and include small country towns with the rural parts to which they virtually belong, the proportion per cent. in urban districts will be 37 as compared with 73 in rural districts. And the proportion is in inverse ratio to the size of the towns; so that while in towns containing between 10,000 and 20,000 inhabitants, the proportion is 66; in towns containing between 20,000 and 50,000 it is 60; in those containing between 50,000 and 100,000 it is 47, and in those containing upwards of 100,000 it is 34. (*See* Table F.F., in the SUMMARY TABLES, *post*, p. 134.) This view suggests with singular force the mixture of sentiments which led to the erection of the greater portion of our sacred edifices. Piety and local attachments—benevolence and longing for perpetual remembrance—principally, doubtless, a sincere desire to honour God, and yet, with this, a natural desire to raise a lasting monument to themselves,—these were the mingling motives to the influence of which may be attributed the existence of some thousands of our churches. Hence, it was in the very spot where the founder had his dwelling that his church was built: no other neighbourhood possessed such hold on his affections. Thus arose our village churches, and a multitude of structures in those ancient towns and cities where, in former times, the merchants were accustomed to reside. But our modern populous towns,—erected more for business than for residence—mere aggregates of offices and workshops and over-crowded dwellings of the subordinate agents of industry,—are inhabited by none whose means permit them to reside elsewhere. The wealthy representatives of those whose piety supplied our ancient towns with churches fly from the unwholesome atmosphere of our new cities, and dispense their charity in those suburban or more rural parishes in which their real homes are situated and their local sympathies are centred. The innumerable multitudes who do and must reside within the compass of the enormous hives in which their toil is daily carried on, are thus the objects of but little of that lively interest with which benevolent men regard the inhabitants of their immediate neighbourhood, and which produces, in our small-sized country parishes, so many institutions for their physical and moral benefit. The masses, therefore, of our large and growing towns—connected by no sympathetic tie with those by fortune placed above them—form a world apart, a nation by themselves; divided almost as effectually from the rest as if they spoke another language or inhabited another land. What Dr. Chalmers calls "the influence of locality," is powerless here: the area is too extensive and the multitude too vast. It is to be hoped that the influence of trade-connexion may ere long sufficiently accomplish what the influence of locality is now too feeble to secure; that heads of great industrial establishments, the growth of recent generations, may perform towards the myriads connected with them by community of occupation, those religious charities or duties which the principal proprietors in rural parishes perform towards those connected with them by vicinity of residence. Much, doubtless, has already been effected in this way;* but the need for more is manifest and urgent. The following Table (4.) shows the present accommodation in seventy-two large towns or boroughs, and the additional amount required, if 58 per cent. of the population ought to have within their reach the means of public worship. It will here be interesting to compare the ancient towns with those which have been called into existence or activity by modern enterprise and industry.

---

* See an interesting account of the various measures—including the provision of a church and chaplain—adopted for the benefit of their workpeople, by Price's Patent Candle Company.—Report to the Shareholders, 1852. Mr. Peto, I believe, supplies the numerous labourers engaged in executing his extensive contracts, with a library and means of religious worship and instruction. Doubtless many other cases might be mentioned of a warm regard displayed by masters for the moral welfare of their men.

TABLE 4.

RELIGIOUS ACCOMMODATION in LARGE TOWNS.*

TOWNS.	Population, 1851.	Number of Sittings provided by all Religious Bodies.	Proportion per Cent. of Sittings to Population.	Additional Number of Sittings required to accommodate 58 per Cent. of the Population.	TOWNS.	Population, 1851.	Number of Sittings provided by all Religious Bodies.	Proportion per Cent. of Sittings to Population.	Additional Number of Sittings required to accommodate 58 per Cent. of the Population.
Ashton-under-Lyne	30,676	11,828	38·6	5,064	Macclesfield	39,048	16,461	42·2	6,187
					Maidstone	20,740	9,787	47·2	2,242
Bath	54,240	33,149	61·1	..	Manchester	303,382	95,929	31·6	80,083
Birmingham	232,841	66,812	28·7	68,236	*Marylebone	370,957	100,208	27·0	114,947
Blackburn	46,536	18,483	39·7	8,508	*Merthyr Tydfil	63,080	36,815	58·4	..
Bolton	61,171	21,801	35·6	13,678					
Bradford	103,778	32,827	31·6	27,364	Newcastle	87,784	30,319	34·5	20,596
*Brighton	69,673	24,098	34·6	16,312	Newport (Monmouth)	19,323	10,706	55·4	501
Bristol	137,328	72,516	52·8	7,134	Northampton	26,657	14,268	53·5	1,193
*Bury	31,262	13,434	43·0	4,698	Norwich	68,195	30,807	45·2	8,746
					Nottingham	57,407	27,261	47·5	6,035
Cambridge	27,815	14,807	53·2	1,326					
Carlisle	26,310	11,407	43·4	3,853	Oldham	52,820	16,976	32·1	13,660
*Chatham	28,424	13,089	46·0	3,397	Oxford	27,843	16,768	60·2	..
*Cheltenham	35,051	19,819	56·5	511					
Chester	27,766	14,176	51·1	1,928	Plymouth	52,221	23,805	45·6	6,483
Colchester	19,443	14,234	73·2	..	Portsmouth	72,096	26,606	36·9	15,206
Coventry	36,208	15,537	42·9	5,464	Preston	69,542	24,642	35·4	15,692
Derby	40,609	20,338	50·1	3,215	Reading	21,456	11,401	53·1	1,043
*Devonport	50,159	23,372	46·6	5,720	Rochdale	29,195	13,583	46·4	3,400
*Dover	22,244	11,636	52·3	1,266					
Dudley	37,962	15,911	41·9	6,107	Salford	63,850	24,772	38·8	12,261
					Sheffield	135,310	45,889	33·9	32,591
Exeter	32,818	19,586	59·7	..	Southampton	35,305	17,959	50·9	2,518
					South Shields	28,974	14,198	49·0	2,607
*Finsbury	323,772	94,165	29·1	93,623	*Southwark	172,963	50,237	29·1	50,024
					Stockport	53,835	22,588	42·0	8,636
Gateshead	25,568	9,081	35·5	5,748	*Stoke-upon-Trent	84,027	40,723	48·5	8,013
Gravesend	16,633	6,532	39·3	3,115	Sunderland	63,897	31,264	48·9	5,796
Great Yarmouth	30,879	14,223	46·1	3,687	Swansea	31,461	18,539	58·9	..
*Greenwich	105,784	35,497	33·6	25,858					
					*Tower Hamlets	539,111	137,921	25·6	174,763
Halifax	33,582	10,192	30·3	9,286	Tynemouth	29,170	12,854	44·1	4,065
*Huddersfield	30,880	15,787	51·1	2,127					
Hull	84,690	37,413	44·2	11,707	Wakefield	22,065	15,649	70·9	..
					Walsall	25,680	10,503	40·9	4,391
Ipswich	32,914	16,017	48·7	3,073	Warrington	22,894	10,083	44·0	3,196
					*Westminster	241,611	76,181	31·5	63,953
Kidderminster	18,462	9,829	53·2	879	Wigan	31,941	9,777	30·6	8,749
King's Lynn	19,355	9,502	49·1	1,724	*Wolverhampton	119,748	48,455	40·5	20,999
					Worcester	27,528	16,174	58·7	..
*Lambeth	251,345	62,307	24·8	83,473					
Leeds	172,270	79,266	46·0	20,651	York	36,303	23,650	65·1	..
Leicester	60,584	25,008	41·3	10,131					
Liverpool	375,955	125,002	31·4	93,052					
London (City) †	127,869	68,330	53·4	18,706					
London (Metropolis)‡	2,362,236	713,561	29·7	669,514	Total §	6,239,099	2,329,416	37·3	1,332,992

* The *Municipal* limits of the Towns here mentioned have been generally taken; an asterisk (*) indicates the exceptions—where the *Parliamentary* boundaries have been followed. Estimates have been made of the number of sittings in those places of worship the Returns for which omit to give this information. For other particulars relating to these towns, see *post*, SUMMARY TABLES, p. 113.

† This is the Municipal and Parliamentary City of London; comprising the three Poor Law Unions of East London, West London, and City of London (within the walls). The latter Union corresponds with the ancient City of London, and contains accommodation for 81 per cent. of the inhabitants, or for 13,338 more than could at any one time attend.

‡ This proportion of sittings to population for the Metropolis is calculated upon the number which remains after deducting 13,338 sittings, a surplus existing in the City of London (within the Walls) over and above the number requisite for 58 per cent. of the population of the district.

§ In dealing with *London* in this total, the entire Metropolis has been taken: the figures therefore which relate to the Boroughs of *Finsbury, Greenwich, Lambeth, London City, Marylebone, Southwark, Tower Hamlets,* and *Westminster* have not been noticed in the addition; being included in the numbers which represent the Metropolis.

This Table clearly shows how great and overwhelming a proportion of the whole deficiency of England is assignable to our great modern towns, since thus it seems that out of the total number of 1,644,734 additional sittings reckoned to be necessary, 1,332,992 or 80 per cent. are required for these seventy-two boroughs, or rather for sixty of the most recent, the remainder, for reasons obvious when their names are seen, being fortunately blessed with more than adequate provision. This gives a vivid picture of the destitute condition of our great-town population, and speaks loudly of the need there is for new and energetic plans of operation having special reference to towns. The absence of that local interest which leads to individual benevolence, and the evident inadequacy of all that can be reasonably expected from the great employers of industry, appear to call for the combined exertions either of the whole inhabitants of a particular neighbourhood, or of the Christian Church at large, as the only other method for relieving such deplorable deficiency. And this has been to some extent perceived and acted on. With reference to the Church of England, many churches have been raised by the united liberality of the inhabitants of populous town parishes, encouraged by assistance from the funds of central bodies, such as the Incorporated Church Building Society; and amongst the Dissenters many chapels have been reared in similar manner. But it cannot, it is feared, be said that these mere local efforts promise to diminish very sensibly the grievous lack of accommodation for the *masses* of our civic population. Hitherto the action of those central bodies which dispense the bounties of the general Christian public has been made dependent on the previous action of the local bodies in whose midst the additional church or chapel is to be erected; and unfortunately it but rarely happens that such local action is aroused, except to obtain accommodation for an increase of the middle classes, who already appreciate religious ordinances and are able and disposed to bear the pecuniary burden requisite in order to obtain them. The effect has been that the considerable addition made in recent years to the religious edifices of large towns has been in very near proportion to the rapid growth, in the same interval, of the prosperous middle classes; but the far more rapid increase in this period in the number of artizans and labourers has taken place without a corresponding increase of religious means *for them.* The only prominent example, within my knowledge, of a vigorous effort to relieve a local want without waiting for local demand, is the movement which, some years ago, the Bishop of London originated and successfully, beyond anticipation, prosecuted, for providing fifty new churches for the metropolitan parishes. And yet it really seems that, without some missionary enterprises similar to this, the mighty task of even mitigating spiritual destitution in our towns and cities hardly can be overcome.*

A most important question is, the rate at which, with our existing modes of operation, fresh accommodation is provided, as compared with the continual increase in the numbers of the people. To display this accurately we require correct accounts of the provision in existence at particular former periods. No authentic records are available, however, of the state of each religious body in preceding years. The nearest estimate that can be made is furnished by the information which the present returns afford with reference to the *dates* at which existing edifices were erected, or appropriated to religious uses; but, for several

Rate at which the supply is increasing.

---

* I am not aware of any special agencies, connected with the various Dissenting bodies, which attain the objects here described. The necessarily self-supporting character of all the institutions founded by Dissenters renders it, in their case, almost indispensable to make the erection of a chapel dependent on the prospect of an adequate pecuniary return. Hence, though the Congregational and Baptist bodies have established recently their " Chapel Building Societies," the operation of these central boards is practically limited, if not by an actual local demand, yet by the prospect of a speedy local sympathy among the middle classes.

reasons, the conclusions to be drawn from this source must be subject to a certain degree of hazard. In the first place, as the facts relate entirely to *existing* buildings, there is no account of those which may have been in use in former times and since abandoned. In the second place, in consequence of an oversight in the framing of the question, several places (parts of buildings), *erected* in former years, but only latterly employed for religious services, have been returned with the earlier date. And thirdly, with respect to as many as 4,546, out of the 34,467, no date whatever is inserted in the returns. Fortunately, for the purpose of an approximate inference, the errors arising from these three sources do not all tend in the same direction, so that there is some probability that an error in the one direction may be counteracted by an error in the other. Thus the influence of the first of these inaccuracies is to make the earlier periods seem to have less than their correct accommodation; while the influence of the second error is, upon the contrary, to attribute to the earlier periods a greater, and to the recent periods a less, amount of accommodation than is really due to them. Of the 4,546 buildings without dates assigned, 2,118 belong to the Church of England, and of these the greater portion probably were built in the earlier periods; while, on the other hand, the larger number of the 2,428 which belong to the Dissenting bodies were erected probably in recent years. Perhaps the best course therefore to pursue, in order to present a tolerably accurate statement of these dates, will be to distribute the 4,546 places of worship over the six intervals, according to the proportion which the number actually assigned to each of these intervals bears towards the total number having dates assigned at all. If this be done, and if the average numbers, as now ascertained, of sittings to a place of worship (viz. 377 for places belonging to the Church of England, and 240 for those belonging to Dissenters), be supposed to have been the average number at each former interval *, we obtain the results which appear in Table 5.

TABLE 5.

AMOUNT of ACCOMMODATION at different Periods, in the whole of ENGLAND and WALES.

Periods.	Population at each Period.	Number of Places of Worship at each Period.	Estimated Number of Sittings at each Period.	Rate of Increase between the Periods of Population and Sittings respectively.		Number of Sittings to 100 Persons at each Period.
				Population.	Sittings.	
				per Cent.	*per Cent.*	
1801	8,892,536	15,080	5,171,123	..	..	58·1
1811	10,164,256	16,490	5,524,348	14·3	6·8	54·4
1821	12,000,236	18,796	6,094,480	18·0	10·3	50·3
1831	13,896,797	22,413	7,007,091	15·8	15·0	50·4
1841	15,914,148	28,017	8,554,636	14·5	22·5	53·8
1851	17,927,609	34,467	10,212,563	12·6	19·4	57·0

* It will not do to apply the general average (296); as the relative position of the different bodies was not the same in the early portion of the century as now; the Church of England having in 1801 (according to the estimate from dates) as many as 11,379 churches, whereas the Dissenters then (according to same estimate) had only 3701. This, however, is scarcely probable, and seems to prove that many Dissenters' buildings, existing in former years, have since become disused or have been replaced by others. As so much depends upon the extent to which this disuse and substitution have prevailed, these calculations, in the absence of any facts upon those points, must necessarily be open to some doubts.

From this it appears that, taken in the gross, our rate of progress during the last thirty years has not been altogether unsatisfactory. Previous to 1821, the population increased faster than accommodation for religious worship, so that while, from 1801 to 1821, the former had increased from 8,892,536 persons to 12,000,236 (or 34·9 per cent.), the latter, during the same interval, had only increased from 5,171,123 sittings to 6,094,486 (or 17·8 per cent.), and the proportion of sittings to population, which in 1801 was 58·1 per cent., had declined in 1821 to less than 51 per cent. But from 1821 to the present time the course of things has changed: the rate of increase of the population has continually declined, while that of religious accommodation has steadily advanced; so that while the number of the people has been raised from 12,000,236 to 17,927,609 (an increase of 49·4 per cent.), the number of sittings has been raised from 6,094,486 to 10,212,563 (or an increase of 67·6 per cent.), and the proportion of sittings to population, which in 1821 was 50·8 per cent., had risen in 1851 to 57 per cent.

As far then as regards the increase of accommodation *in the aggregate*, there seems to be some cause for gratulation; but in the matter of our rate of increase as well as in that of our actual existing supply, the question of distribution is important; and we want to know how far the progress thus manifested in the gross, is taking place in those parts of the country shown to be behind the rest. It is therefore necessary to inquire to what extent the great towns have participated in this augmentation, and the following Table (6.), constructed in the same way as the last, will show the respective rates at which the population and religious provision are increasing in the registration districts which contain large towns, and, compared with this, the same information as to all the rest of England:—

[marginal note:] Comparative increase in towns and other parts.

TABLE 6.

INCREASE of ACCOMMODATION at different Periods in Large-Town Districts,* as compared with the Residue of England and Wales.

| | LARGE TOWN DISTRICTS. | | | | | | | RESIDUE OF ENGLAND. | | | | | |
| Periods. | Population at each Period. | Estimated Number of Places of Worship and Sittings at each Period. | | Rates of Increase of Population and Sittings respectively. | | No. of Sittings to 100 Persons at each Period. | Periods. | Population at each Period. | Estimated Number of Places of Worship and Sittings at each Period. | | Rates of Increase of Population and Sittings respectively. | | No. of Sittings to 100 Persons at each Period. |
		Places of Worship.	Sittings.	Population.	Sittings.				Places of Worship.	Sittings.	Population.	Sittings.	
				per Cent.	*per Cent.*						*per Cent.*	*per Cent.*	
1801	3,608,024	3,500	1,506,922	..	..	41·8	1801	5,284,512	11,580	3,664,201	..	..	69·3
1811	4,269,846	3,805	1,638,240	18·1	8·7	38·5	1811	5,908,496	12,685	3,886,108	11·7	6·1	65·8
1821	5,241,895	4,501	1,927,901	23·0	18·3	37·0	1821	6,758,341	14,295	4,156,585	14·5	7·0	61·5
1831	6,465,953	5,670	2,441,213	23·8	26·0	38·0	1831	7,460,844	16,743	4,565,878	10·4	9·8	61·2
1841	7,785,136	7,391	3,182,186	20·2	30·3	41·1	1841	8,179,012	20,626	5,372,448	9·6	17·7	65·7
1851	9,229,120	9,586	4,127,244	19·3	29·7	44·7	1851	8,698,489	24,881	6,085,319	6·3	13·3	70·0

It hence appears that the Towns have by no means had a share proportionate to their need, in the liberality which, during the last half century, has added 19,387 places of worship and 5,041,440 sittings to the accommodation existing in 1801. For although the increase of provision in towns has been 174 per cent. in the 50 years, while the increase in the country parts has not exceeded 66 per cent., yet such has been the more rapid increase of *population* in the

* The Town Districts included in this Table are all such as contain Towns having upwards of 10,000 inhabitants.

former than in the latter (156 per cent. against 65 per cent.) that the accommodation in towns in proportion to the population is scarcely less deficient than it was in 1801—viz. 45 sittings to every 100 persons instead of 42; while the accommodation for the rest of England will still suffice for as many as 70 out of every 100 of the rural population.

Extent to which the accommodation is actually available.

The result of the previous course of observation, as to the amount of present accommodation, seems to be this: Assuming that all religious sects, whatever their variety, are to have their share in ministering to the people; and applying to the absolute total number of sittings a correction for unequal distribution; the existing provision furnished by the entire religious community is adequate to supply the spiritual wants of 8,753,279 persons, or 48·8 per cent. of the whole; *i.e.*, there are places of worship *within the reach* of that number, and capable of holding them. It is obvious, however, that a church or chapel may be within the reach of a neighbourhood, as far as proximity is concerned, and yet not available for the use of those by leisure able to frequent it: *it might not be open*. The practical value therefore of these 8,753,279 sittings, computed to be within the reach of that same number of persons, is dependent on the extent to which they are offered for the occupation of the public. Now, many places of worship are opened only once upon the Sunday: and where this is the case, although there might be sittings in them equal to 58 per cent. of the population, this supply would practically be inadequate; for it is only on the supposition that persons necessarily detained at home at one period of the day are enabled, by the system of *relief*, to worship in another period of the day—it is only upon this supposition that a proportion of sittings to population of 58 per cent. can be considered adequate; for it must be recollected that 58 per cent. is not an estimate of the total number of persons able to worship *at all* upon the Sunday, but of the total number able to worship *at one time* on the Sunday. The *aggregate* number of people who might worship on the Sunday—some at one period, and some at another—is probably as great as 70 per cent. of the entire community. If, therefore (to suppose a case), in any district, all the churches should have only a *single* service in the day, the accommodation in that district would be, practically, less by some 12 or 15 per cent. than in another district where the actual number of sittings might be just the same, but where in all the churches *two* services a day were held. We must, therefore, before assuming that the state of things would be satisfactory if a certain number of sittings (58 per cent.) were furnished, ask to what extent they would, when furnished, be available. The following Table (7.) will afford a view of the extent to which the present accommodation is made use of:—

TABLE 7.
AVAILABLE ACCOMMODATION in ENGLAND and WALES.

Total Number of Places of Worship and Sittings.		Number of Places *open for Worship*, at each Period of the Day, on Sunday, March 30, 1851; and Number of Sittings thus made available.					
		Places of Worship open.			Available Sittings.*		
Places of Worship.	Sittings.*	Morning.	Afternoon.	Evening.	Morning.	Afternoon.	Evening.
34,467	10,212,563	23,669	21,371	18,055	8,498,520	6,267,928	5,723,000

* Including an estimate for Returns which omitted to mention the number of sittings.

So that, while the actual number of sittings is 10,212,563, there is never at any one time that number available to the public. In the morning, 1,714,043 of them, in the afternoon 3,944,635, in the evening 4,489,563, are withdrawn from public use.

But here no allowance has been made for the effects of unequal distribution, and unless we can assume that all the places closed were situate in districts where there was a surplus of accommodation, equalling exactly the number of their sittings, there must be a slight deduction made from the numbers given in this table, ere we can arrive at a correct account of the available provision of the country; i.e., sittings both *open for worship* and *within reach* of parties able to make use of them. This deduction will take place wherever the number of available sittings in a district exceeds 58 per cent. of the population, and the amount of such deduction will precisely correspond with such excess. The result is, to reduce the number of sittings available for *morning* service to 8,322,066; the number available for *afternoon* service to 6,192,061; and the number available for *evening* service to 5,712,670.

Of course, the number of services *per diem* is mainly affected by the situation of the place of worship, whether it be in town or country. The effect of this is seen in Table 8.; from which it appears that the 34,467 places of worship were made available for the holding of 63,095 services; being an average of not quite two services to each place of worship. In the towns, more use was made of the accommodation than in the country: every 100 places in the former being used for 208 services, while 100 places in the latter were not used for more than 175 services.

TABLE 8.

NUMBER of SERVICES per Day in the Town and Rural Portions respectively, of ENGLAND and WALES.

	Total Number of Places of Worship.	Number of Places of Worship open at different Periods of the Day.						
		Morning only.	Afternoon only.	Evening only.	Morning and Afternoon.	Morning and Evening.	Afternoon and Evening.	Morning, Afternoon, and Evening.
ENGLAND AND WALES -	34,467	3802	3579	2534	9031	6760	4685	4076
Town Portion * - -	7,463	488	277	277	1077	3048	622	1674
Rural Portion - -	27,004	3314	3302	2257	7954	3712	4063	2402

An important question meets us now: how much of the accommodation proved to be existing is available for the use of that great part of the community most needing spiritual education, and least able, by pecuniary outlay, to procure it? What proportion of our present provision is at the service of the poorer classes, without price? For the purpose of ascertaining this, inquiry was made, as to every place of worship, how many of the sittings were "free;" the meaning of the term being "free to any persons wishing, without payment, to occupy them." The answers to this question were, unfortunately, not in every instance framed in accordance with this interpretation. In the case of ancient parish churches, sometimes *all* the sittings were returned as free—the meaning evidently

What proportion of the accommodation is free?

---

* The "Town Portion" here given comprehends every place which, either from possessing a market or from some other cause, is entitled to be called a "Town."

being that no money payment was received from the occupants; but, as many of them were, no doubt, *appropriated*, either by custom or the authority of church officers, to particular persons, it is clear they would not be available indiscriminately to the poor, so as to make them "free sittings" in the sense above referred to. And with reference to Dissenters' chapels, it seems not unlikely that the term "free sittings" has been taken as including sittings merely *unlet*, and not confined to sittings specially and permanently set apart for the use of the poorer classes. In the case of the Church of England, a correction (as explained in the Appendix) was made for the erroneous construction of the question; so that the number of sittings now assigned to that community as "free," will probably express with tolerable accuracy the accommodation provided by the Church of England expressly for the poor; but, no materials existing for a similar correction in the case of Nonconformist chapels, the statement of free sittings given in the Tables as provided in such chapels will be subject to this drawback. So that, probably, the view presented in these Tables of the means of worship specially provided for the poor is somewhat too favourable. However, taking it subject to this reservation, the result of the information is as follows: out of the total of 10,212,563 sittings, 8,390,464 were distinguished into the two classes of "free" and "appropriated," while the remaining 1,822,099 were not distinguished at all. Of the 8,390,464 which were distinguished, 3,947,871 were described as *free*, and 4,443,093 were described as *appropriated*. If, therefore, we assume that the undescribed 1,822,099 were apportioned between the two classes in the same degree as were the 8,390,464 which were properly described, the estimated statement as to all the sittings will be thus:—

Free sittings - - - -	4,804,595
Appropriated sittings - -	5,407,968
Total -	10,212,563

But here again, of course, the element of *distribution* is important in determining how far these 4,804,595 free sittings are available to those requiring them. The previous observations as to distribution, in connexion with the *total* number of sittings, seem to show that out of an apparent supply of 10,212,563, only 8,753,279 are in fact available, as being within reach of those who might use them. If, therefore, we assume that the proportion of "free" to "other" sittings is the same in one part of the country as another, it will follow that, from unequal distribution, 686,535 of the 4,804,595 free sittings will be unavailable, as being beyond the reach of those requiring them; thus leaving only 4,118,060 practically useful. Table 9., however, will convey some information of the comparative provision of free sittings in the town and rural portions of the land respectively:—

TABLE 9.

PROPORTION of FREE SITTINGS in TOWN DISTRICTS, compared with the Proportion in RURAL DISTRICTS.

	Population.	Number of Sittings.			Proportion per Cent. of Sittings which are	
		Free.	Appropriated.	Total.	Free.	Appropriated.
Town Districts *	9,229,120	1,799,879	2,327,365	4,127,244	43·6	56·4
Rural Districts †	8,698,489	3,004,716	3,080,603	6,085,319	49·4	50·6
Total - -	17,927,609	4,804,595	5,407,968	10,212,563	47·0	53·0

Provision made by each Religious Body.

Hitherto the question of accommodation has been treated as if *all* the various churches were to be accepted as appropriate contributors towards the spiritual teaching of the people. Such a view, however, can be evidently satisfactory to none; for while, with reference to *some* communities, a concord on essential points prevails to such extent that neither of them would depreciate the labours of the rest, yet certainly the differences between some bodies are so fundamental that the widest charity could not look favourably on all, nor help regarding the provision furnished by a certain few as utterly to be ignored in any estimate of the religious destitution of the country. But, of course, it is not *here* that any judgment can be given on such delicate and dubious questions. Every reader must for himself select the churches whose exertions he may think commendable and those whose efforts he may fear to be upon the whole injurious. The proper aim of this Report is merely to supply to every reader the facilities for making such selection, and for ascertaining what is the amount of accommodation afforded by each individual sect, and what the rate at which each sect, if active, is advancing.

The precise amount of the provision made by each Religious Body will be seen in Table 10.; in considering which it must, of course be recollected that a striking difference prevails between the *kind* of accommodation provided by the Church of England and that provided by many of the Dissenting bodies; the former almost always consisting of substantial fabrics and commodious pews or seats, while much of the latter is composed of rooms in dwelling houses, with temporary seats or benches. Thus, only 223 out of 14,077 places of worship in connexion with the Church of England were "not separate buildings;" while the number under this head out of 20,390 places of worship in connexion with Dissenting churches was as many as 3,285; and probably this number is below the fact, since the published statistics issued by these various communities make mention of a greater number. Not that this diminishes the value of such provision as affording opportunities of spiritual instruction: rather, perhaps, the character of this accommodation has a special fitness for the classes who avail themselves of it; but it is a fact that must be borne in mind

Apportionment of accommodation amongst the various Churches.

* The districts taken as *Town* Districts, for the purpose of this Table, are all such as contain Towns having upwards of 10,000 inhabitants.
† The districts taken as *Rural* Districts, for the purpose of this Table, are all that remain in England and Wales besides those taken as *Town* Districts.

when considering in other aspects the comparative accommodation furnished by the different churches.

This Table (10.) then, shows the *aggregate* provision made by every individual sect; and what proportion the provision made by each sect bears towards the total accommodation (58 per cent.) conceived to be essential. So that, if it be thought desirable that any particular church (the Church of England, for example,) should provide for the religious teaching of the whole community, this table will afford a view of the extent to which the provision made falls short of that which would on such a supposition be required: and so of other churches.

But, of course, the questions just discussed with reference to all the sects unitedly are equally important with respect to each sect individually: the question of *distribution* must be answered ere the true amount of accommodation can be settled; and a reference to dates, to special localities, to the

TABLE 10.

PROPORTION of ACCOMMODATION provided by each RELIGIOUS BODY.

RELIGIOUS DENOMINATIONS.	Number of Places of Worship and Sittings.		Proportion per cent. of Sittings.		RELIGIOUS DENOMINATIONS.	Number of Places of Worship and Sittings.		Proportion per cent. of Sittings.	
	Places of Worship.	Sittings.*	To Population.	To total number of Sittings provided by all Bodies.		Places of Worship.	Sittings.*	To Population.	To total number of Sittings provided by all Bodies.
PROTESTANT CHURCHES:					PROTESTANT CHURCHES—*continued.*				
Church of England -	14,077	5,317,915	29·7	52·1	Calvinistic Methodists:				
					Welsh Calvinistic Methodists -	828	211,951	1·2	2·1
Scottish Presbyterians:					*Lady Huntingdon's Connexion* -	109	38,727	·2	·4
Church of Scotland -	18	13,789	·1	·1	Sandemanians -	6	956	..	..
United Presbyterian Church -	66	31,851	·2	·3	New Church -	50	12,107	·1	·1
Presbyterian Church in England -	76	41,552	·2	·4	Brethren -	132	18,529	·1	·2
					Isolated Congregations -	539	104,481	·6	1·0
Reformed Irish Presbyterians -	1	120	..	..	Lutherans -	6	2,606	..	..
					French Protestants -	3	560	..	..
Independents - -	3244	1,067,760	6·0	10·5	Reformed Church of the Netherlands -	1	350	..	..
Baptists:					German Protestant Reformers -	1	200	..	..
General - -	93	20,539	·1	·2					
Particular -	1947	582,953	3·3	5·7	OTHER CHRISTIAN CHS.:				
Seventh Day -	2	390	..	..	Roman Catholics -	570	186,111	1·0	1 8
Scotch -	15	2,547	..	..	Greek Church -	3	291	..	..
New Connexion General	182	52,604	·3	·5	German Catholics -	1	300	..	..
Undefined -	550	93,310	·5	·9	Italian Reformers -	1	150	..	..
Society of Friends -	371	91,599	·5	·9	Catholic and Apostolic Church -	32	7,437	..	·1
Unitarians -	229	68,554	·4	·7	Latter Day Saints -	222	30,783	·2	·3
Moravians - -	32	9,305	..	·1	*Jews* - -	53	8,438	..	·1
Wesleyan Methodists:									
Original Connexion -	6579	1,447,580	8·1	14·1					
New Connexion -	297	96,964	·5	1·0					
Primitive Methodists -	2871	414,030	2·3	4·0					
Bible Christians -	482	66,834	·4	·7					
W. M. Association -	419	98,813	·5	1·0					
Independent Methodists -	20	2,263	..	..					
Wesleyan Reformers -	339	67,814	·4	·7	TOTAL - -	34,467	10,212,563	57·0†	100

* Including an estimate for defective Returns.
† This column casts only to 56·9—the remaining 0·1 per cent. belonging chiefly to the *Moravians,* the *Catholic and Apostolic Church,* and the *Jews;* neither of which bodies singly provides accommodation for so much as a tenth per cent. of the population.

frequency of services, and to the number of free sittings, must be made before we can determine, with regard to every church, its rate of progress, its peculiar strongholds, its *available* provision, and its conduct towards the *poor*. The necessary limits of this Report will not, however, suffer me to notice in this manner more than two or three great bodies.

First, the CHURCH OF ENGLAND. We have seen already that the National Church provides, in the gross, accommodation for 5,317,915 persons out of the 10,398,013 able to attend at one time a religious service. But, upon the theory of *distribution*, as explained before, 21,673 of these sittings are superfluous, being situate in districts where there is accommodation in connexion with the Established Church for a greater number than 58 per cent. of the district population*; so that, practically, the *accessible* provision made by the Established Church is enough for only 5,296,242 persons, or but 29·5 per cent. of the inhabitants of England and Wales. To enable the Church of England to provide for all the population, an additional accommodation to the extent of 5,101,771 sittings would be requisite, nearly doubling the present supply; but, probably, considering the hold which several other churches, not extremely differing from the Church of England, have upon the affections of the people, few will advocate the present necessity of so extensive an addition. There exist, however, if the previous course of argument be accurate, as many as 1,644,734 persons wholly unprovided, by the agency of any church whatever, with the means of religious worship; and to this extent, at all events, there is an urgent claim upon the Church of England for augmented effort. Without doubt, the destitute condition of this vast proportion of our countrymen appeals to the benevolence of Christians indiscriminately; but the claim for sympathy and succour is preferred with special force upon the Church of England, to whose care the spiritual welfare of these myriads is peculiarly entrusted, and whose labours for their benefit need not be limited by any courteous fear of trespassing on ground already occupied by other Christian agents. Not that this number constitutes the *only* class for whom the Church should furnish additional accommodation; doubtless, the *ill*-taught and the *wrongly*-taught demand her aid as well as the *un*-taught, but the utterly neglected evidently claim her *first* exertions; not to mention that they form a class which is much more easily defined than are the other two.

Confining our attention, therefore, to the wholly uninstructed multitude in whom the Church of England has an incontestible possession, the inquiry is suggested—Where, principally, are these claimants on her ministrations to be found? To what localities must her attention chiefly be directed, and her measures of relief applied? The previous tables have prepared us to expect that *towns*, especially *large* towns, will prove to be the scenes of most of that deplorable privation of religious means, the formidable aggregate of which has just been mentioned; and the following Table (11.) will show that this anticipation is abundantly correct.

Marginal note: Accommodation provided by the Church of England.

---

* These districts, where the Established Church alone provides room for more than could at any one time be present, are—Alresford; Beaminster; Billesdon; Bosmere; Brackley; Bridge; Bridgnorth; Brixworth; Catherington; Docking; Dorchester; Erpingham; Market Harborough; Marlborough; Melton Mowbray; Meriden; Oakham; Pershore; Romney Marsh; Samford; Skirlaugh; Steyning; Tetbury; Thakeham; Thingoe; Tisbury; Tunstead; Westhampnett; and Winchcomb.

TABLE 11.

ACCOMMODATION furnished by the CHURCH OF ENGLAND in Town and Country Districts respectively.

	Population.	Accommodation.		Proportion per cent. of Sittings to Population.	Number of Persons able to attend Worship at one time, but not provided for by any Religious Body.
		Churches.	Sittings.†		
LARGE TOWN DISTRICTS *	9,229,126	3,457	1,995,729	21·6	1,226,646
COUNTRY DISTRICTS *	8,698,489	10,620	3,322,186	38·2	415,608
ENGLAND AND WALES	17,927,609	14,077	5,317,915	29·7	1,641,254

To come to a more specific mention of localities: in Table 12. will be found a collection of districts in which the Church of England, if determined to provide for all now unprovided for, will have the hardest task.

TABLE 12.

DISTRICTS in which there is most need of further Accommodation.‡

DISTRICTS.	Number of Sittings already provided by the Church of England.	Additional Sittings required, in order to provide for those not accommodated by any Religious Body.	DISTRICTS.	Number of Sittings already provided by the Church of England.	Additional Sittings required, in order to provide for those not accommodated by any Religious Body.
20. Shoreditch	9,214	43,755	34. Rotherhithe	4,420	4,812
23. St. George-in-the-East	5,880	18,019	461. Liverpool	38,021	69,542
30. Newington	6,878	22,194	394. Birmingham	36,796	46,573
26. St. Saviour	3,717	12,017	8. St. George Hanover Square	19,590	19,405
15. Clerkenwell	5,805	21,506	472. Salford	11,163	22,969
439. Radford	2,801	8,862	471. Chorlton	15,687	32,866
31. Lambeth	22,589	45,991	14. Holborn	9,153	13,128
22. Whitechapel	10,368	26,857	465. Wigan	12,426	19,311
7. Marylebone	23,389	51,551	473. Manchester	33,216	56,674
25. Poplar	4,852	15,365	475. Oldham	12,689	21,491
24. Stepney	11,242	35,672	35. Greenwich	16,907	24,413
28. Bermondsey	5,313	15,459	4. Westminster	16,766	15,774
1. Kensington	22,506	38,046	552. Newcastle	10,865	20,692
13. Strand	6,858	13,794	29. St. George Southwark	6,345	11,840
6. St. James Westminster	5,364	11,218	17. East London	7,999	9,982
18. West London	7,331	8,723	546. Chester-le-Street	3,531	4,608
21. Bethnal Green	14,851	26,568	508. Sheffield	16,837	22,067
2. Chelsea	10,693	16,513	96. Portsea Island	12,230	15,225
16. St. Luke	6,500	15,649	85. Brighton	13,491	12,667
10. Islington	15,548	27,639	379. Wolverhampton	21,813	21,280
395. Aston	11,520	18,966	468. Bolton	20,018	23,015
12. St. Giles	9,592	15,305	462. West Derby	33,305	30,638
33. Camberwell	11,212	15,215	27. St. Olave, Southwark	4,170	3,887
393. King's Norton	5,962	8,587	194. West Ham	9,148	6,839
9. St. Pancras	32,190	45,559			
507. Ecclesall Bierlow	5,829	10,335			

* The Large Town Districts referred to in this Table are the Districts which contain Towns having more than 10,000 inhabitants: the Country Districts are the remainder of England and Wales.

† Including an estimate for defective Returns.

‡ The districts are arranged according to their destitution as compared with the population, commencing with the most destitute.

The entire list of districts in which additional accommodation is needed will be found in the SUMMARY TABLES.

Position of the Church of England in relation to other bodies.

This much as to the position of the Church of England in relation to our wholly unaccommodated population. It will now be interesting to observe the position of the Church, in different portions of the country, in relation to the other churches. In Table K., (SUMMARY TABLES, post, p. 139) is given a comparative view of the provision furnished by the Church and by Dissenting Bodies in each county of England and Wales; from which it will be seen what portions of the country are peculiar strongholds of any particular body. Dissenters most abound in *Wales, Monmouthshire, Yorkshire, Cornwall, Cheshire, Lancashire, Derbyshire, Northumberland, Nottinghamshire,* and *Bedfordshire;* in all which counties their sittings exceed in number those provided by the Church of England; while in *Wales* and *Monmouthshire* they are more than double. In all the other counties the Establishment has a preponderance,—most conspicuous in *Herefordshire, Sussex,* and *Oxfordshire,* where the sittings of the Church are more than double those of the Dissenters. The two parties are very nearly balanced in *Lincolnshire, Staffordshire, Leicestershire, Cumberland,* and *Cambridgeshire.* On the whole of England and Wales, for every 100 sittings provided by the Church of England, Dissenters furnish 93.

General rate of progress during the half century

The rate at which the Church of England is advancing in the path of self-extension, so far as this question can be settled by a reference to the dates at which existing churches were erected, is displayed in Table 13, the method of constructing which has been explained before (p. 65, where also will be found some other explanations applicable to this Table). It is probable that an inference as to the position of affairs in former times can be drawn from the dates of existing buildings with more correctness in the case of the Church of England, as the edifices are more permanent and less likely to change hands than are the buildings used by the Dissenters. Still there is a possibility that too great an amount of accommodation has been ascribed to the earlier periods. Subject to a certain degree of qualification from this cause, the Table shows that in the last half century the Church of England has increased her provision by 24 per cent.; but the rapid growth of population in the same time (101.6 per cent.) has materially altered her position as compared with the whole community; for, whereas, in 1801, she supplied accommodation for very nearly half the people (48.2 per cent.), she now contributes less than a third (29.6 per cent). The increase between 1841 and 1851, however, is very striking, being no less than 11.3 per cent., and nearly equal to the whole increase of population in that interval (12.6 per cent).

TABLE 13.

COMPARATIVE INCREASE of POPULATION and CHURCH PROVISION in the whole of ENGLAND AND WALES, during the past Half Century.

Periods.	Population at each Period.	Number of Churches and Sittings at each Period.		Rate per cent. at which the Population increased.	Rate per cent. at which the Sittings increased.	Number of Sittings to 100 People at each Period.
		Churches.	Sittings.			
1801	8,892,536	11,379	4,289,883	..	..	48.2
1811	10,164,256	11,444	4,314,386	14.3	.6	42.4
1821	12,000,236	11,558	4,357,366	18.0	1.0	36.3
1831	13,896,797	11,883*	4,481,891	15.8	2.9	32.3
1841	15,914,148	12,668	4,775,836	14.5	6.6	30.0
1851	17,927,609	14,077	5,317,915	12.6	11.3	29.7

*This number approaches very near to that returned in the Population Abstract of 1831 (viz. 11,883); and, considering that the latter number referred exclusively to separate consecrated buildings, while the number given above includes an estimate for licensed rooms, &c., it seems probable that these estimates are not far from the truth.

The rate of progress in large town districts, where the additional accommodation is so much required, will be shown in Table 14; which, if accurate, displays in a striking manner the continually increasing activity of the Church in recent times.

TABLE 14.

RATE at which CHURCH ACCOMMODATION has increased in LARGE TOWN DISTRICTS, as compared with the RATE of INCREASE in the REST of ENGLAND.

	LARGE TOWN DISTRICTS.				RESIDUE OF THE COUNTRY.			
Periods.	Population at each period.	Number of Churches and Sittings at each period.		Rate of Increase per cent. at each period.	Population at each period.	Number of Churches and Sittings at each period.		Rate of Increase per cent. at each period.	
		Churches.	Sittings.	Popu-lation.	Sit-tings.		Churches.	Sittings.	Popu-lation.	Sit-tings.
1801 -	3,608,024	2,163	1,246,702	..	..	5,284,512	9,216	2,882,983	..	..
1811 -	4,260,846	2,188	1,263,134	18·1	1·2	5,903,406	9,256	2,895,495	11·7	·4
1821 -	5,241,895	2,246	1,296,618	23·0	2·7	6,758,341	9,312	2,913,013	14·5	·6
1831 -	6,435,953	2,436	1,406,305	22·8	8·5	7,460,844	9,447	2,955,243	10·4	1·4
1841 -	7,735,136	2,784	1,607,206	20·2	14·2	8,179,012	9,884	3,091,949	9·6	4·7
1851 -	9,229,120	3,457	1,995,729	19·3	24·2	8,698,489	10,620	3,322,186	6·3	10·7

Number of services.

Pursuing still with respect to the Church of England the inquiries made already with respect to all the churches in the aggregate, the next point is—How much of the accommodation shown to have been belonging to the Church of England on the Census Sunday (viz. 14,077 churches and 5,317,915 sittings) was *available to the public* on that day? or, in other words, how many of the buildings were *open for worship* at each period of the day? The answer is, that, out of 14,077 buildings, 11,794 were open for service in the morning; 9,933 in the afternoon; and 2,439 in the evening. The number of *sittings* thus available was—Morning, 4,852,645; afternoon, 3,761,812; evening, 1,739,275. The much larger proportion of sittings to churches in the evening than in the other periods of the day is itself sufficient to suggest that the *evening* services must have been held in the *towns*, where the edifices are much larger than are those in rural districts; but the following Table (15.) shews at once the frequency with which services were held, and the influence of locality in aiding or diminishing this frequency.

TABLE 15.

FREQUENCY of SERVICES per DAY in the TOWN and COUNTRY PORTIONS of ENGLAND respectively.

	Population, 1851.	Number of Churches in which Services were held in the							TOTAL.
		Morning only.	After-noon only.	Evening only.	Morning and After-noon.	Morning and Evening.	After-noon and Evening.	Morning, After-noon, and Evening.	
Town Portion *	8,294,240	185	110	43	637	765	7	466	2,213
Country Portion - -	9,633,369	2,325	1,855	222	6,526	604	46	286	11,864
ENGLAND AND WALES }	17,927,609	2,510	1,965	265	7,163	1,369	53	752	14,077

* The " Town Portion " referred to in this Table includes *all* Towns without regard to size.

This presents a singular contrast with the usage in regard to Protestant Dissenters' services, which are generally held in the later portion, rather than the earlier, of the day. This will be seen more clearly in Table 16.

TABLE 16.

		Morning only.	After-noon only.	Evening only.	Morning and After-noon.	Morning and Evening.	After-noon and Evening.	Morning, After-noon, and Evening.	TOTAL.
TOWN PORTION	Church of England	8	5	2	29	35	..	21	100
	Dissenting Churches	5	3	5	7	45	12	23	100
COUNTRY PORTION	Church of England	19	17	2	55	5	..	2	100
	Dissenting Churches	6	10	14	8	21	27	14	100
ENGLAND AND WALES	Church of England	18	14	2	51	10	..	5	100
	Dissenting Churches	6	8	12	8	27	23	16	100

Number of Places of worship, out of every 100, in which Services were held in the

The effect of this upon the *available* number of sittings at each portion of the day is, that while the available accommodation provided by the Church of England was highest in the *morning*, lower in the *afternoon*, and lowest in the *evening*, that provided by Dissenters was highest in the *evening*, lower in the *morning*, and lowest in the *afternoon*; as will be seen by reference to the following figures:

	Sittings available in connexion with		
	Church of England.	Other Protestant English Churches.	Total Protestant English Churches.
Morning	4,852,645	3,428,665	8,281,310
Afternoon	3,761,812	2,367,379	6,129,191
Evening	1,739,275	3,855,394	5,594,669

The way to show how much (to use a familiar expression) is *got out of* their buildings by the Church of England and by Dissenters, comparatively, is to take an average 1,000 of the sittings belonging to each, and ascertain how many of them were available at each period of the day. The result is this:

Use made of their buildings by Churchmen and Dissenters comparatively.

	Sittings available (out of an average 1,000) in connexion with		
	Church of England.	Other Protestant English Churches.	Total Protestant English Churches.
Morning	912	736	830
Afternoon	708	508	614
Evening	327	837	561
TOTAL	649	690	668

So that on the whole the Dissenters make rather more of their accommodation than does the Established Church; for while the latter, in the morning and afternoon, makes use of its buildings to a greater extent than do the former (most of the Dissenting chapels being used in the afternoon for Sunday School instruction), yet the very limited extent to which the churches are thrown open for worship in the *evening*, when the chapels of Dissenters are most occupied, gives to Dissenters an enormous superiority for that part of the day, and even makes their *total* accommodation (adding the three columns together) exceed by a little the total available accommodation provided by the Church of England. That is, proportionally to the total accommodation belonging to each; for, absolutely, the Church of England had, in all three portions of the day, 10,353,732 sittings available against 9,651,438 belonging to Protestant Dissenters.

Summary view of the position occupied by the Church of England.
The general result as regards the accommodation furnished by the Church of England is that in 14,077 buildings there are 5,317,915 sittings, equal to 29·6 per cent. of the population; that, of these, 21,673 are practically superfluous as being out of the reach of any persons who could fill them; that the residue (5,296,242) is equal to the wants of only 29·5 per cent. of the population; and that, in consequence of a number of places not being open, there are only 4,852,645 sittings *available* for morning, 3,761,612 for afternoon, and 1,739,375 for evening service. — Of the total number of 5,317,915 sittings, 1,803,773 were described as "free"; and 2,123,395 as "appropriated"; 1,390,747 being altogether undescribed. — The inference to be drawn from the information as to the periods at which existing churches were erected shows a rate of progress not unsatisfactory altogether, but inadequate in *towns*.

Chief Protestant Dissenting Bodies.
The most numerous religious bodies, next to the Established Church, are the Wesleyan Methodists, the Independents or Congregationalists, and the Baptists. The first and the last of these denominations are respectively dispersed into several sections; but the Independents form a compact and undivided body. If we consider the Wesleyans and the Baptists in their aggregate combined capacity, the three denominations will contribute each as follows towards the general religious accommodation of the country:—

	Places of Worship.	Sittings.
Wesleyan Methodists	11,007	2,194,298
Independents	3,244	1,067,760
Baptists	2,789	752,343

Many of these places of worship are, however, merely *parts of buildings*, rooms in houses used as mission stations in poor neighbourhoods unable to support a regular chapel. The number mentioned in the returns as "not separate buildings" is,—Wesleyan Methodists, 2,155; Independents, 284; and Baptists, 804; but there seems to be some reason for conjecturing that these are under-statements, that the number of "separate and entire" religious edifices has been somewhat exaggerated, and the number of rooms, &c. correspondingly reduced.* The WESLEYAN METHODISTS are found in greatest

* Mr. E. Baines, in his evidence before the Select Committee on Church Rates, gave an estimate of the chapels belonging to these bodies as follows:—

	Chapels.	Preaching Stations.	Total.
Wesleyan Methodists	7130	4979	12,109
Independents	2572	1000	3572
Baptists	1943	1384	3327

force in *Cornwall, Yorkshire, Lincolnshire, Derbyshire, Durham,* and *Nottinghamshire;* their fewest numbers are in *Middlesex, Surrey, Sussex, Essex, Warwickshire,* and *Hertfordshire.* The INDEPENDENTS flourish most in *South Wales, North Wales, Essex, Dorsetshire, Monmouthshire,* and *Suffolk;* least in *Northumberland, Durham, Herefordshire,* and *Worcestershire.* The BAPTISTS are strongest in *Monmouthshire, South Wales, Huntingdonshire, Bedfordshire, Northamptonshire, Leicestershire,* and *Buckinghamshire;* weakest in *Cumberland, Northumberland, Westmorland, Cornwall, Staffordshire,* and *Lancashire.*

Increase of the Bodies during the Half Century.

The following statement, derived from the column of *dates,* will show, as far as can be gathered from that source, the rate at which each body has progressed in the present century. But great reliance cannot safely be reposed in inferences from dates in the case of dissenting places of worship, since a certain number (merely rooms) have undoubtedly, though only occupied in *recent* years for religious purposes, been returned with the date of their erection—not that of their first appropriation to such uses.* So, too, of chapels which have passed from one denomination to another: the date supplied has frequently been that of the original construction of the edifice. The effect, as explained already, is to throw upon the earlier years a number of chapels which should properly be reckoned as the offspring of our own day. The chance of possible accuracy is the probability that several places used in former times have since been discontinued. This would act as a counterpoise in some sort to the former error. Subject to whatever reservation may be thought essential, Table 17. will display the progress of these three bodies since 1801.

TABLE 17.

RATE OF INCREASE, in Decennial Periods, of the WESLEYAN METHODISTS, INDEPENDENTS, and BAPTISTS respectively, in the whole of ENGLAND and WALES.

	WESLEYAN METHODISTS. (All branches.)			INDEPENDENTS.			BAPTISTS. (All branches.)		
	Number of Places of Worship and Sittings at each Period.		Rate of Increase per cent. at each Period.	Number of Places of Worship and Sittings at each Period.		Rate of Increase per cent. at each Period.	Number of Places of Worship and Sittings at each Period.		Rate of Increase per cent. at each Period.
PERIODS.	Places of Worship.	Sittings.		Places of Worship.	Sittings.		Places of Worship.	Sittings.	
1801	825	165,000	..	914	299,792	..	652	176,692	..
1811	1465	296,800	80·0	1140	373,920	24·7	858	232,518	31·6
1821	2746	540,600	85·0	1478	484,784	29·2	1170	317,070	36·4
1831	4689	924,400	68·2	1999	655,872	35·2	1613	497,123	37·9
1841	7819	1,563,900	69·2	2606	854,768	30·4	2174	569,154	34·7
1851	11,007	2,194,298	40·3	3244	1,067,760	24·9	2789	752,343	27·7

From this it appears that neither of these bodies is advancing at a rate so rapid as formerly. But then it must also be remembered, that neither is there *room* for such a rapid increase, since the aggregate rate of increase during the half century has been so much more rapid than the increase of the population that; whereas, in 1801, the number of sittings provided for every 1,000 persons was—by Wesleyans 18, by Independents 34, and by Baptists 20; in 1851, the provision was—by Wesleyans 123, by Independents 59, and by Baptists 42.

---

* Instances of this may be seen in the case of the Wesleyan Reformers: 111 of their places of worship being returned as erected prior to 1841, although the movement out of which the party originated did not commence till 1849. So, the *Primitive Methodists,* who did not appear till after 1810, have returned 222 of the chapels before that period; the *Bible Christians,* who arose in 1815, return 27 chapels as erected before 1811; and the *Wesleyan Methodist Association* (which was formed in 1836) reports 86 chapels as existing prior to 1831. In the Table (17.) a correction has been made for these conspicuous errors; and the chapels have been distributed over the period subsequent to the formation of these sects.

We have seen how far the Christian churches generally and the Church of England in particular provide for the religious teaching of the masses in large towns. A similar view of the achievements of the three important bodies named above is presented in Table (18).

TABLE (18).

COMPARATIVE VIEW of the ACCOMMODATION in Rural and Large Town Districts, provided by the WESLEYAN METHODISTS, INDEPENDENTS, and BAPTISTS respectively.

	WESLEYAN METHODISTS.			INDEPENDENTS.			BAPTISTS.		
	Number of Places of Worship and Sittings.		Propor-tion per cent. of Sittings to Popu-lation.	Number of Places of Worship and Sittings.		Propor-tion per cent. of Sittings to Popu-lation.	Number of Places of Worship and Sittings.		Propor-tion per cent. of Sittings to Popu-lation.
	Places of Worship.	Sittings.		Places of Worship.	Sittings.		Places of Worship.	Sittings.	
Large Town Districts -}	3050	896,372	9·7	936	454,729	4·9	839	318,013	3·5
Country Dis-tricts - -}	7957	1,297,926	14·9	2308	613,031	7·1	1950	434,330	5·0
England and Wales - -}	11,007	2,194,296	12·2	3244	1,067,760	6·0	2789	752,343	4·2

With respect to the use which these three bodies made of the accommodation they possessed, it will be found, that out of a total number of 11,007 places of worship belonging to the various sections of *Wesleyan Methodists*, only 4,990 were open for morning worship, 6,796 in the afternoon, and 8,930 in the evening. The *Independents*, out of a total of 3,244 places of worship, opened 2,261 in the morning, 1,406 in the afternoon, and 2,539 in the evening. The *Baptists*, out of 2,789 places of worship, had morning service in 2,055, afternoon service in 1,550, and evening service in 2,127. A general view of the extent to which these bodies severally use their chapels will be seen in the following Table (19).

TABLE (19).

EXTENT to which the ACCOMMODATION provided by the WESLEYAN METHODISTS, INDEPENDENTS, and BAPTISTS respectively, is made available.

	Absolute Number of Places of Worship and Sittings.		Number of Places open for Worship at each period of the day; and Number of Sittings thus available.						Number of Sittings available out of every 1,000 provided.		
	Places of Wor-ship.	Sittings.*	Places of Worship.			Sittings.*					
			Morn-ing.	After-noon.	Even-ing.	Morn-ing.	After-noon.	Even-ing.	Morn-ing.	After-noon.	Even-ing.
Wesleyan Methodists }	11,007	2,194,296	4990	6796	8930	1,367,324	1,257,798	1,924,455	52	58	83
Independents	3,244	1,067,760	2261	1406	2539	901,352	447,300	861,762	85	42	83
Baptists -	2,789	752,343	2055	1550	2127	636,864	397,168	619,804	85	53	82

* Including an Estimate for defective Returns.

The number of *free* sittings provided by these denominations, and the **Free provision.**
proportion which the free sittings bear to the whole number, are as follows :

	Actual Number of Sittings.		Proportion per cent. of Free Sittings to Total Sittings.
	Total.	Free.*	
Wesleyan Methodists - - -	2,194,298	1,066,312	48·6
Independents - - -	1,067,760	438,211	41·0
Baptists - - -	752,343	377,571	50·2

This, however, must be taken, subject to the possibility already hinted, that under the term of *free* sittings may be included sittings merely *unlet*.

Next to these three denominations of Dissenters † come, in the order of **Minor Protestant** magnitude, the *Calvinistic Methodists*, divided into two classes, the Welsh and **Churches.** the English—the latter being known as the *Countess of Huntingdon's Connexion*. Together they supply 250,678 sittings, mostly in Wales. The remaining Protestant sects thus range themselves :

	Places of Worship.		Sittings.
Society of Friends -	- 371	-	91,559
Scottish Presbyterians	- 160	-	86,692
Unitarians - -	- 229	-	68,554
Brethren - -	- 132	-	18,529
New Church - -	- 50	-	12,107
Moravians - -	- 32	-	9,305
Sandemanians -	- 6	-	956
Reformed Irish Presbyterians	1	-	120

And then a great crowd of what are called, for want of a better term, " Isolated Congregations," refusing to acknowledge connexion with any particular sect, make up together as many as 539 places of worship with 104,481 sittings.

In the aggregate, the Protestant Dissenting churches of England provide **Aggregate pro-** accommodation for 4,657,422 persons, or for 26 per cent. of the population, **vision made by** and 45·6 per cent. of the aggregate provision of the country. The proportion **Dissenting** of this accommodation which is *available* at each period of the day is—*morning,* **Churches.** 3,428,665 sittings, ; *afternoon,* 2,367,379 sittings ; *evening,* 3,855,394 sittings ; making a total, at all three portions of the day, of 9,651,438 sittings.

Of the Christian churches not Protestant, the most important is the ROMAN **OTHER CHRIS-** CATHOLIC, which provides 570 places of worship, containing 186,111 sittings. **TIAN CHURCHES:** This, however, represents a greater amount of accommodation than would the **Roman Catholics.** same number of sittings in a Protestant body, inasmuch as, by the custom of Roman Catholic worship, many persons stand. ‡ Out of these 186,111 sittings

---

* Of the total number of sittings belonging to these Bodies there were undistinguished as to this point—170,268 belonging to the Wesleyan Methodists ; 86,032 belonging to the Independents ; and 59,571 belonging to the Baptists. It has been assumed that the proportion of " Free" to " Appropriated" is the same amongst these undescribed sittings as amongst those actually distinguished.
 † Some of the Wesleyan Methodists, however, though far from conforming with the Church of England, object to be called Dissenters from it.
 ‡ There was a column in the Schedule for the numbers who could be accommodated by standing ; but it was thought better not to make use of it in the Abstracts. The above number therefore (186,111) will be strictly *sittings*.

there were, in the churches which were *open* on the Census Sunday as many as 175,309 (or 94 per cent.) in the *morning*, 103,042 (or 55 per cent.) in the *after-noon*, and 89,258 (or 48 per cent.) in the *evening*. The number of sittings described as *free* is 77,200; the number mentioned as *appropriated* is 73,210, and 35,701 are undistinguished.—The following Table shows in what parts of the country the Roman Catholics most and least abound.

TABLE. 20.

ACCOMMODATION provided by the ROMAN CATHOLIC CHURCH in each County of England, in Wales, and in certain large Towns.

COUNTIES.	Number of Places of Worship and Sittings.		Proportion per Cent. of Sittings to Population.	COUNTIES AND LARGE TOWNS.	Number of Places of Worship and Sittings.		Proportion per Cent. of Sittings to Population.
	Places of Worship.	Sittings.*			Places of Worship.	Sittings.*	
ENGLAND AND WALES	570	186,111	1·0	Rutlandshire	..	..	..
				Shropshire	11	1837	·8
Bedfordshire	1	21	..	Somersetshire	8	2382	·5
Berkshire	6	1192	·7	Staffordshire	34	9756	1·6
Buckinghamshire	4	527	·3	Suffolk	4	544	·1
Cambridgeshire	3	350	·2	Surrey	14	8046	1·2
Cheshire	17	6196	1·3	Sussex	8	1216	·4
Cornwall	7	1445	·4	Warwickshire	26	6891	1·5
Cumberland	8	2877	1·5	Westmorland	2	700	1·2
Derbyshire	8	2454	·9	Wiltshire	3	790	·3
Devonshire	8	1250	·2	Worcestershire	12	2834	1·0
Dorsetshire	7	1752	·9	Yorkshire	65	16,420	·9
Durham	20	4816	1·2				
Essex	9	2354	·7	North Wales	5	885	·2
Gloucestershire	14	4109	·9	South Wales	7	1938	·3
Hampshire	13	2904	·7				
Herefordshire	5	900	·8	London	85	24,355	1·0
Hertfordshire	4	455	·3	Liverpool	16	14,532	3·9
Huntingdonshire	..	..	..	Manchester	7	6850	2·2
Kent	13	3651	·6	Birmingham	4	1549	·7
Lancashire	114	58,747	2·9	Leeds	2	1220	·7
Leicestershire	12	2537	1·1	Bristol	6	2354	1·7
Lincolnshire	13	2333	·6	Sheffield	1	950	·7
Middlesex	32	17,846	·9	Wolverhampton	4	1896	1·6
Monmouthshire	8	2764	1·7	Bradford	1	380	·4
Norfolk	6	1456	·8	Newcastle	2	1744	2·0
Northamptonshire	6	705	·3	Hull	1	628	·7
Northumberland	20	4914	1·6	Bath	3	770	1·4
Nottinghamshire	5	1982	·7	Brighton	1	400	·6
Oxfordshire	8	1335	·8	Oldham	1	490	·9

Increase of the Roman Catholics during the half century.
The rate at which the Roman Catholics have increased in the last half century will best be seen by reference to the statistics for the period since 1824, given *ante*, page 44. instead of relying upon the doubtful indication supplied by the dates at which existing edifices were erected. From this source it appears that in 1824 there were 346 Roman Catholic chapels in England and Wales, while in 1853 the number had increased to 616. If we assume that the proportion of sittings to a chapel was the same (314) at each of these periods as in 1851, the number in 1824 would be 108,644, and the number in 1853 would be 193,424;

* Including an Estimate for defective Returns.

the rate of increase in the 30 years being 87·2 per cent. During very nearly the same interval (viz. from 1821 to 1851) the sittings of all Protestant bodies, unitedly, increased from 5,985,842 to 9,982,533, the rate being 66·8 per cent. For every 1000 of the population, the Roman Catholics provided 8 sittings in 1824, and 10 sittings in 1853. The Protestants provided for every 1000 persons, 499 sittings in 1821, and 557 sittings in 1851. The proportion of sittings belonging to Roman Catholics to those belonging to Protestants was 1·8 to 100 at the former period, and 1·9 to 100 at the latter.

The only other prominent sect which appears to possess a noticeable degree of influence, is the "Church of the Latter Day Saints," known better by the name of *Mormons*. Within the short period since the introduction of this singular creed, as many as 222 chapels or stations have been established, with accommodation for 30,783 worshippers or hearers. The activity of the disciples of this faith is evidenced by the frequency with which they occupy these meeting-places: out of the total number of 222, as many as 147 (or 66 per cent.) were open in the morning, 187 (or 84 per cent.) were open in the afternoon, and 193 (or 87 per cent.) were open in the evening. Comparison with similar statistics of the other churches will show that this is much above the average frequency of services. — *Mormons.*

The summary result of this inquiry with respect to accommodation is, that there are in England and Wales 10,398,013 persons able to be present at one time in buildings for religious worship. Accommodation, therefore, for that number (equal to 58 per cent. of the population) is required. The *actual* accommodation in 34,467 churches, chapels, and out-stations is enough for 10,212,563 persons. But this number, after a deduction, on account of ill-proportioned distribution, is reduced to 8,753,279, a provision equal to the wants of only 49 per cent. of the community. And further, out of these 8,753,279 sittings, a certain considerable number are rendered *unavailable* by being in churches or chapels which are *closed* throughout some portion of the day when services are usually held. There is therefore wanted an additional supply of 1,644,734 sittings, if the population is to have an extent of accommodation which shall be undoubtedly sufficient.* These sittings, too, must be provided *where* they are wanted; *i. e.* in the *large town districts* of the country,—more especially in London. To furnish this accommodation would probably require the erection of about 2,000 churches and chapels; which, in towns, would be of larger than the average size. This is assuming that all churches and sects may contribute their proportion to the work, and that the contributions of each may be regarded as by just so much diminishing the efforts necessary to be made by other churches. If, as is probable, this supposition be considered not altogether admissible, there will be required a further addition to these 2,000 structures; the extent of which addition must depend upon the views which may be entertained respecting what particular sects should be entirely disregarded. — *General result as to accommodation.*

Of the total existing number of 10,212,563 sittings, the Church of England contributes 5,317,915, and the other churches, together, 4,894,648.

If we inquire what steps are being taken by the Christian church to satisfy this want, there is ample cause for hope in the history of the twenty years just terminated. In that interval the growth of population, which before had far — *What is being done to supply existing wants?*

* It may be said that this contemplates an optimist condition of society; but it has been thought better to take as a standard the actual *wants* of the people, rather than their probable conduct. Readers can make their own deductions.

outstripped the expansion of religious institutions, has been less, considerably, than the increase of accommodation,—people having multiplied by 29 per cent., while sittings have increased by 46 per cent.; so that the number of sittings to 100 persons, which was only *fifty* in 1831, had risen to *fifty-seven* in 1851. And although this increase has not been confined to one particular church, it will scarcely less perhaps be matter for rejoicing; since, no doubt, the augmentation has occurred in bodies whose exertions cannot fail to have a beneficial influence, whatever the diversities of ecclesiastical polity by which, it may be thought, the value of these benefits in some degree is lessened. Doubtless, this encouraging display of modern zeal and liberality is only part of a continuous effort which—the Christian Church being now completely awakened to her duty—will not be relaxed till every portion of the land and every class of its inhabitants be furnished with at least the *means and opportunities* of worship. The field for future operations is distinctly marked: the *towns*, both from their present actual destitution and from their incessant and prodigious growth, demand almost a concentration of endeavours—the combined exertions of the general Church. Without an inclination for religious worship—certainly without ability to raise religious structures—the inhabitants of crowded districts of populous cities are as differently placed as possible from their suburban neighbours, who, more prosperous in physical condition, possess not only the desire to have, but also the ability to get, an adequate provision for religious culture. New churches, therefore, spring up naturally in those new neighbourhoods in which the middle classes congregate; but, all spontaneous efforts being hopeless in the denser districts peopled by the rank and file of industry, no added churches, evidently, can be looked for there, except as the result of *missionary* labours acting from without. No agency appears more suited to accomplish such a work than that of those societies, possessed by most religious bodies, which collect into one general fund the offerings of the members of each body for church or chapel extension. The Established Church is represented in this way by the Incorporated Society, the Metropolis Churches' Fund, and by several diocesan societies; the Independents, and the Baptists also, each possess their Building Funds; but the support which these societies receive must be enormously increased if any vigorous attempt is to be made to meet and conquer the emergency. Compared with the amount contributed for *foreign* missionary operations, the support received by organized societies for church and chapel extension here at home appears conspicuously inadequate*. The hope may probably be reasonably entertained, that while the contributions to the former work continue undiminished, the disparity between the treatment of the two may speedily disappear.

More frequent services.

Next only in importance to the question, how new churches are to be provided, is the question whether any increased advantage may be got from existing structures. When it is considered that there are probably as many as 25,000 edifices specially devoted to religious worship,—that the vast majority of these unfold their doors on one day only out of every seven,—that many even then are only opened for perhaps a couple of hours,—there seems to be a prodigality of means as compared with ends which forcibly suggests the idea of waste. Of course, in many cases this cannot be helped, and nothing more

	Annual Income.		Annual Income.
	£		£
* Society for the Propagation of the Gospel in Foreign Parts	83,000	Incorporated Society for Church Building	16,000
Church Missionary Society	120,000	Congregational Chapel Building Society	3,365
London Missionary Society	65,000		
Baptist Missionary Society	19,000	Baptist Building Fund	795

Of course, some addition (probably as much as 20,000*l.*) must be made to the sums here mentioned as applicable to Church Building, on account of Diocesan and other local funds; but even allowing for this addition, the contrast will be sufficiently striking.

could be accomplished than is done; but where the population gathers thickly, as in towns and cities, it is thought that greater frequency of services would answer nearly the same purpose as a multiplication of churches. If, where *two* services are held, a *third* should be established, with the special understanding that the working class alone is expected to attend, and that the sittings upon that occasion are to be all free, it is considered that the buildings would be worthily employed, and that accommodation would be thus afforded to probably a third beyond the present ordinary number. So, too, upon *week-days*, it is thought that many opportunities are lost of attracting to religious services no inconsiderable number of those who rarely or never enter church or chapel on a Sunday. Week evening services, undoubtedly, are common now; but they are principally of a character adapted mainly to the regular attendants, and they generally terminate about the hour at which the workmen leave their labour. It appears that in the Church of England daily prayers are read in somewhat upwards of 600 churches in England and Wales.*

Amongst the Dissenters—who attribute no peculiar sanctity to buildings in which worship is conducted, nor regard a consecrated or other specially appropriated edifice as necessary for public service—an opinion has been gaining ground in favour of the plan of holding services in such of the public halls and rooms as are of general use for other purposes. To these, it is expected, working men will much more readily resort than to the formal chapel. The experiment has been repeatedly tried : it is reported with complete success.† *[marginal note: Religious services in secular buildings.]*

Whether, by these various means,—the erection of more churches—the increased employment of the present buildings—and the use of places not expressly dedicated to religious worship; whether by an increase of *accommodation* merely, without other measures, the reluctant people can be gained to practical Christianity, is what will be in some degree decided by inquiring, next, what number of *attendants*, on the Census-Sunday, used the accommodation actually then existing. *[marginal note: Would an increase of accommodation merely be sufficient?]*

---

* Masters's Guide to the Daily Prayers of England, Wales, and Scotland.
† Exeter Hall, during the period of the Exhibition, was engaged for this purpose, and was generally crowded with hearers. Recently (in February and March, 1853) a series of such services was held at Norwich, in St. Andrew's Hall, with similar results. Other instances are not uncommon.

2. ATTENDANCE.

Attendance at religious services a better test of religious disposition, than amount of accommodation.

Thus far, in considering the aspect of the English people towards religious institutions, our regard has been directed wholly to that proof of the existence or the absence of religious feeling, which is furnished by the ample or inadequate supply of the means of public worship. It is scarcely, however, with this evidence that one, desirous of obtaining a correct idea of the extent to which religious sentiments prevail among the masses of our population, would be satisfied. For, though the existence of a *small* provision, only may be fairly taken as a proof of feeble spiritual life, since a people really governed by religious influences will not long remain without the means of outward worship; yet the converse of this proposition cannot be maintained, since much of the provision at the service of one generation may be owing to the piety of a former, whose religious zeal may not perhaps have been inherited by its posterity along with its rich legacy of churches. Even, too, a great *contemporary* addition to the number of religious edifices does not positively indicate the prevalence of a religious spirit in the body of the people: it may merely show the presence of a missionary spirit in a portion of the general Church. An inquirer, therefore, anxious to discover more precisely the extent to which religious sentiments pervade the nation, would desire to know not merely the amount of accommodation *offered* to the people, but also what proportion of the means at their command is actually *used*. A knowledge, therefore, of the number of ATTENDANTS on the various services of public worship is essential.

Number of attendants to be compared both with accommodation and population.

We have seen that, in the gross, there are 34,467 places of worship in England and Wales, with 10,212,563 sittings. But, as many of these places of worship were closed upon each portion of the day, and the sittings in them consequently unavailable, it is with the provision in the *open* buildings that we must compare the number of attendants. In those open for the *morning* service there were (including an estimate for defective returns) 8,498,520 sittings; in those open in the afternoon, 6,267,928 sittings; in those open in the evening, 5,723,000 sittings. The total number of *attendants* (also including estimates for omissions) was, in the morning, 4,647,482; in the afternoon, 3,184,135; in the evening, 3,064,449. From this it seems that, taking the three services together, less than half of the accommodation actually available is used. But here, again, the question of *distribution* is important. For if, in any locality, the amount of accommodation existing should be larger than that required, we cannot expect to find the number of attendants bearing there so large a proportion to the sittings as in other localities where the accommodation may be insufficient. There may really be a better attendance in a district where the churches are half empty than in one in which they are completely filled: that is, a greater number out of a given population may attend in the former case than in the latter. Therefore, before we can assume a lax attendance in particular districts, the number of the *population* must be brought into account. To prove a disregard of spiritual ordinances, there must be exhibited not merely a considerable number of vacant sittings, but also a corresponding number of persons by whom, if so disposed, those sittings might be occupied. But if, according to the previous computation, 58 per cent. of the population is the utmost that can ever be attending a religious service at one time, it is evident that where, as in some districts, the available accommodation is sufficient for a *greater* number, there must *necessarily* exist, whatever the devotional spirit of the people, an excess of sittings over worshippers. If, for example, we refer to the City of London (within the walls), which, with a population of 55,932, has sittings for as many as 45,779—or for 13,339 more than could possibly, at any one time, attend—it is obvious that a great many sittings must inevitably be unoccupied; and this without regard to the question whether, in fulfilling their religious duties, the inhabitants be zealous or remiss. The best plan, therefore, seems to be, to compare the attendants, in the first place, with the population; and then, secondly, with the sittings. The former view will give us an approximate idea of the extent to which religion has a practical influence over the community—exhibiting the numbers who appreciate or neglect religious services; the latter view will show in what degree neglect, if proved, may be occasioned or excused by the supply of insufficient means of worship. If, for instance, in a certain district, the proportion of the population found attending some religious service should be small, while at the same time there should be within the district ample room for the remainder: this would show conclusively that in that district a considerable number of the people were without religious habits, and indifferent to public worship. And the same conclusion might be drawn, although the actual provision were inadequate, if even this inadequate accommodation were but sparely used.

Returning, then, to the total of England and Wales, and comparing the number of actual attendants with the number of persons *able* to attend, we find that out of 10,398,013 (58 per cent. of the total population) who would be at liberty to worship at one period of the day, there were actually worshipping but 4,647,482 in the morning, 3,184,135 in the afternoon, and 3,064,449 in the evening. So that, taking any one service of the day, there were actually attending public worship less than half the number who, as far as physical impediments prevented, *might* have been attending. In the *morning* there were absent, without physical hindrance, 5,750,531; in the *afternoon*, 7,213,878;* in the *evening*, 7,333,564. There exist no *data* for determining how many persons attended twice, and how many three times on the Sunday; nor, consequently, for deciding how many altogether attended on *some* service of the day; but if we suppose that half of those attending service in the afternoon had not been present in the morning, and that a third of those attending service in the evening had not been present at either of the previous services, we should obtain a total of 7,261,032 separate persons who attended service either once or oftener upon the Census-Sunday.† But as the number who would be able to attend at *some* time of the day is more than 58 per cent. (which is the estimated number able to be present *at one and the same time*)—probably reaching 70 per cent.—it is with this latter number (12,549,326) that this 7,261,032 must be compared, and the result of such comparison would lead to the conclusion

Number of non-attendants.

---

* Many of these, no doubt, were teachers and scholars engaged in Sunday schools; which partake, indeed, of the character of religious services. The number of Sunday scholars on the Census-Sunday was about 2,280,000; and the number of teachers was about 302,000. Of these, a considerable proportion must have been engaged during the time for Afternoon service.

† The calculations in the latter part of this paragraph are mainly conjectural. The extent to which the congregations meeting at different portions of the day are composed of the *same persons*, can be ascertained only by a series of observations not yet made, so far as I am aware. We know, from the actual Returns, that the number could not be less than 4,647,482 (the number of attendants in the morning), nor more than 10,896,066 (the aggregate of all the services); and these are the limits within which must lie the number of attendants at *some* service. The mean of these extremes is 7,771,774, which is not considerably different from the result of the previous estimates. Opinions have been expressed that the number of individual *attendants* is about *two thirds* of the number of *attendances*. The latter number is, as above, 10,896,066; two-thirds of which are 7,264,044. Another supposition is, that, taking the number attending the most frequented service in each church or chapel, the addition of *one-third* would give the number of persons probably attending the other services of the day but not *that*. From Table N. (*post* p. 142) we see that the former number (including Sunday Scholars attending service) is 6,356,222, which, increased by a third, amounts to 8,474,693. From this of course a considerable deduction must be made on account of those places of worship in which only *one* service was held; the number of such places being as many as 9,915. So that there appears to be some ground for thinking that the computation hazarded above is not far from the fact.—I believe that 70 per cent. of the total population may be taken as a fair estimate of the number able to worship at one period *or another* of the day.

G 4

that, upon the Census-Sunday, 5,288,294 persons, able to attend religious worship once at least, neglected altogether so to do.*

Is there sufficient accommodation for the non-attendants? This being then the number of persons failing to attend religious services, we now inquire how far this negligence may be ascribed to an inadequate accommodation. If there were not in all the various churches, chapels, and stations, *room* for more than those who actually attended, it is clear there would be no sufficient reason for imputing to the rest indifference to public ordinances : they might answer, they were quite inclined to worship, but were not provided with the means. Upon the other hand, if sittings, within reach of any given population, and available for their acceptance, were provided in sufficient number to accommodate (say) 58 per cent., it is no less manifest that absence in such case could only be attributed to non-appreciation of the service. In the latter case, however, the provision made must evidently be *within the reach* of the people and *open to their use*—accessible and available; for otherwise a portion of it might as well not be at all. As said before, a surplus of accommodation in one district cannot be regarded as supplying a deficiency in another. Therefore, before we can,—in order to compute the numbers who neglect religious worship, spite of opportunities for doing so,—compare attendance with accommodation, we must, when dealing with the whole of England in the gross, deduct from the total number of sittings, the number which in any district may exist *above* the number requisite for 58 per cent. of the district-population;—the excess beyond that number being, if the supposition is correct, entirely unavailing both to the dwellers in the district and to the inhabitants of other districts : to the former, since no more than 58 per cent. could possibly attend ; to the latter, because out of reach. The number thus assumed to be superfluous is 1,459,284; and this deducted from the total number (10,212,563) leaves a residue of 8,753,279. This will be the number of sittings which, *if all the churches and chapels were open*, might be occupied at once each Sunday if the people within reach of them were willing; and whatever deficiency is shown by a comparison between this number and the total number of attendants may be safely asserted to consist of persons who, possessing the facilities, are destitute of the inclination to attend religious worship. The gross number of attendants being 4,647,482 in the morning, 3,184,135 in the afternoon, and 3,064,449 in the evening, it would follow, if the places of worship were all open, that 4,105,797 persons were, without excuse of inability, absent from the morning, 5,569,144 from the afternoon, and 5,688,830 from the evening service. But, as the churches and chapels are *not* all open every Sunday at each period of the day ; 10,798 with 1,714,043 sittings being closed in the morning, 13,096 with 3,944,635 sittings being closed in the afternoon, and 16,412 with 4,489,563 sittings being closed in the evening ; we are met by the question whether we should consider that the churches are closed because no congregations could be gathered, or that the people are absent because the churches are closed. If the former, the attendants may be properly compared with the total number of sittings in *all* places of worship (after making the deduction for unequal distribution) whether open or not ; but, if the latter, the attendants cannot be compared with any but the number of sittings in the places of worship *open* at each period of the day. Perhaps as this is a question not to be decided here, the better course will be to make the comparison upon *both* hypotheses. The result will be observed in Table 21.

---

* It must not, however, be supposed that this 5,288 294 represents the number of *habitual* neglecters of religious services. This number is absent every Sunday; but it is not always composed of the *same persons.* Some may attend *occasionally* only ; and if the number of such occasional attendants be considerable, there will always be a considerable number of absentees *on any given Sunday.* The number of *habitual* non-attendants cannot be precisely stated from these Tables.

TABLE 21.

	1. All Places of Worship.				2. Places of Worship *open.*			
	Morn-ing.	After-noon.	Even-ing.	Total.	Morn-ing.	After-noon.	Even-ing.	Total.
Total Number of Sittings within reach *	8,753,279	8,753,279	8,753,279	26,259,837	8,322,066†	6,192,061†	5,712,670†	20,226,797 †
Total Number of Persons able to attend	10,396,013	10,396,013	10,396,013	12,549,326 ‡	10,396,013	10,396,013	10,396,013	12,549,326 ‡
Number of Sittings within reach {Occupied	4,647,482	3,184,135	3,064,449	10,896,066	4,647,482	3,184,135	3,064,449	10,896,066
{Unoccupied	4,105,797	5,569,144	5,688,830	15,363,711	3,674,584	3,007,926	2,648,221	9,330,731
Number of Persons able to attend {Attending	4,647,482	3,184,135	3,064,449	7,261,032 ‡	4,647,482	3,184,135	3,064,449	7,261,032 ‡
{Absent	5,750,531	7,213,878	7,333,564	15,288,294 ‡	5,750,531	7,213,878	7,333,564	15,288,294 ‡
Excess or Deficiency of unoccupied Sittings as compared with the Number of Persons absent {Excess	..	..	..	10,075,417	..	..	..	4,042,437
{Deficiency	1,644,734	1,644,734	1,644,734	..	2,075,947	4,205,952	4,685,343	..

This shows that if all who were absent from each service desired to attend that service, there would not be room for them on either supposition. On the first hypothesis (assuming that the buildings would all be open if the people wished to attend), there would be wanted 1,644,734 additional sittings; and the number of those who, in excuse for non-attendance, might plead absence of accommodation would be just that number; leaving, however, destitute of that excuse, 4,105,797 persons who neglected morning service, 5,569,144 who neglected afternoon service, and 5,688,830 who neglected evening service. On the second hypothesis (assuming that the churches closed are closed from necessary circumstances, and could not be opened even if it were desired), there would be wanted an additional supply of sittings to the extent of 2,575,947 in the morning, 4,205,952 in the afternoon, and 4,685,343 in the evening; and the number of persons who could plead the above excuse for non-attendance would be just as many. But this assumes that at *every* service 58 per cent. of the population would attend: a state of things which, however desirable, is scarcely likely to be realized. If we refer to the fourth and eighth columns of the Table, we shall see the computed number (7,261,032) who at the close of every Sunday can say that they have during the day attended a religious service; some thrice, some twice, but all at least *once.* As this would leave 5,288,294 *altogether absent* every Sunday, and as the aggregate of sittings is in the one case 26,259,837, and in the other 20,226,797, of which only 10,896,066 would be occupied; it is clear that, unless they should all select the *same service,* there is ample room for all the 70 per cent. who, according to the estimate, are able to attend at least *once* upon the Sunday. So that it is tolerably certain that the 5,288,294 who every Sunday, neglect religious ordinances, do so of their own free choice, and are not compelled to be absent on account of a deficiency of sittings.

* See *ante,* page 88.   † See *ante,* page 87.
‡ These numbers are not the aggregate of the three preceding columns; but the computed number of separate persons who either attended at *some* service on the Census-Sunday, or were *altogether* absent.

Nor will this conclusion be invalidated by a reference to the portion of accommodation which is *free*. We have seen that out of a total of 10,212,563 sittings, 4,804,595 are thus described; and the very fact that the others are, in greatest measure, *paid* for (and therefore likely to be used), appears to indicate that it is principally these "free" sittings that are thus unoccupied.

If therefore we were to measure the required additional supply of accommodation by the extent of the present demand for it, the use now made of our existing provision, as revealed by these few statements of attendance, would appear to indicate that very little more is wanted. The considerable number of available sittings which are every Sunday totally unoccupied, might be adduced as proof so manifest of unconcern for spiritual matters on the part of a great portion of the people, that, until they are impressed with more solicitude for their religious culture, it is useless to erect more churches. It will probably, however, be considered that, from various causes, many persons might attend new churches who would never attend the old; and that church and chapel extension is the surest means of acting on the neighbouring population—bringing into contact with it an additional supply of Christian agency, intent upon securing an increased observance of religious ordinances.

Comparative frequency of attendance in Town and Country.

The frequency and regularity with which the people should attend religious services might naturally be expected to depend considerably upon locality. In rural, thinly-peopled districts, where the distances to be traversed are often long, with many impediments to locomotion, we should not anticipate so constant an attendance as in towns, where churches are within an easy walk of everybody's house. It seems, however, that facts will scarcely justify this supposition. The following Table (22.) will exhibit the comparative proportion of attendants in the thinly and the densely populated portions of the land:—

TABLE 22.

	Actual Number of Attendants (including an Estimate for defective Returns).			Proportion per cent. of Attendants to Population.			Proportion per cent. of Attendants to the Total Number of Sittings.		
	Morning.	Afternoon.	Evening.	Morning.	Afternoon.	Evening.	Morning.	Afternoon.	Evening.
Rural Districts * -	2,444,539	2,213,995	1,547,203	28·1	25·5	17·8	40·1	36·4	25·4
Large Town Districts * - -	2,202,943	970,140	1,517,246	23·9	10·5	15·3	53·4	23·5	36·8

Number of Attendants in connexion with each religious body.

The estimated number of attendants at the service of *each religious body* will be found in the SUMMARY TABLES (*post*, page 109). The statement given there supplies the number attending at each period of the day; and if we may accept the supposition previously hazarded, that one-half of those attending in the afternoon and one-third of those attending in the evening are entirely new, the 7,261,032 individual persons who attended *some* religious service on the Census-Sunday will be thus distributed among the various bodies: (Table 23.)

---

* The Large Town Districts are those containing Towns of more than 10,000 inhabitants; the Rural Districts are the residue of the country.

TABLE 23.

	Estimated Total Number of Attendants.	Proportion per 1000.			Estimated Total Number of Attendants.	Proportion per 1000.	
		Of the Population.	Of the Number of all Attendants of all Denominations.			Of the Population.	Of the Number of Attendants of all Denominations.
PROTESTANT CHURCHES :				PROTESTANT CHURCHES —continued.			
Church of England -	3,773,474	210	520	Calvinistic Methodists :			
Scottish Presbyterians :				*Welsh Calvinistic Methodists*	151,046	8	21
Church of Scotland -	8,712	1	1	*Lady Huntingdon's Connexion* -	29,679	2	4
United Presbyterian Church -	23,207	1	3	Sandemanians -	587	..	..
Presbyterian Church in England -	28,212	2	4	New Church -	7,062	..	1
				Brethren - -	10,414	1	1
Independents - -	793,142	44	109	Isolated Congregations -	63,572	4	9
Baptists :				Lutherans - -	1,234	..	..
General - -	12,323	1	2	French Protestants -	291	..	..
Particular -	471,283	26	65	Reformed Church of the Netherlands -	70	..	..
Seventh Day -	52	..	..	German Protestant Reformers -	140	..	..
Scotch - -	1,246	..	..				
New Connexion General -	40,027	2	5	OTHER CHRISTIAN CHS.			
Undefined -	63,047	4	9	Roman Catholics	305,393	17	42
Society of Friends -	18,172	1	3	Greek Church -	240	..	..
Unitarians - -	37,156	2	5	German Catholics -	587	..	..
Moravians - -	7,864	1	1	Italian Reformers -	20	..	..
Wesleyan Methodists :		•		Catholic and Apostolic Church - -	4,908	..	1
Original Connexion -	907,313	51	125	Latter Day Saints -	18,800	1	3
New Connexion -	61,319	3	8	*Jews* - - -	4,150	..	1
Primitive -	266,555	15	37	Total - -	7,261,032	405	1000
Bible Christians -	38,612	2	5				
Wesleyan Association	56,430	3	8				
Independent Methodists - -	1,659	..	..				
Wesleyan Reformers	53,494	3	7				

The comparative *frequency* with which the members of the various sects attended service will be found illustrated in Tables L. and M., among the Tabular Results (*post*, pp. 140, 141), from which it appears that while, in the aggregate, out of every 100 sittings, 45 are occupied in the morning, 31 in the afternoon, and 30 in the evening, considerable difference exists between the different bodies both as to the total number of their attendances, and as to the periods of the day at which they most attend. Thus, while the Table just presented shows that the Church of England has attending its three services more *persons* than all the other bodies put together, (3,773,474 against 3,487,558,) it appears from the Table on page 109, that the number of *attendances* given by the 3,773,474 persons is actually less than the number given by the 3,487,558 ; the former having attended 5,292,551 times, while the latter attended 5,603,515 times. Or, if we assume that a service, on an average, occupies *an hour and three-quarters*, it would seem that the 3,773,474 Churchmen devoted 9,261,962 hours to religious worship, (or two hours and a half each,) while the 3,487,558 Dissenters devoted 9,806,151 hours to a similar duty (or two hours and three-quarters each). If we come to particular bodies, we find from Table M. that, of those bodies whose size is sufficient to justify an inference, the

Comparative frequency of attendance in each religious body.

most assiduous in attending public worship are the *Wesleyan Reformers*—45 per cent. of their accommodation (assuming that the chapels *might* be open for three services) being used in the course of the Sunday; next to whom, in diligence, are the *Particular Baptists*, using 42 per cent. of their provision; and the scale falls gradually till we come to the *Society of Friends* who only avail themselves of 8 per cent. of their accommodation. The following List contains the principal Bodies, arranged in the order of their frequency of attendance (the *Roman Catholics*, however, being omitted, as the greater number of their services prevents comparison):

RELIGIOUS DENOMINATION.	Proportion per cent. of Attendants to Sittings.
Wesleyan Reformers	45
Particular Baptists	42
Welsh Calvinistic Methodists	41
Primitive Methodists	41
General Baptist, New Connexion	41
Moravians	39
Independents	38
Lady Huntingdon's Connexion	38
Mormons	38
Bible Christians	37
General Baptists	36
Wesleyan Original Connexion	35
„ New Connexion	34
Catholic and Apostolic Church	34
United Presbyterian Church	34
Church of England	33
Wesleyan Methodist Association	32
Brethren	32
Presbyterian Church in England	30
Church of Scotland	28
New Church	28
Unitarians	24
Jews	24
Society of Friends	8

Portions of the day at which attendants are most numerous.   With reference to the particular periods of the day preferred by different bodies, Table M. will show that the members of the Church of England choose the earlier, while the members of the principal dissenting churches choose the later portion of the Sunday for attendance at religious worship. Thus, while the number of sittings out of every 100 occupied by the former is 48 in the morning, 36 in the afternoon, and only 16 in the evening; the number, out of every 100, occupied by the other Protestant Churches in the aggregate, is 40 in the morning, 26 in the afternoon, and 45 in the evening. This fact exhibits strikingly the different social habits of the members of these bodies; and, even if we did not know as much already, would suffice to prove their difference of social station.

If must not be overlooked, when considering the amount of *afternoon* attendance, that, amongst Dissenters more especially, that period is occupied to very great extent by *Sunday-school instruction*. Of the number of children thus instructed at this portion of the day we have no account but as the total number of Sunday Scholars in attendance every Sunday is as many as 1,800,000, the number present every Sunday afternoon must be considerable. The religious knowledge thus administered to children is by no means ineffective:

probably, indeed, this mode of spiritual teaching is far better suited to a child's capacity than is the more elaborate service of the church or chapel.

The most important fact which this investigation as to attendance brings before us is, unquestionably, the alarming number of the non-attendants. Even in the least unfavorable aspect of the figures just presented, and assuming (as no doubt is right) that the 5,288,294 absent every Sunday are not always the same individuals, it must be apparent that a sadly formidable portion of the English people are habitual neglecters of the public ordinances of religion. Nor is it difficult to indicate to what particular class of the community this portion in the main belongs. The middle classes have augmented rather than diminished that devotional sentiment and strictness of attention to religious services by which, for several centuries, they have so eminently been distinguished. With the upper classes, too, the subject of religion has obtained of late a marked degree of notice, and a regular church-attendance is now ranked amongst the recognized proprieties of life. It is to satisfy the wants of these two classes that the number of religious structures has of late years so increased. But while the *labouring* myriads of our country have been multiplying with our multiplied material prosperity, it cannot, it is feared, be stated that a corresponding increase has occurred in the attendance of this class in our religious edifices. More especially in cities and large towns it is observable how absolutely insignificant a portion of the congregations is composed of artizans. They fill, perhaps, in youth, our National, British, and Sunday Schools, and there receive the elements of a religious education; but, no sooner do they mingle in the active world of labour than, subjected to the constant action of opposing influences, they soon become as utter strangers to religious ordinances as the people of a heathen country. From whatever cause, in them or in the manner of their treatment by religious bodies, it is sadly certain that this vast, intelligent, and growingly important section of our countrymen is thoroughly estranged from our religious institutions in their present aspect. Probably, indeed, the prevalence of *infidelity* has been exaggerated, if the word be taken in its popular meaning, as implying some degree of intellectual effort and decision; but, no doubt, a great extent of negative, inert indifference prevails, the practical effects of which are much the same. There is a sect, originated recently, adherents to a system called "Secularism"; the principal tenet being that, as the fact of a future life is (in their view) at all events susceptible of *some* degree of doubt, while the fact and the necessities of a present life are matters of direct sensation, it is therefore prudent to attend exclusively to the concerns of that existence which is certain and immediate—not wasting energies required for present duties by a preparation for remote, and merely possible, contingencies. This is the creed which probably with most exactness indicates the faith which, virtually though not professedly, is entertained by the masses of our working population; by the skilled and unskilled labourer alike—by hosts of minor shopkeepers and Sunday traders—and by miserable denizens of courts and crowded alleys. They are *unconscious Secularists*—engrossed by the demands, the trials, or the pleasures of the passing hour, and ignorant or careless of a future. These are never or but seldom seen in our religious congregations; and the melancholy fact is thus impressed upon our notice that the classes which are most in need of the restraints and consolations of religion are the classes which are most without them.

As was to be expected, in an age so prone to self-inquiry and reform, this attitude of our increasing population towards religion and religious institutions has occasioned much solicitude and many questions; and the Christian church has not been backward to investigate the causes of her ill-success with these the

[margin note:] Most important result of this inquiry as to attendance.

[margin note:] Causes of the neglect of religious Institutions:—

more especial objects of her mission. It is only purposed here to point out some of the more prominent results of this investigation.

1. Social distinctions.

1. One chief cause of the dislike which the labouring population entertain for religious services is thought to be the maintenance of those distinctions by which they are separated as a class from the class above them. Working men, it is contended, cannot enter our religious structures without having pressed upon their notice some memento of inferiority. The existence of pews and the position of the free seats are, it is said, alone sufficient to deter them from our churches; and religion has thus come to be regarded as a purely middle-class propriety or luxury. It is therefore, by some, proposed to abandon altogether the pew system, and to raise by voluntary contributions the amount now paid as seat rents. The objection and proposal come from churchmen and dissenters too; but from the former much more strenuously than from the latter; and with this addition in their case—that they point out the *offertory*, prescribed by the Rubric, as the specific mode in which the voluntary contributions should be gathered.—To other minds, the prevalence of social distinctions, while equally accepted as a potent cause of the absence of the working classes from religious worship, is suggestive of a different remedy. It is urged that the influence of that broad line of demarcation which on week days separates the workman from his master cannot be effaced on Sundays by the mere removal of a physical barrier. The labouring myriads, it is argued, forming to themselves a world apart, have no desire to mingle, even though ostensibly on equal terms, with persons of a higher grade. Their tastes and habits are so wholly uncongenial with the views and customs of the higher orders, that they feel an insuperable aversion to an intermixture which would bring them under an intolerable constraint. The same disposition, it is said, which hinders them from mixing in the scenes of recreation which the other classes favour, and induces their selection preferably of such amusements as can be exclusively confined to their own order, will for ever operate to hinder their attendance at religious services, unless such services can be devised as shall become exclusively *their own*. An argument in favour of such measures is supposed to be discovered in the fact that the greatest success amongst these classes is obtained where, as amongst the Methodists, this course is (more perhaps from circumstances than design) pursued. If such a plan were carried out by the Church of England, and by the wealthier Dissenting bodies, it is thought that some considerable advantage would result. It has consequently been proposed to meet so far the prejudices of the working population; and to strive to get them gradually to establish places of worship for themselves. Experiments have been already put in operation with the persons lowest in the social scale; and RAGGED CHURCHES* are in several places making a successful start. In several places, too, among Dissenters, special services in halls and lecture rooms are being held, intended wholly for the working class; and the success of these proceedings seems to prove that multitudes will readily frequent such places, where of course there is a total absence of all class distinctions, who would never enter the exclusive-looking chapel.

2. Indifference of the churches to the social condition of the poor.

2. A second cause of the alienation of the poor from religious institutions is supposed to be an insufficient sympathy exhibited by professed Christians for the alleviation of their social burdens—poverty, disease, and ignorance. It is argued that the various philanthropic schemes which are from time to time originated, though certainly the offspring of benevolent minds, are not associated with the Christian church in such a manner as to gain for it the

---

* The objections to this term are felt as much by the founders of these institutions as by others; but considerable difficulty is felt in providing any substitute.

gratitude of those who thus are benefited. This cause, however, of whatever force it may have been as yet, is certainly in process now of mitigation; for the clergy everywhere are foremost in all schemes for raising the condition of the poor, and the ministers and members of the other churches are not backward in the same good labour.

3. A third cause of the ill-success of Christianity among the labouring classes is supposed to be a misconception on their part of the motives by which Christian ministers are actuated in their efforts to extend the influence of the Gospel. From the fact that clergymen and other ministers receive in exchange for their services pecuniary support, the hasty inference is often drawn, that it is wholly by considerations of a secular and selfish kind that their activity and zeal are prompted.* Or, even if no sordid motives are imputed, an impression is not seldom felt that the exhortations and the pleadings of the ministry are matters merely of professional routine—the requisite fulfilment of official duty. It is obvious that these misapprehensions would be dissipated by a more familiar knowledge; but the evil of the case is, that the influence of such misapprehensions is sufficient to prevent that closer intimacy between pastors and their flocks from which alone such better knowledge can arise. The ministers are distrusted— the poor keep stubbornly aloof: how shall access to them be obtained? The employment of LAY-AGENCY has been proposed as the best of many methods by which minds, indifferent or hostile to the regular clergy, can be reached. It is thought by some that that unfortunate suspicion, by the poor, of some concealed and secretly inimical design, by which the regular ministers are often baffled in their missionary enterprises, might be much allayed if those who introduced the message of Christianity were less removed in station and pursuits from those whom it is sought to influence.

4. Another and a potent reason why so many are forgetful of religious obligations is attributable to their *poverty;* or rather, probably, to certain conditions of life which seem to be inseparable from less than moderate incomes. The scenes and associates from which the poor, however well disposed, can never, apparently, escape; the vice and filth which riot in their crowded dwellings, and from which they cannot fly to any less degraded homes; what awfully effective teaching, it is said, do these supply in opposition to the few infrequent lessons which the Christian minister or missionary, after much exertion, may impart! How feeble, it is urged, the chance, according to the course of human probabilities, with which the intermittent voice of Christianity must strive against the fearful never-ceasing eloquence of such surrounding evil!—Better dwellings, therefore, for the labouring classes are suggested as a most essential aid and introduction to the labours of the Christian agent.† And, indeed, of secondary influences, few can be esteemed of greater power than this. Perhaps no slight degree of that religious character by which the English middle classes are distinguished is the consequence of their peculiar isolation in distinct and separate houses—thus acquiring almost of necessity, from frequent opportunities of solitude, those habits of reflection which cannot be exercised to the entire exclusion of religious sentiments; but, certainly, however this may be, no doubt can be admitted that a great obstruction to the

Side notes:

3. Misconceptions of the motives of ministers.

4. Poverty and crowded dwellings.

---

* "A very common objection taken against ministers by men of this [the labouring] class is, that they would not preach or lecture if they were not paid for it; attributing the most sordid motives to all who call the attention of their fellow men to religious subjects. Absurd and untrue as is this objection, yet it is extensively entertained and avowed."—Twenty-seventh Annual Report of the Society for Promoting Christian Instruction.

† The "Metropolitan Association for Improving the Dwellings of the Industrious Classes" has already expended 60,000*l.* in providing better residences for the poor, and has realized a dividend upon its capital.

progress of religion with the working class would be removed if that condition which forbids *all* solitude and *all* reflection were alleviated.

Inadequate supply of Christian agency.

Probably, however, the grand requirement of the case is, after all, a multiplication of the various *agents* by whose zeal religious truth is disseminated. Not chiefly an additional provision of religious *edifices*. The supply of these perhaps, will not much longer, if the present wonderful exertions of the Church of England (aided in but little less degree by other Churches) be sustained, prove very insufficient for the wants of the community. But what is eminently needed is, an agency to bring into the buildings thus provided those who are indifferent or hostile to religious services. The present rate of church-and-chapel-increase brings before our view the prospect, at no distant period, of a state of things in which there will be small deficiency of structures where to worship, but a lamentable lack of worshippers. There is indeed already, even in our present circumstances, too conspicuous a difference between accommodation and attendants. Many districts might be indicated where, although the provision in religious buildings would suffice for barely half of those who might attend, yet scarcely more than half of even this inadequate provision is appropriated. Teeming populations often now surround half empty churches, which would probably remain half empty even if the sittings were all free.* The question then is mainly this: By what means are the multitudes thus absent to be brought into the buildings open for their use? Whatever impeding influence may be exerted by the prevalence of class distinctions, the constraints of poverty, or misconceptions of the character and motives of the ministers of religion, it is evident that absence from religious worship is attributable *mainly* to a genuine repugnance to religion itself. And, while this lasts, it is obvious that the stream of Christian liberality, now flowing in the channel of church-building, must produce comparatively small results. New churches and new chapels will arise, and services and sermons will be held and preached within them ; but the masses of the population, careless or opposed, will not frequent them. It is not, perhaps, sufficiently remembered that the process by which men in general are to be brought to practical acceptance of Christianity is necessarily

Necessity of aggressive measures.

aggressive. There is no attractiveness, at first, to them in the proceedings which take place within a church or chapel: all is either unintelligible or disagreeable. We can never then, expect that, in response to the mute invitation which is offered by the open door of a religious edifice, the multitudes, all unprepared by previous appeal, will throng to join in what to them would be a mystic worship, and give ear to truths which, though unspeakably beneficent, are also, to such

---

* Dr. Chalmers thus narrates the fate of an endeavour to induce, by the offer of sittings at a low rate, and even gratuitously, a better attendance of the working classes:—" An experiment may often be as instructive by its failure, as by its success. We have here to record the fate of a most laudable endeavour, made to recal a people alienated from Christian ordinances to the habit of attendance upon them. The scene of this enterprise was Calton and Bridgeton, two suburb districts of Glasgow which lie contiguous to each other, bearing together a population of above 29,000, and with only one chapel of ease for the whole provision which the establishment has rendered to them. It was thought that a regular evening sermon might be instituted in this chapel, and that for the inducement of a seat-rent so moderate as from 6d. to 1s. 6d. a year, to each individual, many who attended nowhere through the day might be prevailed upon to become the regular attendants of such a congregation. The sermon was preached, not by one stated minister, but by a succession of such ministers as could be found; and as variety is one of the charms of a public exhibition, this also might have been thought a favourable circumstance. But besides, there were gentlemen who introduced the arrangement to the notice of the people, not merely by acting as their informants, but by going round among them with the offer of sittings; and in order to remove every objection on the score of inability, they were authorized to offer seats gratuitously to those who were unable to pay for them. Had the experiment succeeded, it would have been indeed the proudest and most pacific of all victories. But it is greatly easier to make war against the physical resistance of a people, than to make war against the resistance of an established moral habit. And, accordingly, out of 1,500 seats that were offered, not above 50 were let or occupied by those who before had been total non-attendants on religious worship; and then about 150 more were let, not, however, to those whom it was wanted to reclaim, but to those who already went to church through the day, and in whom the taste for church-going had been already formed. And so the matter moved on, heavily and languidly, for some time, till, in six months after the commencement of the scheme, in September 1817, it was finally abandoned."—Christian and Economic Polity, vol. i. p. 128.

persons, on their first announcement, utterly distasteful. Something more, then, it is argued, must be done. The people who refuse to hear the gospel in the church must have it brought to them in their own haunts. If ministers, by standing every Sunday in the desk or pulpit, fail to attract the multitudes around, they must by some means make their invitations heard beyond the church or chapel walls. The myriads of our labouring population, really as ignorant of Christianity as were the heathen Saxons at Augustine's landing, are as much in need of missionary enterprise to bring them into practical acquaintance with its doctrines; and until the dingy territories of this alienated nation are invaded by *aggressive* Christian agency, we cannot reasonably look for that more general attendance on religious ordinances which, with many other blessings, would, it is anticipated, certainly succeed an active war of such benevolent hostilities.

Nor, it is urged in further advocacy of these missionary efforts, are the people insusceptible of those impressions which it is the aim of Christian preachers to produce. Although by natural inclination adverse to the entertainment of religious sentiments, and fortified in this repugnance by the habits and associations of their daily life, there still remain within them that vague sense of some tremendous want, and those aspirings after some indefinite advancement, which afford to zealous preachers a firm hold upon the conscience even of the rudest multitude. Their native and acquired disinclination for religious truth is chiefly of a negative, inert description—strong enough to hinder their spontaneous seeking of the passive object of their dis-esteem—too feeble to present effectual resistance to the inroads of aggressive Christianity invading their own doors. In illustration, the conspicuous achievements of the patriarchs of Methodism are referred to; and a further proof is found in the success of Mormon emissaries. It is argued that the vast effect produced upon the populace by Wesley and Whitfield, in the course of their unceasing labours, shows that the masses are by no means inaccessible to earnest importunity; while the very progress of the Mormon faith reveals the presence in its votaries of certain dim, unsatisfied religious aspirations, which, to be attracted to an orthodox belief, need only the existence, on the part of orthodox evangelists, of zeal and perseverance similar to those displayed by Mormon "prophets" and "apostles."

The masses no inaccessible.

Various are the schemes proposed in order to accomplish this more constant and familiar intercourse of Christian teachers with the multitude. The Church of England is at present considerably restricted in its efforts this way by canonical or customary regulations. Nevertheless, so deep is the impression of the urgent nature of the case, that propositions have been made for adapting to the purpose of religious services a greater number of *rooms*, licensed by the bishops; and it has even been suggested that "street-preaching," under proper sanction and control, would not be a too energetic measure for the terrible emergency. The employment of additional agents, over and above the augmentation which is necessarily occasioned by the building of additional churches, is also urged; but hitherto not much has been achieved in this direction as compared with what is needed. The necessity, if proper pastoral supervision in town districts is to be accomplished, of a greater number of agents than of churches will be evident on very slight reflection. For many reasons the churches in large towns are constructed of considerable size, and rarely with accommodation for less than 1,000 persons. Under present circumstances, a congregation which should moderately fill an edifice of such dimensions, must be drawn from a neighbourhood containing 4,000 or 5,000 persons. But it evidently is impos-

Different schemes suggested

C.　　　　　　　　　　H

sible for any minister, compatibly with the severe exertions which the present age imposes on him in respect of pulpit-duties, to perform with reference to any large proportion of these 4,000 or 5,000 persons, that perpetual visitation which is necessary first to gather, and then to retain, them within the Church's fold. The choice, then, seems to be—either a much minuter subdivision of existing districts, with the erection of much smaller churches; or (if large churches are to be retained) the employment, in each district, of a number of additional agents as auxiliaries to the regular incumbent. Both of these plans have been adopted in different portions of the country. Under the various Acts for creating ecclesiastical districts and new parishes, 1,255 such subdivisions have been legally effected; and many "conventional" districts have been formed by private understanding. Of the 1,255 legal districts many are still of very considerable size, and clearly quite beyond the management of any one incumbent. The varying populousness of the whole (excepting three, of which the population has not been ascertained) is seen as follows:—

Sub-division of parishes.

Districts containing				Districts containing		
Less than	100 persons	1		1500 and less than 2000 persons	86
100 and less than 200	,,	6		2000 ,, 3000 ,,	196
200 ,, 300	,,	18		3000 ,, 4000 ,,	160
300 ,, 400	,,	28		4000 ,, 5000 ,,	104
400 ,, 500	,,	33		5000 ,, 10,000 ,,	217
500 ,, 750	,,	101		10,000 ,, 15,000 ,,	53
750 ,, 1000	,,	91		15.000 ,, 20,000 ,,	20
1000 ,, 1500	,,	127		20,000 persons and upwards -	14

So that many of these districts are themselves too large, and need to be again the subjects of partition. But this plan of subdivision, so unquestionably useful in wide country parishes and very large town parishes, becomes perhaps of doubtful application to a moderate-sized town parish (4,000 or 5,000 inhabitants), where a single church with 1,500 sittings will suffice for all who would attend. The erection of another church in such a case would seem to be an injudicious measure; and yet, in such a parish, the exertions of a single clergyman, however active, cannot but be far from adequate. The awkwardness arises from the fact that the area which a minister can cover in the course of pastoral oversight is far from co-extensive with the sphere which he can influence by his ministrations in his church: he can preach to 1,500 people, but he cannot visit and effectually supervise the third of such a number. If this be correct, we seem to be driven to the employment, in such cases, of additional *agents* rather than the erection of additional churches. These additional agents may, of course, be of two kinds—*clerical* and *lay*: and vigorous efforts have been made, of late years, to provide a satisfactory supply of both. The "Society for Promoting the Employment of Additional Curates in Populous Places," founded in 1836, with a present income of 18,000l. per annum, aids in providing 323 such curates. By Sir Robert Peel's Act (6 & 7 Vict. c. 37.) the Ecclesiastical Commissioners have power to assign new districts, and provide by endowment for the appointment of clergymen to minister therein without churches; and these Commissioners have made 232 such districts; but all these appointments are *in contemplation* of a church being sooner or later provided. There appears to be no scheme for giving to a clergyman the cure of souls, within a small and definite locality, apart from the very onerous duties which attach to the possession of a church.

Lay-agency in the Church of England

The employment of *lay-agency* has been a measure forced upon the Church both by the clear impossibility of worthily supporting, if entirely clerical, so numerous a body as is requisite for any really effective visitation of the poor, and also by the evidently readier access which at first is granted by that class to overtures from persons of their own condition, having no professional garb. It has been thought that by employing in each populous town parish, in subordination to the clergyman, and with his sanction, a considerable staff of such assistants, much impression might be made upon that part of his parishioners which unavoidably eludes his personal attentions; that considerable numbers might be thus allured within the circle of his influence, and prepared for his maturer teaching, who would otherwise continue utterly untaught; and that this might be effectually accomplished without even in the least infringing on the ministerial office. Probably the force of these suggestions was assisted by the practical experience of such a plan afforded by the Methodist community, in which some ten or fifteen thousand laymen are employed not merely in the work of visitation, but also in that of preaching; and it might have been concluded that if such a wide responsibility could be conferred on Methodist lay-agents, while the regular Methodist ministers lost none of their prerogatives, but rather gained augmented influence, the benefits which must result to the poorer classes from the efforts of lay visitors and Scripture readers in connection with the Church of England, were not likely to be counterbalanced by the least depreciation of the functions of the regular clergy. And the actual result appears, according to the testimony of incumbents who have tried the plan, to justify these expectations.—The *extent* to which lay-agency is now adopted by the Church of England is not easily computed. There are two Societies by which such agents are supported or assisted—the *Pastoral Aid Society* and the *Scripture Readers Association :*—the former aiding 128 lay agents and the latter 323. Independently of these, however, there are doubtless many supported by individual and local funds. There are also many District Visitors. The Lay Assistants and the Scripture Readers are expected to devote six hours per day to their engagements. They are limited to conversation and the reading of the Bible and Prayer Book. They are not, on any account, to *preach*.[*]

By the various Protestant Dissenting churches too, the question of the readiest way to reach the working classes has of late had much attention. Lectures, specially addressed to them, and services conducted in the public halls or rooms with which they are familiar and to which they will resort without objection though deterred from church or chapel, are (as we have seen) amongst the means adopted to attract them to religious habits. In these various operations lay exertion is of course encouraged; but—excepting by the Methodists, with whom it has been long adopted to the utmost—not to that extent which, from the views which most Dissenting bodies entertain upon the subject of the ministerial office, might have been expected. The Independents and the Baptists have each a "Home Missionary Society;" and the members of these bodies aid in supporting such undenominational societies as the "London City Mission." But the amount of lay exertion proceeding from individual churches (congregations), though considerable, is much less, especially in large towns, than might, from their professed opinions on the nature of the Christian ministry[†], have been anticipated. This has not been unobserved by some amongst them-

Side note: Lay-agency amongst Dissenters.

[*] The *London City Mission* (founded in 1835) occupies a space midway between the Church of England and the Protestant Dissenting churches. Supported by a combination of the two, its operations are conducted without reference to the peculiarities of either. Its 300 missionaries visit the dwellings of the poor—distribute tracts—and hold religious conversations: services for prayer and exposition of the Scriptures, too, are held in rooms (not licensed or consecrated) from time to time.

[†] "So, neither does our polity reject the labours, in preaching the Gospel, of brethren not in the ministerial office. The order of the ministry, and the benefits of that order, are not destroyed because some are preachers who are not ministers. The world, the church, the ministry itself, need the zealous labours of all who can aid to diffuse the truth of God and to save the souls of men. We deem the order of the ministry to be in excess and in abuse when to it must be sacrificed all gifts and all activities not within its range — when no man may say to his neighbour, 'know the Lord,' if he belong not to an exclusive order of teachers."—Congregational Union Tract Series, No. X.

selves*; and recently considerable agitation has been manifested on this subject in a portion of the Independent body. It is urged that ministers, especially in the larger congregations, have assumed too much authority, appropriated too exclusively the work of spiritual teaching, and discouraged rather than assisted the development and exercise of those abilities and gifts which, though abundantly possessed, are little exercised by members of the Congregational churches. This monopoly of teaching, it is argued, has considerably hindered the diffusion of the truth amongst the masses; as the single pastor of each congregation, overburdened with those duties which a proper oversight of his already gathered flock demands, has neither time nor strength nor aptitude for those incursions on neglected portions of his neighbourhood which might with safety and with ease be undertaken and accomplished by selected members of his church. This party, therefore, urges a return to what is thought to have been the custom in the primitive church,—*plurality of elders:* thus, without depriving pastors of their present influence, relieving them from their excess of toil, and greatly multiplying the amount of Christian agency available for spreading Christianity.

At present, the grand employers of lay agency, amongst Dissenters, are the Methodists, who, in the aggregate, possess perhaps as many as 20,000 preachers and class leaders not belonging to the ministerial order. Nothing, probably, has more contributed than this to their success amongst the working population. The community whose operations penetrate most deeply through the lower sections of the people is the body called the *Primitive Methodists;* whose trespasses against what may be thought a proper order will most likely be forgiven when it is remembered that perhaps their rough, unformal energy is best adapted to the class to which it is addressed, and that, at all events, for every convert added to their ranks, society retains one criminal, one drunkard, one improvident the less.†

Lay-agency of Sunday School Teachers. In estimating the extent and power of lay exertion for religious objects, we must not forget the vast amount of Christian zeal and influence displayed and exercised by *teachers in Sunday Schools.* Of these there were, at the time of the Census, more than 250,000, instructing every Sunday in religious knowledge as many as 1,800,000 children.‡ It is difficult to overstate the value of these voluntary labours, much as the effect of them, unhappily, is lost, when, verging on maturity, the scholar ceases to attend the school without commencing or continuing to frequent the church. Few questions can be more momentous than the one which all the friends of Sunday Schools are anxiously endeavouring to answer,—By what means can the salutary influence exerted on so many in the period of their youth be still exerted on them when they shall become adults? Some have suggested that the bond which unites a teacher with his

---

* " Let me touch, as lightly and delicately as possible, upon another mischievous product of the professional sentiment—the strong temptation it sometimes presents to repress or impede the development of lay talent and enterprise. * * * Wonderful, most wonderful, is the dearth of genius, of talent, of peculiar aptitude, of striking character, of plodding industry, of almost everything indicative of mind on the alert, in connexion with the spiritual action of the unofficial bulk of evangelical churches. In no equally extensive area of human interest, perhaps, can such a level uniformity of unproductiveness be discovered. How is this? we ask. What will account for it? There cannot but be the influence of an unfriendly system constantly at work. I attribute the result to what I have designated professionalism—the monopoly, on principle, of spiritual functions by a special order deemed to have received their prerogative from the Head of the Church, and indisposed therefore, not necessarily from jealousy, but from deference to mistaken notions of polity, to call out lay-agency in the prosecution of strictly spiritual objects."—The British Churches in Relation to the British People. By E. Miall, M.P.

† It may not be unworthy of consideration, also, whether the labours of such agents do not practically operate to prepare the classes which they influence, for the more refined and less exciting worship of the other churches. It is certain that the progress of the Church of England in attracting to herself the affections of the multitude has been contemporaneous with the increase of Dissent; and it may not be improbable that many, who would not have been originally won by her advances, have, through the agency of such Dissenting teachers, as by a sort of preliminary education, been enabled to appreciate her services.

‡ The total number of Sunday Scholars, *on the books* of the Schools, was about 2,400,000; the number given above is about the number *attending* every Sunday. There are about *two* teachers to every *fifteen* scholars.

scholars need not be dissolved by their departure from the school; but that the more experienced instructors—thus becoming a superior order of lay-agents—might erect, midway between the school and the congregation, a new species of religious institution, which, while the school would be for it a natural preparation, would itself be no less natural an introduction to more regular and formal worship.

Mention ought not perhaps, when noticing the need of further agency, to be omitted of an increase thought to be desirable in the higher kinds of spiritual officers. The extension of the episcopate is thought to have been rendered necessary by the great increase of churches, clergymen, and population which has taken place since most of the existing sees were formed.

Extension of the episcopate.

The practical result of this feeling has been principally shown in the creation (by 6 & 7 Wm. IV. cap. 77.) of the two additional sees of Manchester and Ripon. The other efforts of legislation on the subject have been directed more toward the equalization than the multiplication of the sees, as the following Table (24) of the changes which have been effected since 1831 will show. It will be observed that some of the sees are still as large and populous as several continental principalities. Not fewer than 60 has been named as the number of bishops neccessary for a really effective superintendence of this aggregate population ; but in contemplation of some difficulties in the way of such a large extension of the present episcopate, suggestions have been made for the revival of *suffragan bishops* *.

TABLE 24.

DIOCESE.	Population.		DIOCESE.	Population.	
	1831.	1851.		1831.	1851.
St. Asaph - -	191,156	236,296	Lincoln - - -	899,468	677,649
Bangor - - -	163,712	192,964	Llandaff - -	181,244	337,526
Bath and Wells -	403,795	424,492	†London - - -	1,722,685	2,558,718
Bristol - -	232,026	—	Manchester - -	..	1,395,404
Canterbury -	405,272	417,099	Norwich - -	690,138	671,583
†Carlisle - -	135,002	272,306	Oxford - - -	140,700	503,042
†Chester - - -	1,883,958	1,066,124	Peterborough - -	194,339	465,671
Chichester - -	254,400	336,844	Ripon - - -	..	1,033,457
St. Davids - -	358,451	407,758	Rochester - -	191,875	577,298
Durham - -	469,933	701,381	Salisbury - -	384,683	379,296
Ely - - -	133,722	482,412	Sodor and Man -	..	52,387
Exeter - - -	795,416	922,656	†Winchester - -	729,607	665,034
Gloucester - -	315,512	538,109	Worcester - -	271,687	752,376
Hereford - -	206,327	216,143	York - - -	1,496,538	764,538
Lichfield -	1,045,481	1,022,080	TOTAL - -	13,897,187	18,070,735

* " In the 26 Henry VIII. c. 14. twenty-six places are mentioned for which bishops suffragan may be appointed. The archbishop or bishop is to present two persons to the king, of whom he is to nominate one to be a suffragan. The authority of such suffragans shall be limited by their commissions, which they shall not exceed on pain of *præmunire*. These commissions are to be given by the bishop's presentation.—This Act was repealed by 1 & 2 Philip and Mary, c. 8. and revived by 1 Eliz. c. 1.—Bishops suffragan are spoken of in the 35th Canon of 1604. It would be very desirable that in populous dioceses they should be appointed now, and there seems no legal reason why they should not be."—Short's History of the Church of England, p. 484.

† The population of these dioceses is given within the limits which are to belong to them on the next avoidance of the sees of Carlisle and Winchester. For the population, within *existing* limits, see *post*, SUMMARY TABLES, page 112.

Prominent Facts elicited by the whole Inquiry.

Prominent facts elicited by the whole Inquiry.

The great facts which appear to me to have been elicited by this inquiry are,—that, even taking the accommodation provided by all the sects, including the most extravagant, unitedly, there are 1,644,734 inhabitants of England who, if all who might attend religious services were willing to attend, would not be able, on account of insufficient room, to join in public worship : that this deficiency prevails almost exclusively in *towns*, especially *large* towns : that, if these 1,644,734 persons are to be deprived of all excuse for non-attendance, there must be at least as many additional sittings furnished, equal to about 2,000 churches and chapels, and a certain number more if any of the present provision be regarded as of doubtful value; and that even such additional accommodation will fall short of the requirement if the edifices are so often, as at present, closed. Further, it appears that as many as 5,288,294 persons able to attend, are every Sunday absent from religious services, for all of whom there is accommodation for at least one service : that neglect like this, in spite of opportunities for worship, indicates the insufficiency of any mere addition to the number of religious *buildings :* that the greatest difficulty is to fill the churches when provided; and that this can only be accomplished by a great addition to the number of efficient, earnest, religious *teachers*, clerical or lay, by whose persuasions the reluctant population might be won.

Ability of the Church to provide for the emergency.

That, having thus displayed before it the precise requirements of the times, the Christian Church will fail in adequately meeting the emergency, is what the many recent proofs of its abounding liberality and zeal forbid us in the least to fear. The means, though latent, are at hand; the agents, though unknown, are ready : nothing more is wanted than the action of the rulers of the Church to gather and direct them. If the following pages serve to make the task less difficult of properly directing such exertions, no small portion will have been attained of the advantages which you considered would result from this inquiry.

These, Sir, are the observations which have occurred to me in introducing these statistics. I am conscious that, although in illustration of the Tables I have been compelled, in order to secure an early publication, to shorten my remarks, they have upon the whole been too extended ; and I cannot expect that, in the unavoidable haste with which they have been written, by one previously unacquainted with the subject, they are free from error. But I do indulge a hope that they are free from bias. It has been my study strictly to fulfil the task of a *reporter*,—pointing out results, but not constructing arguments; describing fairly the opinions of others, but not presuming to express my own. It is, however, in the facts and figures which succeed that any value which belongs to this inquiry will be found; and these—much labour having been bestowed upon them—are, I think, sufficiently complete to justify whatever inferences may, by those accustomed to statistical investigations, fairly be deduced. If this should be the case, the public will assuredly be grateful, Sir, to you for undertaking, and to Government for sanctioning, as part of the decennial Census, an inquiry which must certainly reveal important facts relating to that most important of all subjects—the religious state of the community. Inquiry upon such a subject will not, surely, be considered as beneath the notice or beyond the province of a Government, if only it be recollected that, apart from those exalted and immeasurable interests with which religion is connected in the destinies of all—on which it is the office rather of the Christian preacher to dilate—no inconsiderable portion of the secular prosperity and peace of individuals and states depends on the extent to which a pure religion is professed and practically followed. If we could imagine the effects upon a people's temporal condition of two different modes of treatment—education separate from religion, and religion separate from education*—doubtless we should gain a most impressive lesson of the inappreciable value of religion even to a nation's physical advancement. For, whatever the dissuasive influence, from crime and grosser vice, of those refined ideas which in general accompany augmented knowledge, yet undoubtedly it may occur that, under the opposing influence of social misery, increased intelligence may only furnish to the vicious and the criminal increased facilities for evil. But the wider and more penetrating influence exerted by religious principle—controlling conscience rather than refining taste—is seldom felt without conferring, in addition to its higher blessings, those fixed views and habits which can scarcely fail to render individuals prosperous and states secure. Applying to the regulation of their daily conduct towards themselves and towards society the same high sanctions which control them in their loftier relations, Christian men become, almost inevitably, temperate, industrious, and provident, as part of their religious duty ; and Christian citizens acquire respect for human laws from having learnt to reverence those which are divine. The history of men and states shows nothing more conspicuously than this—that in proportion as a pure and practical religion is acknowledged and pursued are individuals materially prosperous† and nations orderly and free. It is thus that religion " has the promise of the life that now is, as well as of that which is to come."

I have the honour to be,

Sir,

Your very faithful Servant,

HORACE MANN.

Census Office,
8 December 1853.

---

* That is, using the term " Education " with its popular meaning.
† The founders of religious sects have generally been so conscious of the tendency of religion to increase the temporal riches of their followers, that they have often expressed their apprehensions of a future when prosperity should be the cause of their declension. The Quakers, amidst all the persecutions of their early days, advanced so rapidly in wealth that Fox gave frequent utterance to his fears on that account. John Wesley, too, had similar misgivings with respect to his societies.

SUMMARY TABLES

AND

TABULAR RESULTS.

TABLE A.—ACCOMMODATION

Popul

RELIGIOUS DENOMINATION.	Number of Places of Worship.			Number of Sittings.*				Number of Attendan at Public Worship on Su March 30, 1851.		
	Separate Buildings.	Not separate Buildings.	Total.	Free.	Appropriated.	Not distinguished.	TOTAL.	Morning.	Afternoon.	
TOTAL - -	30,959	3,508	34,467	3,947,371	4,443,093	1,077,274	9,467,738	4,426,338	3,030,280	2,9
PROTESTANT CHURCHES.										
BRITISH :										
Church of England and Ireland -	13,854	223	14,077	1,805,773	2,123,295	993,344	4,922,412	2,371,732	1,764,641	3
Scottish Presbyterians—										
Church of Scotland - -	17	1	18	2,422	9,492	1,000	12,914	6,949	960	
United Presbyterian Church -	64	2	66	5,275	19,856	5,270	30,401	17,188	4,361	
Presbyterian Church in England	73	3	76	5,669	33,899	1,890	40,458	22,607	3,345	
Reformed Irish Presbyterians -	1	..	1	120	..	..	120	..	..	
Independents, or Congregationalists -	2,960	284	3,244	402,905	578,823	20,779	1,002,507	515,071	228,060	4
Baptists—										
General - - - -	96	6	96	10,596	6,869	1,060	18,532	5,296	7,965	
Particular - - -	1,776	171	1,947	290,596	361,459	8,720	660,775	296,944	172,145	2
Seventh Day - - -	2	..	2	390	..	..	390	27	40	
Scotch - - -	11	4	15	2,021	16	..	2,037	649	966	
New Connexion General -	170	12	182	24,135	26,268	766	51,159	23,888	15,545	
Baptists (not otherwise defined) -	441	109	550	49,900	30,415	2,355	82,770	36,525	22,826	
Society of Friends - -	343	28	371	80,683	920	7,948	89,551	14,016	6,458	
Unitarians - - -	217	12	229	23,153	37,787	2,830	63,770	27,612	8,610	
Moravians, or United Brethren -	29	3	32	7,768	455	500	8,723	4,681	2,512	
Wesleyan Methodists—										
Original Connexion - -	5,625	954	6,579	626,434	729,928	5,081	1,361,443	482,753	376,202	6
New Connexion - -	269	28	297	36,630	55,066	..	91,716	36,428	22,391	
Primitive Methodists - -	2,039	832	2,871	201,965	165,057	2,174	369,216	98,001	172,584	2
Bible Christians - -	387	95	482	30,164	29,502	675	60,341	14,655	24,002	
Wesleyan Methodist Association	340	79	419	44,585	45,894	310	90,789	31,929	20,888	
Independent Methodists §	15	5	20	1,693	451	..	2,144	871	1,245	
Wesleyan Reformers - -	177	162	339	42,105	14,576	445	57,126	30,018	15,841	
Calvinistic Methodists—										
Welsh Calvinistic Methodists	792	36	828	76,223	120,730	1,289	198,242	79,738	89,140	3
Countess of Huntingdon's Connexion -	98	11	109	13,694	21,461	55	35,210	19,963	4,090	
Sandemanians, or Glassites -	5	1	6	610	28	..	638	489	256	
New Church - - -	42	8	50	3,782	7,833	300	11,865	4,623	2,308	
Brethren - - -	77	55	132	14,216	1,623	30	15,869	5,613	4,441	
Isolated Congregations ¶ -	372	167	539	64,862	21,549	3,637	90,048	34,706	22,726	
FOREIGN :										
Lutherans - - -	5	1	6	931	1,241	..	2,172	960	290	
French Protestants - -	3	..	3	560	..	..	560	150	21	
Reformed Church of the Netherlands -	1	..	1	350	..	..	350	70	..	
German Protestant Reformers -	1	..	1	140	60	..	200	120	..	
OTHER CHRISTIAN CHURCHES :										
Roman Catholics - - -	506	64	570	77,200	73,210	14,254	164,664	240,792	51,406	
Greek Church - - -	3	..	3	291	..	..	291	240	..	
German Catholics - -	..	1	1	100	200	..	300	500	..	
Italian Reformers - -	..	1	1	150	..	..	150	..	20	
Catholic and Apostolic Church -	29	3	32	6,460	373	240	6,973	3,077	1,807	
Latter Day Saints, or Mormons -	88	134	222	22,255	264	432	22,951	7,212	11,016	
Jews - - - - -	42	11	53	2,608	5,353	..	7,961	2,848	1,043	

* The Returns afford no information as to the number of *sittings* in 2,524 of the above-mentioned 34,467 places of worship. The distri these defective Returns among the various Denominations is as follows:—Church of England, 1,026 ; Church of Scotland, 1 ; United terian Church, 2 ; Presbyterian Church in England, 2 ; Independents, 185 ; General Baptists, 9 ; Particular Baptists, 109 ; Scotch [Ba General Baptists, New Connexion, 5 ; Baptists (not otherwise defined), 82 ; Society of Friends, 8 ; Unitarians, 16 ; Moravians, 2 ; W Original Connexion, 306 ; Methodist New Connexion, 16 ; Primitive Methodists, 309 ; Bible Christians, 42 ; Wesleyan Methodist Associa Independent Methodists, 2 ; Wesleyan Reformers, 80 ; Welsh Calvinistic Methodists, 53 ; Countess of Huntingdon's Connexion, 5 ; manians, 2 ; New Church, 1 ; Brethren, 19 ; Isolated Congregations, 72 ; Lutherans, 1 ; Roman Catholics, 45 ; Catholic and Apostolic C Latter Day Saints, 52 ; Jews, 3. For an estimate of the number of sittings in these places, see *post*, page 109.

† The number of *attendants* is not stated in the case of 1,394 of the above 34,467 places of worship. Of these 1,392 there belong to the C England, 989 ; United Presbyterian Church, 2 ; Presbyterian Church in England, 1 ; Reformed Irish Presbyterians, 1 ; Independents, 59 ; Baptists, 3 ; Particular Baptists, 36 ; General Baptists, New Connexion, 3 ; Baptists (not otherwise defined), 23 ; Society of Friends,

...ANCE IN ENGLAND AND WALES.

...,609.

...of Places open *for Worship*, at each period ...the day, on Sunday, March 30, 1851, ...Number of Sittings thus *available*.					Dates at which the Buildings were erected or appropriated to religious purposes.								RELIGIOUS DENOMINATION.
...Worship.		Sittings.											
Afternoon.	Evening.	Morning.	Afternoon.	Evening.	Before 1801.	1801 to 1811.	1811 to 1821.	1821 to 1831.	1831 to 1841.	1841 to 1851.	Not stated.	TOTAL.	
22,371	16,065	8,026,595	5,946,120	5,486,617	18,094	1,224	2,603	3,141	4,966	5,504	4,366	34,467	**TOTAL.**
													PROTESTANT CHURCHES. *BRITISH ·*
14,863	9,489	4,546,521	3,498,289	1,701,575	9,667	55	97	276	667	1,197	2,118	14,077	Church of England and Ireland.
													Scottish Presbyterians—
4	12	12,914	2,180	9,196	8	1	..	2	3	2	1	18	*Church of Scotland.*
19	40	39,314	7,908	18,823	26	2	10	9	9	5	5	66	*United Presbyterian Church.*
20	44	40,358	7,250	27,540	27	1	4	6	10	24	4	76	*Presbyterian Church in England.*
1	..	120	120	..	..	..	..	..	..	..	1	1	Reformed Irish Presbyterians.
1,405	2,530	871,176	426,964	544,705	849	210	314	484	564	593	230	3,244	Independents, or Congregationalists.
													Baptists—
44	70	9,455	12,569	15,127	30	7	8	15	8	16	9	93	*General.*
1,190	1,532	490,479	394,449	456,535	419	149	205	295	365	380	134	1,947	*Particular.*
1	1	380	300	300	1	..	..	1	..	1	..	2	*Seventh Day.*
14	4	1,611	1,787	1,000	8	..	1	1	7	..	1	15	*Scotch.*
94	140	38,875	22,879	42,335	64	9	18	22	19	38	12	182	*New Connexion General.*
227	380	68,534	43,072	65,946	75	20	51	69	111	123	101	550	*Baptists (not otherwise defined).*
223	21	88,799	60,869	5,781	265	17	14	25	20	17	13	371	Society of Friends.
85	114	56,755	20,528	36,872	147	8	14	12	15	18	15	229	Unitarians.
16	22	8,543	4,563	6,751	18	3	2	4	2	3	..	32	Moravians, or United Brethren.
													Wesleyan Methodists—
4,861	5,268	938,515	738,515	1,911,984	644	523	927	1,075	1,411	1,347	752	6,579	*Original Connexion.*
134	262	74,387	48,290	84,775	34	19	30	59	92	47	16	297	*New Connexion.*
1,910	1,233	178,937	300,996	836,074	196	30	65	332	779	940	527	2,871	*Primitive Methodists.*
279	381	39,405	40,634	61,756	23	4	15	78	164	146	55	483	*Bible Christians.*
331	345	65,908	38,442	94,442	26	12	19	29	178	109	46	419	*Wesleyan Methodist Association.*
16	17	901	1,997	2,053	..	1	1	4	2	9	3	20	*Independent Methodists.*
175	289	49,846	24,353	85,066	44	8	13	18	26	114	114	339	*Wesleyan Reformers.*
													Calvinistic Methodists—
321	690	130,906	77,350	177,530	174	77	109	177	162	108	26	828	*Welsh Calvinistic Methodists.*
28	86	31,449	8,530	31,470	31	10	12	18	20	14	4	109	*Countess of Huntingdon's Connexion.*
4	1	698	438	170	3	..	..	3	..	..	..	6	Sandemanians, or Glassites.
23	20	11,823	4,513	7,518	5	4	2	4	12	15	8	50	New Church.
61	188	13,853	8,080	14,170	12	2	8	5	17	34	41	132	Brethren.
243	388	67,196	42,968	76,861	86	18	34	55	74	149	228	539	Isolated Congregations.
													FOREIGN:
1	1	2,172	1,603	300	5	..	..	..	1	..	..	6	Lutherans.
1	2	530	30	530	2	..	..	..	..	1	..	3	French Protestants.
..	..	350	..	..	1	..	..	..	..	..	..	1	Reformed Ch. of the Netherlands.
..	1	200	..	200	..	..	1	..	..	..	..	1	German Protestant Reformers.
													OTHER CHRISTIAN CHURCHES:
289	510	160,955	94,878	85,804	156	26	29	58	92	151	63	570	Roman Catholics.
..	..	291	..	..	..	..	1	..	..	2	..	5	Greek Church.
..	1	300	..	300	..	1	..	..	..	..	..	1	German Catholics.
1	..	..	150	..	..	..	..	..	..	..	1	1	Italian Reformers.
17	24	6,512	4,253	5,043	3	..	2	2	16	5	4	32	Catholic and Apostolic Church.
187	196	18,523	19,297	30,822	26	5	..	11	13	52	113	222	Latter Day Saints, or Mormons.
21	37	7,788	5,404	5,771	16	3	1	6	7	15	4	53	Jews.

...: Moravians, 2; Wesleyan Original Connexion, 133; Methodist New Connexion, 3; Primitive Methodists, 61; Bible Christians, 5;
...Methodist Association, 5; Independent Methodists, 1; Wesleyan Reformers, 5; Countess of Huntingdon's Connexion, 7; New Church,
...n, 2; Isolated Congregations, 33; Lutherans, 1; French Protestants, 1; Roman Catholics, 27; Catholic and Apostolic Church, 1;
...w Saints, 9; Jews, 7.   For an estimate of the number of attendants in these places of worship, see *post*, page 110.

...33,469 places of worship open in the morning, 1,467 did not return the number of their *sittings*, and a similar omission was made with
...1,424 out of the 21,371 open in the afternoon, and 996 out of the 18,065 open in the evening.   For the particular sects affected by these
...s: and for an estimate of the number of sittings included in the defective Returns, see *post*, page 111.

...numbers for the Independent Methodists are inaccurate.   By a mistake, discovered too late for rectification, some of their congrega-
...s been included with those of other bodies.   The total, however, is very small, and too few to affect the comparative position of these

...the detailed particulars of these Congregations, see the next page.

TABLE A.—continued.

ISOLATED CONGREGATIONS
Included in the preceding Table.

RELIGIOUS DENOMINATION.[*]	Number of Places of Worship and Sittings.		Number of Attendants at Public Worship on Sunday, March 30, 1851.[‡]			Number of Places open for Worship on Sunday, March 30, 1851, and Number of Sittings thus available.					
						Places of Worship.			Sittings.		
	Places of Worship.	Sittings.[†]	Morning.	Afternoon.	Evening.	Morning.	Afternoon.	Evening.	Morning.	Afternoon.	Evening.
TOTAL	539	90,048	34,706	22,726	40,835	338	245	368	67,196	42,963	70,861
I.§											
Independents and Baptists	61	12,113	4,951	4,516	6,120	29	31	46	7,153	6,941	9,610
Independents, Baptists, and Wesleyans	2	250	..	138	320	..	1	2	..	250	250
Independents and Wesleyans	3	210	20	105	130	1	1	2	..	140	210
Independents and Calvinistic Methodists	1	100	20	..	..	1	..	..	100	..	..
Independents and Primitive Methodists	1	..	..	55	41	..	1	1	..	..	..
Baptists and Wesleyans	2	160	20	..	47	..	..	2	120	..	160
Baptists, Wesleyans, and Moravians	1	78	..	80	40	..	1	1	..	78	78
Presbyterians and Particular Baptists	1	336	344	..	404	1	..	1	336	..	336
Wesleyan Christian Union	1	150	..	100	120	..	1	1	..	150	150
Mixed	54	6,739	1,749	2,033	3,346	17	23	44	3,074	3,490	5,335
Neutral	1	500	..	100	160	..	1	1	..	500	500
II.											
Calvinists	81	12,878	6,340	3,455	5,837	69	36	49	11,321	5,622	9,730
Calvinists (Supralapsarian)	1	450	102	30	93	1	1	1	450	450	450
Huntingtonians	1	120	29	..	21	1	..	1	120	..	120
Universalists	2	1,417	675	..	75	2	..	1	1,417	..	667
Millennarians	5	1,370	425	289	415	5	3	3	1,370	970	1,070
Predestinarians	1	30	12	30	..	1	1	..	30	30	..
Trinitarian Predestinarians	1	110	45	..	48	1	..	1	110	..	110
III.											
Christians	96	15,796	6,162	2,134	6,878	79	35	79	13,865	6,045	14,046
Christian Association	8	800	230	185	632	5	3	7	600	280	800
Orthodox Christians	1	40	20	..	20	1	..	1	40	..	40
New Christians	1	120	30	..	35	1	..	1	120	..	120
Christ's Disciples	3	169	19	132	163	1	3	3	84	169	169
Primitive Christians	1	50	..	15	..	..	..	..	..	50	..
New Testament Christians	2	160	15	24	87	1	1	1	100	60	160
Original Christians	1	300	30	10	7	1	1	1	300	300	300
United Christians	1	1,400	950	..	1,000	1	..	1	1,400	..	1,400
Gospel Pilgrims	2	121	42	114	71	1	2	2	121	121	121
Free Gospel Christians	14	2,855	954	960	1,842	9	11	11	2,055	2,105	2,615
Believers	2	1,560	819	..	750	2	..	2	1,560	..	1,560
Non-sectarian	7	2,230	284	905	1,170	3	3	7	1,490	1,140	2,230
No particular Denomination	7	575	268	223	223	3	4	3	280	375	380
Evangelists	4	570	..	..	30	3	1	3	500	..	570
Gospel Refugees	1	160	100	130	160	1	1	1	160	160	160
Freethinking Christians	2	256	54	20	..	1	1	..	216	40	..
IV.											
Protestant Christians	3	440	157	56	280	2	1	3	340	100	440
Evangelical Protestants	1	100	..	..	100	..	..	1	..	..	100
Protestant Free Church	1	80	45	..	80	1	..	1	80	..	80
Trinitarians	1	250	80	31	60	1	1	1	250	250	250
Protestant Dissenters	24	4,518	1,943	1,274	2,067	16	15	16	3,441	2,588	2,884
Dissenters	6	325	280	316	132	4	3	2	125	135	160
Evangelical Dissenters	3	530	125	149	152	1	2	1	290	270	290
Episcopalian Seceders	1	420	226	..	347	1	..	1	420	..	420
V.											
London City Mission	7	470	..	78	141	..	3	4	..	170	260
Railway Mission	1	70	..	..	..	1	..	1	70	..	70
Town Mission	17	1,966	399	591	1,355	9	8	16	718	1,040	1,925
Home Mission	1	150	..	..	45	..	..	1	..	..	150
Mission Society	8	1,010	145	203	249	3	2	3	470	330	410
Seaman's Bethel	11	2,586	402	963	214	4	9	3	1,398	2,016	756
Christian Mission	3	440	209	144	300	3	1	3	440	240	440
VI.											
Free Church	8	3,020	1,700	457	1,862	6	2	5	3,020	370	2,850
Teetotalers	1	50	..	..	..	1	..	1	..	..	50
Doubtful	43	4,888	3,342	996	2,396	28	15	27	4,908	2,156	3,382
Benevolent Methodists	1	150	..	158	207	..	1	1	..	150	150
General	2	130	..	40	86	..	1	1	..	70	130
Israelites	1	30	9	8	..	1	1	..	30	30	..
Christian Israelites	3	1,050	89	160	..	3	1	..	1,050	1,000	..
Stephenites	1	..	..	..	..	1	1	1	..	..	..
Inghamites	9	2,336	758	1,135	320	8	8	6	2,186	2,186	1,670
Temperance Wesleyan	1	50	..	16	33	..	1	1	..	50	50
Temperance Christians	1	246	..	144	137	..	1	1	..	246	246
Free Thinkers	2	125	20	..	37	1	..	1	25	..	100
Rational Progressionists	1	..	..	..	300	..	..	1	..	..	..
Southcottians	4	445	68	5	196	3	1	3	245	100	380

[*] The appellations in this List are given exactly as they were used by the parties making the Returns.
[†] The Returns afford no information as to the number of *sittings* in 71 of the above-mentioned 539 places of worship. The distribution of these defective Returns among the various Denominations is as follows:— Independents and Baptists, 2; Independents, Baptists, and Wesleyans, 1; Independents and Wesleyans, 1; Independents and Primitive Methodists, 1; Mixed, 8; Calvinists, 13; Millennarians, 1; Christians, 13; Christian Society, 2; Gospel Pilgrims, 1; Free Gospel Christians, 3; Evangelists, 1; Protestant Dissenters, 1; Town Mission, 3; Seaman's Bethel, 1; Christian Mission, 1; Free Church, 1; Doubtful, 17; Christian Israelites, 1; Stephenites, 1; Rational Progressionists, 1.
[‡] The number of *attendants* is not stated in the case of 33 of the above 539 places of worship. Of these 33, there belong to Baptists and Wesleyans, 1; Mixed, 1; Calvinists, 7; Christians, 4; Unsectarian, 1; Evangelists 2; Protestant Dissenters, 1; Dissenters, 1; London City Mission, 1; Railway Mission, 1; Mission Society, 1; Teetotallers, 1; Doubtful, 9; Stephenites, 1; Inghamites, 1.
§ For an explanation of the grouping here adopted, see Report, p. 153.

SUPPLEMENT I. to TABLE A.

Showing the total ACCOMMODATION provided by each Religious Body; *including Estimates* for defective Returns.*

	Number of Places of Worship.			Number of Sittings.			Average number of Sittings to one Place of Worship.†
	Returns complete as to Sittings.	Returns defective as to Sittings.	Total.	In the complete Returns.	Estimate for the defective Returns.*	Total.	
TOTAL - -	31,943	2524	34,467	9,467,738	744,825	10,212,563	296
PROTESTANT CHURCHES:							
BRITISH:							
Church of England - - -	13,051	1026	14,077	4,922,412	395,503	5,317,915	377
Scottish Presbyterians :							
Church of Scotland -	17	1	18	12,914	875	13,789	760
United Presbyterian Church	64	2	66	30,401	950	31,351	475
Presbyterian Church in England - -	74	2	76	40,458	1,004	41,552	547
Reformed Irish Presbyterians -	1	..	1	120	..	120	120
Independents, or Congregationalists - -	3,058	186	3,244	1,002,507	65,253	1,067,760	328
Baptists :							
General - - -	82	9	93	18,532	2,007	20,539	223
Particular - - -	1,847	100	1,947	550,775	32,178	82,953	299
Seventh-Day - -	2	..	2	390	..	390	195
Scotch - - -	12	3	15	2,037	510	2,547	170
New Connexion, General	177	5	182	51,159	1,445	52,604	289
Undefined - -	486	64	550	82,770	10,540	93,310	170
Society of Friends - -	362	9	371	89,551	2,048	91,599	247
Unitarians - - -	212	17	229	63,770	4,784	68,554	299
Moravians - - -	30	2	32	8,723	582	9,305	291
Wesleyan Methodists :							
Original Connexion -	6,193	386	6,579	1,361,443	86,137	1,447,580	220
New Connexion -	281	16	297	91,716	5,248	96,964	328
Primitive Methodists -	2,562	309	2,871	369,216	44,814	414,030	144
Bible Christians -	440	42	482	60,341	6,493	66,834	137
Wesleyan Methodist Association - - -	335	34	419	90,789	8,024	98,813	236
Independent Methodists	18	2	20	2,144	119	2,263	119
Wesleyan Reformers -	238	51	330	57,126	10,688	67,814	199
Calvinistic Methodists :							
Welsh Calvinistic Methodists	775	53	828	198,242	13,709	211,951	256
Lady Huntingdon's Connexion - -	104	5	109	35,210	3,517	38,727	339
Sandemanians - - -	4	2	6	638	318	956	159
New Church - - -	49	1	50	11,865	242	12,107	242
Brethren - - -	112	20	132	15,869	2,660	18,529	140
Isolated Congregations -	468	71	539	90,048	14,433	104,481	192
FOREIGN :							
Lutherans - - -	5	1	6	2,172	434	2,606	434
French Protestants - -	3	..	3	560	..	560	187
Reformed Church of the Netherlands - - -	1	..	1	350	..	350	350
German Protestant Reformers -	1	..	1	200	..	200	200
OTHER CHRISTIAN CHURCHES:							
Roman Catholics - - -	522	48	570	164,664	21,447	186,111	314
Greek Church - - -	3	..	3	291	..	291	97
German Catholics - -	1	..	1	300	..	300	300
Italian Reformers - -	1	..	1	150	..	150	150
Catholic and Apostolic Church -	31	1	32	6,973	464	7,437	232
Latter Day Saints - -	169	53	222	22,951	7,832	30,783	135
Jews - - - -	50	3	53	7,961	477	8,438	159

* The method adopted in preparing this estimate has been to take the average number of sittings for each body, for the whole of England and Wales, and apply this average to each defective return, where there is no more specific criterion ; but where the average number of sittings in any case is less than the number of persons actually attending at one service, the plan has been to put down the number of sittings in that case at one fourth more than the number of attendants.

† Calculated wholly from the *complete Returns.*

SUPPLEMENT II. to TABLE A.

Showing the total number of ATTENDANTS at Public Worship, in connection with each Religious Body; *including Estimates* for defective Returns.*

RELIGIOUS DENOMINATION.	Number of Places of Worship.			Number of Attendants						Total Number of Attendances.
	Returns complete as to Attendance.	Returns defective as to Attendance.	Total.	In the Places of Worship sending complete Returns.			In the total Number of Places of Worship (including an Estimate for the Places which sent defective Returns.)*			
				Morning.	After-noon.	Even-ing.	Morning.	After-noon.	Even-ing.	
TOTAL	33,073	1,394	34,467	4,428,338	3,030,230	2,960,772	4,647,482	3,184,135	3,064,449	10,896,066
PROTESTANT CHURCHES:										
BRITISH:										
Church of England	13,138	939	14,077	2,371,732	1,764,641	803,141	2,541,244	1,890,764	860,543	5,292,551
Scottish Presbyterians:										
Church of Scotland	18	..	18	6,949	960	3,849	6,949	960	3,849	11,758
United Presbyterian Church	64	2	66	17,188	4,931	8,551	17,725	5,085	8,818	31,628
Presbyterian Church in England	75	1	76	22,607	3,345	10,684	22,908	3,390	10,836	37,124
Reformed Irish Presbyterians	..	1	1	..	..	..	..	..	..	..
Independents	3,185	59	3,244	515,071	228,060	448,847	524,612	232,285	457,162	1,214,059
Baptists—										
General	90	3	93	5,228	7,865	8,283	5,404	8,130	8,562	22,096
Particular	1,909	38	1,947	286,944	172,145	267,205	292,656	175,572	272,524	740,752
Seventh Day	2	..	2	27	48	16	27	40	16	83
Scotch	15	..	15	649	986	312	649	986	312	1,947
New Connexion, General	180	2	182	23,688	15,545	24,381	23,951	15,718	24,652	64,321
Undefined	526	24	550	36,525	22,826	37,417	38,119	23,822	39,050	100,991
Society of Friends	362	9	371	14,016	6,458	1,459	14,364	6,619	1,495	22,478
Unitarians	222	7	229	27,612	8,610	12,406	28,483	8,881	12,697	50,061
Moravians	30	2	32	4,681	2,312	3,202	4,993	2,466	3,415	10,874
Wesleyan Methodists:										
Original Connexion	6,446	133	6,579	482,763	376,202	654,349	492,714	383,964	667,850	1,544,528
New Connexion	294	3	297	36,428	22,391	39,232	36,801	22,620	39,624	99,045
Primitive Methodists	2,810	61	2,871	98,001	172,684	229,646	100,125	176,435	234,635	511,195
Bible Christians	474	8	482	14,655	24,002	34,088	14,902	24,345	34,612	73,859
W. M. Association	414	5	419	31,923	20,888	40,170	32,308	21,140	40,655	94,103
Independent Methodists	19	1	20	571	1,245	1,148	601	1,311	1,208	3,120
Wesleyan Reformers	334	5	339	30,018	15,841	44,286	30,470	16,080	44,953	91,503
Calvinistic Methodists:										
Welsh Calvinistic Methodists	828	..	828	79,728	59,140	125,244	79,728	59,140	125,244	264,112
Lady Huntingdon's Connexion	102	7	109	19,966	4,099	17,929	21,103	4,380	19,159	44,642
Sandemanians	6	..	6	489	256	61	439	256	61	756
New Church	48	2	50	4,652	2,308	2,978	4,846	2,404	3,102	10,352
Brethren	130	2	132	5,613	4,441	7,272	5,699	4,509	7,384	17,592
Isolated Congregations	506	33	539	34,706	22,726	40,835	36,969	24,208	43,498	104,675
FOREIGN:										
Lutherans	5	1	6	960	220	..	1,152	264	..	1,416
French Protestants	2	1	3	150	21	100	225	32	150	407
Reformed Church of the Netherlands	1	..	1	70	..	..	70	..	..	70
German Protestant Reformers	1	..	1	120	..	60	120	..	60	180
OTHER CHRISTIAN CHS.:										
Roman Catholics	543	27	570	240,792	51,406	73,232	252,783	53,967	76,880	383,630
Greek Church	3	..	3	240	..	..	240	..	..	240
German Catholics	1	..	1	500	..	200	500	..	200	700
Italian Reformers	1	..	1	..	..	..	..	20	..	20
Catholic and Apostolic Church	30	2	32	3,077	1,607	2,622	3,176	1,659	2,707	7,542
Latter Day Saints	213	9	222	7,212	11,016	15,954	7,517	11,481	16,628	35,626
Jews	46	7	53	2,848	1,043	1,673	2,910	1,202	1,918	6,030

* There are various methods of making a computation of the probable number of attendants at places of worship for which no information upon this point was supplied. The plan adopted for this Table has been to assume that each of the places of worship making defective returns would have had as many attendants as the average number shown to have been present at the places of worship making complete returns. Thus, for the Church of England, to discover the probable morning attendance in the 939 churches, the returns from which were silent on that point, the proportion would be—as 13,138 : 2,371,732 :: 939. Similar proportions would give the probable afternoon and evening attendance. The same process has been repeated for each religious body; except for the REFORMED IRISH PRESBYTERIANS, in which case, there being only one chapel and the attendants there not stated, no materials exist for any calculation.

SUPPLEMENT III. to TABLE A.

Showing the Total Number of Sittings in the Places *open for Worship* on Sunday, March 30, 1851; including an Estimate for those Cases in which the Number of Sittings was not returned.*

RELIGIOUS DENOMINATIONS.	Total Number of Sittings in Places *open for Worship*, including an Estimate for defective Returns.			RELIGIOUS DENOMINATIONS.	Total Number of Sittings in Places *open for Worship*, including an Estimate for defective Returns.		
	Morn-ing.	After-noon.	Even-ing.		Morn-ing.	After-noon.	Even-ing.
TOTAL	8,496,520	6,267,988	5,723,000	PROTESTANT CHURCHES— *continued.*			
PROTESTANT CHURCHES:							
Church of England	4,958,645	3,761,812	1,789,275	Calvinistic Methodists :			
Scottish Presbyterians :				*Welsh Calvinistic Methodists*	188,463	98,982	185,978
Church of Scotland	13,674	2,940	9,196	*Lady Huntingdon's Connexion*	32,905	8,609	32,826
United Presbyterian Church	31,389	8,383	19,296	Sandemanians	956	597	170
Presbyterian Church in England	41,552	7,250	28,087	New Church	11,465	5,055	7,818
Reformed Irish Presbyterians	120	120	..	Brethren	14,613	9,590	15,850
Independents	901,352	447,300	881,769	Isolated Congregations	74,876	47,955	78,349
Baptists :				Lutherans	2,172	1,202	300
General	10,125	13,907	16,365	French Protestants	530	30	530
Particular	514,899	309,997	488,571	Reformed Church of the Netherlands	350	..	..
Seventh-Day	390	300	300	German Protestant Reformers	200	..	200
Scotch	2,121	2,297	1,000				
New Connexion, General	39,875	23,835	43,202	OTHER CHRISTIAN CHS.:			
Undefined	49,954	46,832	70,366	Roman Catholics	175,309	103,042	89,258
Society of Friends	94,805	65,127	5,781	Greek Church	201	..	..
Unitarians	60,044	21,887	39,264	German Catholics	300	..	300
Moravians	8,543	4,563	6,751	Italian Reformers	..	150	..
Wesleyan Methodists :				Catholic and Apostolic Church	6,545	4,168	5,275
Original Connexion	952,215	797,915	1,263,364	Latter Day Saints	23,413	24,582	26,697
New Connexion	76,563	46,100	88,383				
Primitive	191,177	293,326	365,154	Jews	8,100	5,563	5,771
Bible Christians	51,595	43,366	55,044				
Wesleyan Methodist Association	67,319	44,106	88,714				
Independent Methodists	1,139	2,116	2,171				
Wesleyan Reformers	47,326	30,864	61,623				

* This Table is compiled from Table A. (page 108)—the summary of England and Wales in the Table of Defective Returns and the average of sittings to a Church or Chapel of each Denomination, as shown in Supplement I. (page 109).

TABLE E.

Number of PLACES of WORSHIP and SITTINGS in the several DIOCESES of England and Wales.

	Population, 1851.	Number of Places of Worship.			Number of Sittings.			Number of Places of Worship for which no Sittings are returned.*	
		Provided by			Provided by				
		The Church of England.	Other Churches.	TOTAL.	The Church of England.	Other Churches.	TOTAL.	The Church of England.	Other Churches.
ENGLAND AND WALES, including the Channel Islands and the Isle of Man	18,070,735	14,152	20,569	34,721	4,959,895	4,589,847	9,549,742	1,037	1,506
Province of CANTERBURY	12,785,048	11,626	15,231	26,857	3,805,925	3,231,014	7,036,939	923	952
Province of YORK	5,285,687	2,526	5,338	7,864	1,153,970	1,358,833	2,512,803	114	554
PROVINCE OF CANTERBURY.									
Bangor	192,964	198	577	775	45,303	121,501	166,804	19	24
Bath and Wells	424,492	550	565	1,115	172,223	108,848	281,071	17	25
Canterbury	417,099	403	407	810	151,204	79,143	230,347	44	20
Chichester	336,844	350	267	617	108,076	52,912	160,988	68	24
Ely	482,412	576	649	1,225	164,941	145,330	310,271	46	13
Exeter	922,656	814	1,587	2,401	286,865	310,418	597,283	96	106
Gloucester and Bristol	538,109	523	612	1,135	181,734	143,068	324,802	42	29
Hereford	216,143	417	355	772	94,678	39,755	134,433	21	31
Lichfield	1,022,080	699	1,260	1,959	297,297	264,604	561,901	16	66
Lincoln	677,649	905	1,226	2,131	213,772	219,236	433,008	67	94
Llandaff	337,526	282	579	861	55,220	160,316	215,536	24	69
London	2,143,340	486	658	1,144	393,825	261,346	655,171	8	21
Norwich	671,583	1,067	971	2,038	264,240	168,387	432,627	81	83
Oxford	503,042	709	757	1,466	196,323	124,960	321,283	56	21
Peterborough	465,671	634	704	1,338	180,011	148,290	328,301	48	10
Rochester	577,298	628	557	1,185	198,396	136,062	334,458	51	21
St. Asaph	236,296	172	716	888	66,159	118,707	184,866	5	60
St. David	407,758	485	935	1,420	103,797	217,999	321,796	40	119
Salisbury	379,296	556	536	1,092	141,489	98,522	240,011	89	46
Winchester	1,080,412	668	764	1,432	286,268	171,982	458,250	69	55
Worcester	752,376	504	549	1,053	204,104	139,628	343,732	21	13
PROVINCE OF YORK.									
Carlisle	154,933	147	225	372	47,341	36,787	84,128	8	32
Chester	1,183,497	518	909	1,427	281,531	232,448	513,979	19	109
Durham	701,381	327	801	1,128	120,554	192,754	313,308	15	77
Manchester	1,395,494	352	844	1,196	256,600	305,747	562,347	9	50
Ripon	1,033,457	478	1,224	1,702	221,055	337,243	558,298	23	141
Sodor and Man	52,387	39	93	132	14,978	18,007	32,985	6	4
York	764,538	665	1,242	1,907	211,911	235,847	447,758	39	141

* An estimate of the probable addition to be made on account of these defective Returns may be readily obtained by using the numbers in these columns in combination with the average number of sittings to a place of worship, as shown in the last column of Supplement I. to Table A. (ante, p. 109).

TABLE F.

RELIGIOUS ACCOMMODATION AND ATTENDANCE

IN

LARGE TOWNS.

(Arranged Alphabetically.)

RELIGIOUS DENOMINATION.	Number of Places of Worship.	Number of Sittings.			Number of Attendants at Public Worship on Sunday, March 30, 1851 [including Sunday Scholars].			Number of Places of Worship.	Number of Sittings.			Number of Attendants at Public Worship on Sunday, March 30, 1851 [including Sunday Scholars].		
		Free.	Appropriated.	Total.	Morning.	Afternoon.	Evening.		Free.	Appropriated.	Total.	Morning.	Afternoon.	Evening.
		ASHTON-UNDER-LYNE. (*Municipal Borough.*) Population, 30,676.							BATH. (*Municipal Borough.*) Population, 54,240.					
TOTAL -	16	5219	5354	10,573	5580	3774	4705	61	14,183	17,300	32,568	21,802	5114	15,070
PROTESTANT CHURCHES:														
Church of England -	3	1955	2066	4021	1879	2300	1465	28	9163	10,477	20,575	13,704	3974	8737
Independents - -	3	980	1470	2450	1738	..	1105	2	470	960	1430	1440	..	1200
Particular Baptists -	1	..	550	550	192	234	92	5	574	1730	2304	1288	100	1645
Society of Friends -	..	..	..	..	..	..	..	1	300	..	300	47	..	21
Unitarians - -	..	..	..	..	..	..	..	1	..	300	300	175	..	120
Moravians - - -	..	..	..	..	..	..	..	1	300	..	300	390	..	200
Wesleyan Methodists -	1	..	..	..	400	..	350	5	782	1654	2436	886	85	962
Methodist New Connex.	2	552	850	1402	598	452	794	..	..	..	..	..	..	..
Primitive Methodists -	1	362	268	630	..	386	253	1	127	305	432	437	..	530
Wesleyan Association -	..	..	..	..	..	..	..	1	80	100	180	95	..	89
Wesleyan Reformers -	..	..	..	..	..	..	..	2	450	441	891	770	70	556
L'Huntingdon'sConnex.	..	..	..	..	..	..	..	3	520	550	1070	500	60	930
New Church - - -	1	100	150	250	90	..	..	1	..	300	300	150	..	..
Brethren - - -	..	..	..	..	..	..	..	1	40	..	40	30	..	12
Isolated Congregations	2	1000	..	1000	50	160	..	3	970	250	1220	1050	..	500
OTHER CHRISTIAN CHS.:														
Roman Catholics -	1	..	..	..	500	..	450	3	70	50	270	645	580	170
Cath. and Apos. Church	..	..	..	..	..	..	..	1	77	153	230	110	96	..
Latter Day Saints -	1	270	..	270	133	242	194	1	250	..	250	70	120	250
Jews - - - -	..	..	..	..	..	..	..	1	10	30	40	15	29	28

ASHTON-UNDER-LYNE.—The returns omit to state the number of *sittings* in one place of worship belonging to the WESLEYAN METHODISTS, attended by a maximum number of 350 persons at a service; and in one place belonging to the ROMAN CATHOLICS, attended by a maximum of 500 at a service.—*Neither sittings nor attendants* are given for one place of worship belonging to an ISOLATED CONGREGATION.

BATH. - The returns omit to state the number of *sittings* in one place of worship belonging to the CHURCH OF ENGLAND attended by a maximum of 65 at a service; and in one belonging to the ROMAN CATHOLICS, attended by a maximum of 400 persons at a service.

C.   I

TABLE F.—*continued.*

BIRMINGHAM (*Municipal Borough.*) Population, 232,841. / BLACKBURN (*Municipal Borough.*) Population, 46,536.

RELIGIOUS DENOMINATION.	No. of Places of Worship	Number of Sittings.			Attendants at Public Worship, March 30, 1851			No. of Places of Worship	Number of Sittings.			Attendants at Public Worship, March 30, 1851		
		Free	Appro-priated	Total	Morn-ing	After-noon	Even-ing		Free	Appro-priated	Total	Morn-ing	After-noon	Even-ing
TOTAL	92	30,503	35,311	66,714	43,544	6877	33,564	26	6997	11,243	18,240	8845	3527	5163
PROTESTANT CHURCHES:														
Church of England	25	14,465	15,378	30,843	20,402	3977	15,142	7	3429	5104	8533	3919	1676	2189
United Presby. Church	..	..	..	..	..	..	..	1	210	590	800	521	574	..
Presby. Ch. in England	1	500	200	700	464	..	277	..	..	..	..	..	..	..
Independents	12	2110	4547	6657	3824	529	3298	4	865	1928	2793	1343	136	937
Particular Baptists	9	2387	4362	6749	3764	1049	3990	3	310	704	1014	304	230	140
Gen. Baptist New Con.	1	212	356	568	460	..	275	..	..	..	..	..	..	..
Baptists (*not otherwise defined*)	..	..	..	..	..	..	..	1	..	..	..	20	..	..
Society of Friends	2	744	..	744	544	318	..	2	600	..	600	64	37	..
Unitarians	5	1634	1450	3064	1852	..	631	..	..	..	..	..	..	..
Wesleyan Methodists	13	3268	4646	7814	4272	336	3775	1	250	660	910	282	..	200
Methodist New Connex.	3	488	900	1388	574	..	585	..	..	..	..	..	..	..
Primitive Methodists	3	428	228	656	400	190	463	1	360	400	760	550	..	500
Wesleyan Association	1	250	350	600	569	..	600	1	150	500	650	530	..	90
Wesleyan Reformers	2	270	..	270	100	..	155	1	400	300	700	320	..	415
Welsh Calv. Methodists	1	10	22	32	130	..	..	..	..	..	..	..	..	..
L'Huntingdon'sConnex.	1	200	..	200	200	..	100	..	..	..	..	..	..	..
New Church	1	180	320	500	298	..	132	1	97	57	154	122	184	112
Brethren	1	..	..	..	100	..	..	..	..	..	..	..	..	..
Isolated Congregations	3	250	1550	1800	1273	..	1350	..	..	..	..	..	..	..
OTHER CHRISTIAN CHS.:														
Roman Catholics	4	847	702	1549	3383	378	1346	2	226	1000	1226	800	600	500
Cath. and Apos. Church	2	600	..	600	85	60	173	..	..	..	..	..	..	..
Latter Day Saints	1	1600	..	1600	665	..	1200	1	100	..	100	70	90	80
Jews	1	60	300	360	185	40	92	..	..	..	..	..	..	..

BOLTON (*Municipal Borough.*) Population, 61,171. / BRADFORD (*Municipal Borough.*) Population, 103,778.

RELIGIOUS DENOMINATION.	No. of Places of Worship	Number of Sittings.			Attendants at Public Worship, March 30, 1851			No. of Places of Worship	Number of Sittings.			Attendants at Public Worship, March 30, 1851		
		Free	Appro-priated	Total	Morn-ing	After-noon	Even-ing		Free	Appro-priated	Total	Morn-ing	After-noon	Even-ing
TOTAL	36	6619	12,597	20,976	11,555	5031	5901	54	11,807	20,658	32,287	20,438	9579	14,288
PROTESTANT CHURCHES:														
Church of England	9	3024	5132	9616	4850	3054	1469	12	4145	5299	10,026	4719	3479	1957
United Presby. Church	..	..	..	..	..	..	..	1	14	625	639	430	..	255
Presby. Ch. in England	1	..	500	500	100	100	..	..	..	..	..	..	..	..
Independents	5	370	2040	2410	1410	90	1098	6	690	2878	3568	2510	1164	2129
General Baptists	..	..	..	..	..	..	..	2	140	460	600	488	96	277
Particular Baptists	2	163	377	540	285	27	240	3	672	2153	2825	2127	852	1242
Society of Friends	1	..	300	300	70	30	..	1	1000	..	1000	167	95	..
Unitarians	1	14	600	614	530	180	..	1	30	460	490	128	..	102
Moravians	..	..	..	..	..	..	..	1	200	86	286	149	156	..
Wesleyan Methodists	5	1608	1792	3400	1860	457	1191	12	1571	5499	7070	3548	2321	3916
Methodist New Connex.	2	600	..	600	68	179	92	1	230	543	773	294	..	285
Primitive Methodists	3	450	306	756	254	355	317	5	640	1340	1980	867	818	976
Wesleyan Association	1	150	350	500	169	..	287	3	225	1215	1440	524	20	396
Wesleyan Reformers	..	..	..	..	..	..	..	3	810	..	810	1061	128	1483
New Church	1	20	350	370	94	..	306	..	..	..	..	..	..	..
Brethren	1	70	..	70	25	..	30	1	..	..	..	..	100	20
Isolated Congregations	2	150	550	700	80	47	165	..	..	..	..	..	..	..
OTHER CHRISTIAN CHS.:														
Roman Catholics	2	..	600	600	1760	482	711	1	280	100	380	3228	..	600
Latter Day Saints	..	..	..	..	..	..	..	1	400	..	400	200	350	450

BIRMINGHAM.—The returns omit to state the number of *sittings* for one place of worship belonging to the BRETHREN, attended by a maximum of 55 at a service; and for one included amongst those of the ISOLATED CONGREGATIONS, attended by a maximum of 23 at a service.—The number of *attendants* was not stated for one place of worship belonging to the CHURCH OF ENGLAND.

BLACKBURN.—The returns omit to state the number of *sittings* in one place of worship belonging to the CHURCH OF ENGLAND, attended by a maximum of 150 persons at a service; in one place belonging to the INDEPENDENTS, attended by a maximum of 94 at a service; and in one place belonging to the BAPTISTS (not otherwise defined), attended by a maximum of 80 at a service.—The number of *attendants* is not given for two places of worship belonging to the CHURCH OF ENGLAND.

BOLTON.—The returns omit to state the number of *sittings* in one place of worship belonging to the ROMAN CATHOLICS, attended by a maximum of 506 persons at a service.—*Neither sittings nor attendants* are given for one place of worship belonging to an ISOLATED CONGREGATION.

BRADFORD.—The returns omit to state the number of *sittings* in one place of worship belonging to the CHURCH OF ENGLAND, attended by a maximum of 127 persons at a service; in one belonging to the INDEPENDENTS, attended by a maximum of 130 at a service; in one belonging to the GENERAL BAPTISTS, attended by a maximum of 85 at a service; in one belonging to the WESLEYAN REFORMERS, attended by a maximum of 630 at a service; and in one belonging to the BRETHREN, attended by a maximum of 100 persons at a service.—The number of *attendants* is not given for one place of worship belonging to the CHURCH OF ENGLAND.

TABLE F.—continued.

RELIGIOUS DENOMINATION.	Number of Places of Worship.	Number of Sittings.			Number of Attendants at Public Worship on Sunday, March 30, 1851 [including Sunday Scholars].			Number of Places of Worship.	Number of Sittings.			Number of Attendants at Public Worship on Sunday, March 30, 1851 [including Sunday Scholars].		
		Free.	Appropriated.	Total.	Morning.	Afternoon.	Evening.		Free.	Appropriated.	Total.	Morning.	Afternoon.	Evening.
	BRIGHTON. (*Parliamentary Borough.*) Population, 69,673.							BRISTOL. (*Municipal Borough.*) Population, 137,328.						
TOTAL -	38	11,067	12,448	24,665	18,568	5954	12,061	119	34,713	32,731	71,944	39,512	4081	34,328
PROTESTANT CHURCHES:														
Church of England -	12	6539	6952	13,491	11,061	4767	6113	42	16,973	15,224	31,884	18,747	2244	13,669
Independents -	7	1175	1680	2855	1825	330	979	19	4581	6521	11,102	5814	240	6261
Particular Baptists -	4	865	1391	2256	1920	132	1865	9	1860	3206	5866	3317	275	2370
Baptists (*undefined*) -	..	..	..	..	..	..	..	1	60	..	60	36	..	50
Society of Friends -	1	..	..	500	135	95	..	1	600	..	600	455	..	200
Unitarians - -	2	450	652	1102	674	..	248	2	320	670	990	690	..	320
Moravians -	..	..	..	..	..	..	..	1	400	..	400	262	..	147
Wesleyan Methodists -	2	500	600	1100	671	35	615	12	3580	4662	8242	2165	90	2168
Primitive Methodists -	2	161	100	261	212	142	286	2	935	134	1069	469	..	650
Bible Christians -	2	240	82	322	120	87	152	1	80	..	80	30	..	50
Wesleyan Reformers -	..	..	..	..	..	..	..	10	4112	540	4652	2555	175	3729
Calvinistic Methodists -	..	..	..	..	..	..	..	1	340	810	1150	702	..	725
L' Huntingdon's Connex. -	1	337	636	973	1000	..	1150	..	..	..	..	..	..	..
Brethren -	..	..	..	..	..	..	..	1	170	..	170	70	..	76
Isolated Congregations -	1	200	..	200	200	..	150	8	2735	150	2885	973	..	1397
OTHER CHRISTIAN CHS.:														
Roman Catholics -	1	100	300	400	520	200	200	6	1620	634	2254	2383	890	1630
Cath. and Apos. Church -	1	300	..	300	150	100	200	..	..	..	..	..	..	..
Latter Day Saints -	1	200	..	200	40	50	70	2	280	..	280	250	150	260
Jews - - -	1	20	55	75	40	16	40	1	80	180	260	95	17	126

RELIGIOUS DENOMINATION.	Number of Places of Worship.	Number of Sittings.			Number of Attendants.			Number of Places of Worship.	Number of Sittings.			Number of Attendants.		
		Free.	Appropriated.	Total.	Morning.	Afternoon.	Evening.		Free.	Appropriated.	Total.	Morning.	Afternoon.	Evening.
	BURY. (*Parliamentary Borough.*) Population, 31,262.							CAMBRIDGE. (*Municipal Borough.*) Population, 27,815.						
TOTAL -	21	3554	7766	12,920	6654	4271	2849	25	5967	7127	13,894	8596	3296	6961
PROTESTANT CHURCHES:														
Church of England -	4	1100	2878	5578	2666	1960	782	16	4140	4444	9384	5616	1436	4246
Independents -	4	130	1720	1850	1213	408	296	1	500	180	680	317	94	220
Particular Baptists -	2	350	400	750	150	414	207	3	512	1658	2170	1668	1053	1462
Unitarians -	1	12	690	702	334	202	..	..	..	..	..	..	..	..
Wesleyan Methodists -	3	736	744	1480	581	100	502	1	400	600	1000	569	250	653
Methodist New Connex. -	1	328	468	796	313	312	100	..	..	..	..	..	..	..
Primitive Methodists -	1	150	150	300	..	150	234	1	35	245	280	130	195	110
Wesleyan Association -	1	118	676	794	411	60	478	..	..	..	..	..	..	..
New Church -	1	80	40	120	60	80	..	..	..	..	..	..	..	..
OTHER CHRISTIAN CHS.:														
Roman Catholics -	1	550	..	550	812	335	..	1	230	..	230	260	200	180
Latter Day Saints -	1	..	..	..	100	250	250	1	150	..	150	38	70	90
Jews - - -	1	..	..	..	14	..	..	1	..	..	..	..	..	..

BRIGHTON.—The returns omit to state the number of *sittings* in one place of worship belonging to the INDEPENDENTS attended by a maximum of 50 persons at a service.

BRISTOL.—The returns omit to state the number of *sittings* in one place of worship belonging to the CHURCH OF ENGLAND attended by a maximum of 14 persons at a service.—The number of *attendants* is not given for three places of worship belonging to the CHURCH OF ENGLAND.—*Neither sittings nor attendants* are given for one place of worship belonging to the WESLEYAN METHODISTS; one belonging to the WESLEYAN REFORMERS; and one belonging to the LATTER DAY SAINTS.

BURY.—The returns omit to state the number of *sittings* in one place of worship belonging to the INDEPENDENTS, attended by a maximum of 146 at a service; in one place belonging to the LATTER DAY SAINTS, attended by a maximum of 250 at a service; and in one place belonging to the JEWS, attended by a maximum of 14 at a service.—The number of *attendants* is not given for one place of worship belonging to the CHURCH OF ENGLAND.

CAMBRIDGE.—The returns omit to state the number of *sittings and attendants* in two places of worship belonging to CHURCH OF ENGLAND, and in one place of worship belonging to the JEWS.

TABLE F.—*continued.*

RELIGIOUS DENOMINATION.	Number of Places of Worship.	Number of Sittings.			Number of Attendants at Public Worship on Sunday, March 30, 1851 [including Sunday Scholars].			Number of Places of Worship.	Number of Sittings.			Number of Attendants at Public Worship on Sunday, March 30, 1851 [including Sunday Scholars].		
		Free.	Appropriated.	Total.	Morning.	Afternoon.	Evening.		Free.	Appropriated.	Total.	Morning.	Afternoon.	Evening.
	CARLISLE. (*Municipal Borough.*) Population, 26,310.							CHATHAM. (*Parliamentary Borough.*) Population, 28,424.						
TOTAL -	18	4629	3089	11,078	5152	674	3376	31	3949	7325	11,962	7558	2283	5607
PROTESTANT CHURCHES:														
Church of England -	5	763	1816	4039	1678	390	948	10	2220	3702	6610	4013	1440	1994
Church of Scotland -	1	..	750	750	160	..	116	..	..	..	..	..	..	..
United Presby. Church -	1	100	370	470	452	..	..	..	..	..	..	..	..	..
Independents -	3	1217	153	1370	439	..	402	3	270	950	1220	915	138	893
General Baptists -	..	..	..	..	..	..	..	1	123	163	286	94	..	85
Particular Baptists -	1	1000	..	1000	30	..	60	2	264	644	908	665	..	873
Society of Friends -	1	360	..	360	94	64	..	..	..	..	..	..	..	..
Wesleyan Methodists -	2	200	800	1000	415	..	463	6	420	1112	1532	1246	340	1140
Primitivo Methodists -	1	..	..	..	120	..	200	..	..	..	..	..	..	..
Bible Christians -	..	..	..	..	..	..	..	4	231	466	697	220	151	324
Wesleyan Association -	1	900	100	1000	680	..	700	2	231	138	369	95	14	98
New Church -	..	..	..	..	..	..	..	1	70	..	70	20	..	40
OTHER CHRISTIAN CHS.:														
Roman Catholics -	1	..	..	1000	1060	180	456	1	..	150	150	250	200	100
Cath. and Apos. Church -	..	..	..	..	..	..	..	1	120	..	120	40	..	60
Latter Day Saints -	1	89	..	89	24	40	31	..	..	..	..	..	..	..

RELIGIOUS DENOMINATION.		Free.	Appropriated.	Total.	Morning.	Afternoon.	Evening.		Free.	Appropriated.	Total.	Morning.	Afternoon.	Evening.
	CHELTENHAM. (*Parliamentary Borough.*) Population, 35,051.							CHESTER. (*Municipal Borough.*) Population, 27,766.						
TOTAL -	27	6942	12,123	19,065	10,900	4248	8067	35	4612	8517	13,529	7112	4022	4801
PROTESTANT CHURCHES:														
Church of England -	7	3398	7457	10,855	6866	3338	3200	15	2878	5069	7547	4242	2830	1540
Presby. Ch. in England -	..	..	..	..	..	..	..	1	..	50	50	60	60	..
Independents -	4	680	1350	2030	1031	45	804	4	580	880	1400	776	40	899
Particular Baptists -	3	800	1400	2200	1190	..	1600	1	88	162	250	71	16	102
Scotch Baptists -	..	..	..	..	..	..	..	1	..	..	..	8	12	..
Baptists (*not otherwise defined*) -	1	100	..	100	30	..	30	..	..	..	..	..	..	..
Society of Friends -	1	100	..	100	21	9	..	2	300	..	600	34	26	..
Unitarians -	1	300	..	300	72	..	35	1	..	250	250	102	..	57
Wesleyan Methodists -	4	489	926	1415	805	107	756	3	428	941	1369	872	357	999
Methodist New Connex. -	..	..	..	..	..	..	..	1	350	620	970	146	..	156
Primitive Methodists -	..	..	..	..	..	..	..	1	200	180	380	177	224	180
Wesleyan Association -	2	130	110	240	44	49	42	..	..	..	..	..	..	..
Calvinistic Methodists -	..	..	..	..	..	..	..	1	100	265	365	120	125	179
L'Huntingdon's Connex. -	1	200	550	750	350	..	700	1	..	..	..	245	..	200
Isolated Congregations -	..	..	..	..	..	..	..	1	150	..	150	39	32	29
OTHER CHRISTIAN CHS.:														
Roman Catholics -	1	100	260	360	325	400	400	1	38	100	138	190	270	210
Latter Day Saints -	1	630	..	630	150	300	500	1	..	..	30	30	..	250
Jews - -	1	15	70	85	16	..	..	..	..	..	..	..	..	..

CARLISLE.—The returns omit to state the number of *sittings* in one place of worship belonging to the WESLEYAN METHODISTS, attended by a maximum number of 63 persons at a service; and in one place belonging to the PRIMITIVE METHODISTS, attended by a maximum of 200 at a service.—The number of *attendants* is not given for one place of worship belonging to the CHURCH OF ENGLAND.

CHATHAM.—The returns omit to state the number of *sittings* in one place of worship belonging to the CHURCH OF ENGLAND, attended by a maximum of 600 at a service.—*Neither sittings nor attendants* are given for one place of worship belonging to the CHURCH OF ENGLAND.

CHELTENHAM.—The number of *attendants* is not mentioned for two places of worship belonging to the CHURCH OF ENGLAND.

CHESTER.—The returns omit to state the number of *sittings* in one place of worship belonging to the INDEPENDENTS, attended by a maximum of 55 persons at a service; in one belonging to the SCOTCH BAPTISTS, attended by a maximum of 12 at a service; in one belonging to LADY HUNTINGDON'S CONNEXION, attended by a maximum of 200 at a service; and in one belonging to the LATTER DAY SAINTS, attended by a maximum of 250 at a service.

TABLE F.—*continued.*

COLCHESTER (Municipal Borough). Population, 19,443. — COVENTRY (Municipal Borough). Population, 36,208.

RELIGIOUS DENOMINATION.	Number of Places of Worship	Number of Sittings. Free.	Appropriated.	Total.	Attendants Morning.	Afternoon.	Evening.	Number of Places of Worship	Number of Sittings. Free.	Appropriated.	Total.	Attendants Morning.	Afternoon.	Evening.
TOTAL	34	6401	4693	13,796	6095	7260	4049	20	6588	8949	15,537	6827	1827	5892
PROTESTANT CHURCHES:														
Church of England	16	2586	1172	6460	3161	4033	1257	6	3714	4267	7981	2871	1214	2563
Independents	6	1480	1185	2665	1510	1631	1278	4	681	1867	2548	1350	251	1244
Particular Baptists	3	440	1170	1610	560	900	457	2	240	620	860	537	..	417
General, Baptists, New Connexion	..	..	..	..	..	..	..	1	50	250	300	397	..	170
Baptists (*not otherwise defined*)	1	300	..	300	30	50	35	..	..	..	..	..	..	..
Society of Friends	1	767	..	767	58	48	..	1	300	..	300	31	5	..
Unitarians	..	..	..	..	..	..	..	1	200	260	460	325	..	110
Wesleyan Methodists	1	270	560	830	500	85	330	1	100	650	750	203	..	242
Primitive Methodists	3	166	256	422	183	283	205	1	92	168	260	193	..	142
New Church	1	150	350	500	20	200	300	..	..	..	..	..	..	..
Isolated Congregations	..	..	..	..	..	..	..	1	361	667	1028	..	..	•
OTHER CHRISTIAN CHS.:														
Roman Catholics	1	140	..	140	73	..	67	1	600	200	800	900	300	1000
Latter Day Saints	1	102	..	102	..	30	120	1	250	..	250	20	57	64

DERBY (Municipal Borough). Population, 40,609. — DEVONPORT (Parliamentary Borough). Population, 50,159.

RELIGIOUS DENOMINATION.	Number of Places of Worship	Number of Sittings. Free.	Appropriated.	Total.	Attendants Morning.	Afternoon.	Evening.	Number of Places of Worship	Number of Sittings. Free.	Appropriated.	Total.	Attendants Morning.	Afternoon.	Evening.
TOTAL	31	7414	11,783	19,647	10,97?	3776	9196	42	9030	12,050	23,180	13,110	2997	12,243
PROTESTANT CHURCHES:														
Church of England	11	3573	4991	8564	4700	2299	2590	18	5005	3327	10,432	5528	1531	3996
Independents	3	498	1090	1588	847	631	780	9	1439	3384	4823	2099	473	2497
Particular Baptists	1	..	500	500	220	111	192	4	667	1547	2214	1409	200	1430
Gen. Baptist New Con.	2	651	599	1250	472	..	510	..	..	..	..	..	..	..
Baptists (*not otherwise defined*)	2	372	1128	1500	570	215	870	..	..	..	..	..	..	..
Society of Friends	1	300	..	300	42	30	..	..	..	..	..	..	..	..
Unitarians	1	..	..	450	217	..	107	1	..	300	300	62	..	40
Moravians	..	..	..	..	..	..	..	1	300	..	300	190	..	230
Wesleyan Methodists	3	750	1499	2249	1041	140	988	5	906	2397	3303	2683	145	2825
Methodist New Connex.	1	150	330	480	256	..	384	1	40	140	180	100	..	180
Primitive Methodists	2	660	532	1192	674	..	1310	..	..	..	..	..	..	..
Bible Christians	..	..	..	..	..	..	..	2	83	397	480	339	16	341
Wesleyan Association	..	..	..	..	..	..	..	1	30	238	268	150	30	140
Wesleyan Reformers	1	360	374	734	543	..	682	1	80	..	80	..	70	..
New Church	1	100	240	340	151	..	85	..	..	..	..	..	..	..
Isolated Congregation	..	..	..	..	..	..	..	2	120	..	120	..	97	75
OTHER CHRISTIAN CHS:														
Roman Catholics	2	..	500	500	1244	350	700	1	60	320	380	500	250	250
Latter Day Saints	..	..	..	..	..	..	..	1	300	..	300	50	40	250

COLCHESTER.—The returns omit to state the number of *sittings* in one place of worship belonging to the CHURCH OF ENGLAND, attended by a maximum of 250 at a service; and in one belonging to the INDEPENDENTS, attended by a maximum of 100 persons at a service.—The number of *attendants* is not given for one place of worship belonging to the CHURCH OF ENGLAND.

COVENTRY.—The returns omit to state the number of *sittings* in one place of worship belonging to the CHURCH OF ENGLAND.—The number of *attendants* is not given for one place of worship belonging to the CHURCH OF ENGLAND; nor for one place belonging to an ISOLATED CONGREGATION.

DERBY.—The returns omit to state the number of *sittings* in one place of worship belonging to the CHURCH OF ENGLAND, attended by a maximum number of 200 persons at a service; and in one place belonging to the ROMAN CATHOLICS, attended by a maximum number of 44 persons at a service.—The number of *attendants* is not stated for two places of worship belonging to the CHURCH OF ENGLAND.

DEVONPORT.—The returns omit to state the number of *sittings* in one place of worship belonging to an ISOLATED CONGREGATION, attended by a maximum number of 30 persons at a service.

TABLE F.—*continued.*

RELIGIOUS DENOMINATION.	Number of Places of Worship.	Number of Sittings.			Number of Attendants at Public Worship on Sunday, March 30, 1851 [including Sunday Scholars].			Number of Places of Worship.	Number of Sittings.			Number of Attendants at Public Worship on Sunday, March 30, 1851 [including Sunday Scholars].		
		Free.	Appropriated.	Total.	Morning.	Afternoon.	Evening.		Free.	Appropriated.	Total.	Morning.	Afternoon.	Evening.
		DOVER. *(Municipal Borough.)* Population, 22,244.							DUDLEY. *(Parliamentary Borough.)* Population, 37,962.					
TOTAL -	21	5436	4413	11,338	6305	3311	4807	32	7367	8044	15,911	9128	4171	7707
PROTESTANT CHURCHES:														
Church of England -	7	4362	2449	7111	4854	2766	2848	5	2994	2700	5694	2511	1745	1211
Presby. Ch. in England	..	..	..	..	..	..	..	1	200	450	650	390	..	300
Independents -	3	279	971	1250	454	..	477	1	420	758	1178	836	..	474
General Baptists -	1	..	..	500	..	..	..	1	50	50	100	224	60	100
Particular Baptists -	1	100	400	500	233	60	319	2	250	500	750	160	60	400
Baptists (*not otherwise defined*) - -	1	..	..	389	294	100	268	1	350	..	350	350	270	250
Society of Friends -	1	180	..	180	18	10	..	1	170	..	170	18	..	..
Unitarians - -	..	..	..	..	..	..	..	1	..	..	500	190	..	182
Wesleyan Methodists -	3	485	584	1069	822	295	705	6	862	1554	2316	1542	795	1290
Methodist New Connex.	..	..	..	..	..	..	..	6	1010	1540	2550	1530	661	1950
Primitive Methodists -	..	..	..	..	..	..	..	4	756	444	1200	737	535	990
OTHER CHRISTIAN CHS.:														
Roman Catholics -	1	..	..	300	..	..	..	1	200	238	438	830	..	500
Latter Day Saints -	2	..	..	..	70	80	130	1	105	..	105	..	85	50
Jews - - - -	1	30	9	39	60	..	60	1	..	10	10	10	10	10
		EXETER. *(Municipal Borough.)* Population, 32,818.							FINSBURY. *(Parliamentary Borough.)* Population, 323,772.					
TOTAL -	40	5984	11,943	18,457	12,235	6448	8992	127	38,175	51,574	89,129	60,899	11,812	47,620
PROTESTANT CHURCHES:														
Church of England -	25	3661	6649	10,840	7852	5438	4655	46	21,415	26,164	48,879	29,694	6891	23,059
Church of Scotland -	..	..	..	..	..	..	..	1	120	480	600	250	..	100
Presby. Ch. in England	..	..	..	..	..	..	..	2	565	935	1500	870	..	718
Independents - -	2	180	892	1072	557	133	507	24	4212	9958	15,070	10,262	1651	10,539
Particular Baptists -	3	140	890	1030	960	290	1050	19	2388	6095	8661	5573	822	5661
Baptists (*not otherwise defined*) - -	..	..	..	..	..	..	..	1	30	..	30	..	..	20
Society of Friends -	1	700	..	700	54	..	37	..	..	..	..	..	..	..
Unitarians - -	1	100	700	800	364	..	250	1	20	180	200	130	..	..
Wesleyan Methodists -	2	250	1130	1380	920	150	980	9	2216	4588	6804	3818	1205	3864
Primitive Methodists -	..	..	..	..	..	..	..	3	268	962	1230	225	93	362
Bible Christians -	1	300	500	800	130	165	220	..	..	..	..	..	..	..
Wesleyan Association -	..	..	..	..	..	..	..	3	305	354	659	517	..	332
Wesleyan Reformers -	1	115	230	345	300	60	345	1	50	150	200	93	..	130
L'Huntingdon's Connex.	..	..	..	..	..	..	..	1	..	..	2000	..	..	..
New Church -	..	..	..	..	..	..	..	1	..	520	520	300	..	126
Brethren - -	1	200	..	200	150	..	120	..	..	..	..	..	..	..
Isolated Congregations	1	200	800	1000	700	200	800	7	1216	550	1766	1882	5	389
OTHER CHRISTIAN CHS.:														
Roman Catholics -	1	100	100	200	250	..	..	4	1370	640	2010	4945	601	1679
Cath. & Apos. Church -	..	..	..	..	..	..	..	1	300	..	300	200	150	180
Latter Day Saints -	..	..	..	..	..	..	..	3	700	..	700	140	194	510
Jews - - - -	1	38	52	90	48	12	28	..	..	..	..	..	..	..

DOVER.—The returns omit to state the number of *sittings* in one place of worship belonging to the LATTER DAY SAINTS, attended by a maximum number of 130 persons at a service.—The number of *attendants* is not given for one place of worship belonging to the GENERAL BAPTISTS, and for one place belonging to the ROMAN CATHOLICS.—*Neither sittings nor attendants* are given for one place of worship belonging to the LATTER DAY SAINTS.

EXETER.—The number of *sittings* is not given for one place of worship belonging to the CHURCH OF ENGLAND, attended by a maximum number of 110 persons at a service; and for one place belonging to the PARTICULAR BAPTISTS, attended by a maximum number of 300 persons at a service.—The number of *attendants* is not given for one place of worship belonging to the CHURCH OF ENGLAND.—*Neither sittings nor attendants* are given for one place of worship belonging to the CHURCH OF ENGLAND.

FINSBURY.—The number of *sittings* is not given for one place of worship belonging to the CHURCH OF ENGLAND, attended by a maximum number of 840 persons at a service; for two places belonging to the PARTICULAR BAPTISTS, attended by a maximum number of 165 persons at a service; for the place of worship belonging to LADY HUNTINGDON'S CONNEXION, attended by a maximum number of 2000 persons at a service; for two places belonging to ISOLATED CONGREGATIONS, attended by a maximum number of 950 persons at a service; and for one place belonging to the ROMAN CATHOLICS, attended by a maximum number of 200 persons at a service.—The number of *attendants* is not given for four places of worship belonging to the CHURCH OF ENGLAND; for one place belonging to the INDEPENDENTS; and for one place belonging to the ROMAN CATHOLICS.

TABLE F.—continued.

RELIGIOUS DENOMINATION.	Number of Places of Worship	Number of Sittings.			Number of Attendants at Public Worship on Sunday, March 30, 1851 [including Sunday Scholars].			Number of Places of Worship.	Number of Sittings.			Number of Attendants at Public Worship on Sunday, March 30, 1851 [including Sunday Scholars].		
		Free.	Appropriated.	Total.	Morning.	Afternoon.	Evening.		Free.	Appropriated.	Total.	Morning.	Afternoon.	Evening.
	GATESHEAD. (Municipal Borough.) Population, 25,568.							**GRAVESEND.** (Municipal Borough.) Population, 16,633.						
TOTAL	24	3890	3841	9681	3519	2424	2467	11	3304	3078	6532	3919	966	3231
PROTESTANT CHURCHES:														
Church of England	7	1605	940	3695	1563	619	1162	4	1036	1114	3350	1945	664	1801
Presby. Ch. in England	1	..	600	600	290	..	100	..	..	..	..	..	..	..
Independents	..	..	..	..	..	..	..	1	428	673	1101	690	..	500
Particular Baptists	..	..	..	..	..	..	..	2	430	540	970	507	200	360
Wesleyan Methodists	6	1078	880	1958	516	255	664	1	230	630	860	461	72	420
Methodists, New Connex.	5	595	1331	1926	630	1006	392	..	..	..	..	..	..	..
Primitive Methodists	4	312	90	402	..	344	149	1	80	100	180	140	..	155
Isolated Congregations	..	..	..	..	..	..	..	1	..	..	50	16	..	..
OTHER CHRISTIAN CHS.:														
Roman Catholics	1	300	..	300	500	200	..	1	..	21	21	140	..	..
	GREAT YARMOUTH. (Municipal Borough.) Population, 30,879.							**GREENWICH.** (Parliamentary Borough.) Population, 105,784.						
TOTAL	21	5699	8532	14,223	7280	4297	5716	70	16,431	17,830	34,685	25,546	6486	13,543
PROTESTANT CHURCHES:														
Church of England	5	3200	3728	6928	3785	2499	2163	21	5611	8134	13,845	14,716	5087	8303
Presby. Ch. in England	..	..	..	..	..	..	..	3	206	1128	1776	1257	..	481
Independents	2	284	816	1100	640	..	519	7	790	2368	3658	2499	125	1906
Particular Baptists	1	150	338	480	316	434	270	9	1100	2514	3614	2702	104	2360
General Baptists, New Connexion	1	..	..	300	200	..	..	..	..	..	..	..	..	..
Baptists (not otherwise defined)	..	..	..	..	..	..	..	2	190	248	438	196	101	187
Society of Friends	1	255	..	255	17	10	..	1	148	..	148	25	11	..
Unitarians	1	50	350	400	210	..	130	..	..	..	..	..	..	..
Wesleyan Methodists	3	400	1050	1450	671	246	689	6	758	1542	2320	1365	26	1169
Methodist New Connex.	1	250	500	750	347	349	333	..	..	..	..	..	..	..
Primitive Methodists	1	300	700	1000	500	600	900	3	255	177	432	180	8	191
Bible Christians	..	..	..	..	..	..	..	2	118	240	358	181	..	156
Wesleyan Association	..	..	..	..	..	..	..	3	373	431	804	536	..	372
Wesleyan Reformers	1	150	250	400	400	..	450	1	..	..	..	111	..	60
Ly Huntingdon's Connex.	1	150	470	620	180	..	150	..	..	..	..	..	..	..
Isolated Congregations	2	460	..	460	..	159	90	7	430	96	540	521	72	536
OTHER CHRISTIAN CHS.:														
Roman Catholics	..	..	..	..	..	..	..	3	350	950	1300	1047	822	740
Latter Day Saints	..	..	..	..	..	..	..	2	100	..	252	212	180	230
Jews	1	30	30	60	14	..	22	..	..	..	..	..	..	..

GATESHEAD.—The number of *attendants* is not given for two places of worship belonging to the CHURCH OF ENGLAND.

GREENWICH.—The returns omit to state the number of *sittings* in one place of worship belonging to the PARTICULAR BAPTISTS, attended by a maximum number of 450 persons at a service ; and in one place belonging to an ISOLATED CONGREGATION, attended by a maximum of 200 persons.—The number of *attendants* is not given for one place of worship belonging to an ISOLATED CONGREGATION.

TABLE F.—continued.

HALIFAX (Municipal Borough. Population, 33,582.) / HUDDERSFIELD (Parliamentary Borough. Population, 30,880.)

RELIGIOUS DENOMINATION.	No. of Places of Worship	Number of Sittings			Attendants March 30, 1851			No. of Places of Worship	Number of Sittings			Attendants March 30, 1851		
		Free	Appropriated	Total	Morning	Afternoon	Evening		Free	Appropriated	Total	Morning	Afternoon	Evening
TOTAL	13	2458	7384	10,192	5650	1442	4816	25	4528	11,259	15,787	8758	3309	6328
PROTESTANT CHURCHES:														
Church of England	6	1380	3081	4811	2996	2588	2270	7	2015	3775	5790	3670	2020	2300
Independents	..	..	..	..	..	..	..	2	460	2450	2910	1717	261	906
Particular Baptists	..	..	..	..	..	..	..	2	40	280	320	62	80	218
General Baptist New Connexion	1	50	300	350	208	..	90	..	..	..	..	..	..	..
Society of Friends	..	..	..	..	..	..	..	1	429	..	429	73	41	..
Unitarians	..	..	..	..	..	..	..	1	100	120	220	120	..	90
Wesleyan Methodists	2	438	1928	2366	973	311	808	5	668	2856	3524	1763	282	1307
Methodists New Connex.	2	110	1500	1610	579	54	681	3	266	946	1212	496	285	523
Primitive Methodists	1	80	575	655	434	239	441	1	200	432	632	348	240	600
Wesleyan Reformers	1	400	..	400	460	200	526	..	..	..	..	..	..	..
Isolated Congregations	..	..	..	.	..	..	..	1	100	..	100	47	70	..
OTHER CHRISTIAN CHS.:														
Roman Catholics	..	..	..	..	..	..	..	1	..	400	400	400	..	300
Latter Day Saints	..	..	..	..	..	..	..	1	250	..	250	40	30	80

HULL (Municipal Borough. Population, 84,690.) / IPSWICH (Municipal Borough. Population, 32,914.)

RELIGIOUS DENOMINATION.	No. of Places of Worship	Free	Appropriated	Total	Morning	Afternoon	Evening	No. of Places of Worship	Free	Appropriated	Total	Morning	Afternoon	Evening
TOTAL	51	12,109	22,906	36,177	20,921	2223	18,828	31	4993	10,274	16,017	9721	7611	6106
PROTESTANT CHURCHES:														
Church of England	15	4850	6818	12,830	7057	611	5164	15	2555	4862	8167	5722	4760	2946
United Presby. Church	1	470	130	600	117	..	89	..	..	..	..	..	..	..
Independents	8	1606	4372	5978	2963	510	2883	2	352	1020	1372	971	997	835
Particular Baptists	2	140	1000	1140	525	..	461	4	546	2460	3006	1880	1414	1150
Baptists (not otherwise defined)	2	..	..	..	50	..	50	..	..	..	..	..	..	..
Society of Friends	1	386	..	386	111	61	..	1	600	..	600	111	71	..
Unitarians	1	90	400	490	220	..	130	1	50	800	850	310	..	450
Wesleyan Methodists	7	1362	6094	7456	4123	..	3983	2	300	555	855	299	72	290
Methodists New Connex.	2	205	875	1080	509	..	380	..	..	..	..	..	..	..
Primitive Methodists	5	620	2130	2750	2714	..	2730	1	100	200	300	80	237	100
Wesleyan Association	..	..	..	..	..	..	..	1	80	270	350	88	60	80
Wesleyan Reformers	1	500	500	1000	650	..	1000	..	..	..	..	..	..	..
Brethren	1	383	327	710	380	400	800	1	60	..	60	20	..	20
Isolated Congregations	2	534	..	534	138	334	137	1	120	..	120	30	..	35
OTHER CHRISTIAN CHS.:														
Roman Catholics	1	428	200	628	1200	..	850	1	200	100	300	200	..	200
Latter Day Saints	1	500	..	500	70	90	150	..	..	..	..	..	..	..
Jews	1	35	60	95	74	17	21	1	30	7	37	10	..	..

HUDDERSFIELD.—The number of *attendants* is not given for one place of worship belonging to the WESLEYAN METHODISTS.

HULL.—The number of *sittings* is not given for one place of worship belonging to the BAPTISTS (not otherwise defined), attended by a maximum number of 50 persons at a service.—*Neither sittings nor attendants* are given for two places of worship belonging to the CHURCH OF ENGLAND; for one place belonging to the BAPTISTS (not otherwise defined); and for one place belonging to the PRIMITIVE METHODISTS.

TABLE F.—*continued.*

RELIGIOUS DENOMINATION.	Number of Places of Worship.	Number of Sittings.			Number of Attendants at Public Worship on Sunday, March 30, 1851 [including Sunday Scholars].			Number of Places of Worship.	Number of Sittings.			Number of Attendants at Public Worship on Sunday, March 30, 1851 [including Sunday Scholars].		
		Free.	Appropriated.	Total.	Morning.	Afternoon.	Evening.		Free.	Appropriated.	Total.	Morning.	Afternoon.	Evening.
	KIDDERMINSTER. (*Municipal Borough.*) Population, 18,462.							KING'S LYNN. (*Municipal Borough.*) Population, 19,355.						
TOTAL -	15	3756	5629	9685	5027	801	4066	15	3257	5145	9502	5076	1767	3202
PROTESTANT CHURCHES:														
Church of England	5	2556	2689	5545	2789	484	2212	4	1324	1640	3714	2090	1314	970
Independents	1	100	1000	1100	533	..	300	1	258	700	958	538	..	386
Particular Baptists	1	120	280	400	224	..	181	2	370	750	1120	740	..	616
Society of Friends	..	..	..	..	..	..	..	1	120	..	120	7	1	..
Unitarians	1	50	500	550	311	..	157	1	146	104	250	120	..	..
Wesleyan Methodists	3	340	550	890	400	167	683	1	276	884	1160	625	100	420
Primitive Methodists	2	110	140	250	210	..	233	1	113	417	530	343	281	360
Wesleyan Association	..	..	..	..	..	..	..	1	150	150	300	102	71	100
Wesleyan Reformers	..	..	..	..	..	..	..	1	400	500	900	281	..	350
L'Huntingdon'sConnex.	1	230	470	700	260	..	300	..	..	..	..	..	..	..
OTHER CHRISTIAN CHS.:														
Roman Catholics	1	250	..	250	300	150	..	1	..	..	350	200	..	..
Latter Day Saints	..	..	..	..	..	..	..	1	100	..	100	30	..	..
	LAMBETH. (*Parliamentary Borough.*) Population, 251,345.							LEEDS. (*Municipal Borough.*) Population, 172,270.						
TOTAL -	96	22,849	36,925	61,664	40,240	5295	32,426	137	33,201	42,804	76,488	39,392	12,922	29,280
PROTESTANT CHURCHES:														
Church of England	36	13,975	22,468	38,223	24,723	2804	17,778	36	9760	10,193	25,436	13,530	6106	8558
Independents	15	2620	7092	9712	6854	1072	5694	11	2050	6255	8305	3428	90	2564
Particular Baptists	12	1078	3216	4374	3568	746	3576	9	1246	2695	3941	1350	608	1080
Scotch Baptists	..	..	..	..	..	..	..	1	150	..	150	35	46	42
General Baptists, New Connexion	..	..	..	..	..	..	..	2	300	850	1150	469	..	477
Baptists (*not otherwise defined*)	1	100	..	100	..	..	35	1	104	436	540	235	..	159
Society of Friends	1	334	..	334	117	72	..	1	..	..	1100	363	169	..
Unitarians	..	..	..	..	..	..	..	3	690	550	1240	506	..	227
Wesleyan Methodists	12	2262	3026	5288	3292	15	3719	26	7604	12,871	20,475	9614	2193	8089
Methodist New Connex.	1	120	462	582	219	..	160	7	642	2075	2717	1573	711	1314
Primitive Methodists	5	400	50	480	105	16	134	13	1607	2293	3900	1507	698	1698
Bible Christians	1	140	116	256	129	..	258	..	..	..	..	..	..	..
Wesleyan Association	1	90	70	160	87	..	52	10	1438	2916	4354	1796	725	1843
Wesleyan Reformers	1	100	25	125	110	..	110	4	200	..	200	650	732	1030
L'Huntingdon'sConnex.	1	100	400	500	340	..	200	..	..	..	..	..	..	..
New Church.	..	..	..	..	..	..	..	1	150	700	850	80	..	110
Brethren	..	..	..	..	..	..	..	2	150	100	250	271	..	330
Isolated Congregations	5	820	..	820	256	60	75	5	280	..	280	195	181	559
OTHER CHRISTIAN CHS.:														
Roman Catholics	..	..	..	..	..	..	..	2	400	820	1220	3644	365	1000
Cath. and Apos. Church	1	400	..	400	250	309	300	..	..	..	..	..	..	..
Latter Day Saints	3	310	..	310	190	210	335	1	240	..	240	100	150	200
Jews -	..	..	..	..	..	..	..	2	90	50	140	46	86	..

KIDDERMINSTER.—The number of *attendants* is not given for one place of worship belonging to the CHURCH OF ENGLAND.—*Neither sittings nor attendants* are given for one place of worship belonging to the PRIMITIVE METHODISTS.

LAMBETH.—The returns omit to state the number of *sittings* in one place of worship belonging to the WESLEYAN METHODISTS, attended by a maximum number of 40 persons at a service; in two places belonging to the PRIMITIVE METHODISTS, attended by a maximum number of 45 persons at a service; and in one place belonging to the LATTER DAY SAINTS, attended by a maximum number of 80 persons at a service.—The number of *attendants* is not given for two places of worship belonging to the ESTABLISHED CHURCH; for one place belonging to the INDEPENDENTS; and for one place belonging to an ISOLATED CONGREGATION.

LEEDS.—The returns omit to state the number of *sittings* in one place of worship belonging to the ESTABLISHED CHURCH, attended by a maximum number of 63 persons at a service; in one place belonging to the PARTICULAR BAPTISTS, attended by a maximum number of 120 persons at a service; in two places belonging to the WESLEYAN METHODISTS, attended by a maximum number of 109 persons at a service; in one place belonging to the WESLEYAN REFORMERS, attended by a maximum number 750 persons at a service; and in three places belonging to ISOLATED CONGREGATIONS, attended by a maximum number of 580 persons at a service.—The number of *attendants* is not given for two places of worship belonging to, the ESTABLISHED CHURCH.

TABLE F.—continued.

RELIGIOUS DENOMINATION.	Number of Places of Worship	Number of Sittings.			Number of Attendants at Public Worship on Sunday, March 30, 1851 [including Sunday Scholars].			Number of Places of Worship	Number of Sittings.			Number of Attendants at Public Worship on Sunday, March 30, 1851 [including Sunday Scholars.]		
		Free.	Appropriated.	Total.	Morning.	Afternoon.	Evening.		Free.	Appropriated	Total.	Morning.	Afternoon.	Evening.
				LEICESTER. (*Municipal Borough*) Population, 60,584.							LIVERPOOL. (*Municipal Borough*.) Population, 375,955.			
TOTAL -	35	11,110	13,598	25,008	16,960	5386	15,522	165	41,672	78,071	122,266	96,218	9983	61,653
PROTESTANT CHURCHES :														
Church of England -	9	4274	4354	8628	6884	4036	6024	59	23,489	37,365	60,545	36,001	4733	26,433
Church of Scotland -	..	..	..	..	..	..	..	2	20	2630	2650	730	310	200
United Presby. Church	..	..	..	..	..	..	..	1	60	1100	1160	666	..	425
Presby. Ch. in England	..	..	..	..	..	..	..	4	70	3830	3900	2588	838	1150
Reformed Irish Presby.	..	..	..	..	..	..	..	1	120	..	120	..	..	..
Independents - -	3	1144	1490	2634	1700	..	1237	10	2437	5505	7942	3590	246	3489
Particular Baptists -	5	1562	1652	3214	2549	200	1715	7	1090	3300	4390	1283	140	1441
General Baptists, New Connexion - -	5	1424	2005	3429	2250	..	2143	..	..	..	..	..	..	..
Baptists (not otherwise defined) - -	..	..	..	..	..	..	..	4	730	1400	2130	475	46	720
Society of Friends -	1	280	..	280	78	41	..	1	..	..	940	239	130	..
Unitarians - -	1	20	450	470	350	..	280	4	181	1610	1791	985	57	328
Wesleyan Methodists -	2	356	1216	1572	750	79	800	17	3192	5752	8944	5941	1063	5647
MethodistNewConnex.	..	..	..	..	..	..	..	3	620	1400	2020	744	..	686
Primitive Methodists -	3	340	781	1121	555	285	960	3	400	900	1300	571	20	557
Wesleyan Association -	1	160	600	760	320	200	500	4	937	1494	2431	803	..	662
IndependentMethodists	1	250	..	250	..	140	40	1	..	..	20	..	..	30
Wesleyan Reformers -	1	250	800	1050	683	..	630	..	..	..	..	..	..	..
Welsh Calv. Methodists	..	..	..	..	..	..	..	5	1118	3123	4241	2240	242	2915
L'Huntingdon'sConnex.	..	..	..	..	..	..	..	1	150	..	150	..	146	150
Sandemanians - -	..	..	..	..	..	..	..	1	..	..	39	32	..	..
New Church - -	..	..	..	..	..	..	..	2	200	400	600	181	..	400
Isolated Congregations	1	600	..	600	175	..	400	14	1308	787	2095	739	37	1118
OTHER CHRISTIAN CHS. :														
Roman Catholics -	1	200	350	550	636	185	497	16	7273	6945	14,218	33,132	1905	15,205
Cath. and Apos. Church	..	..	..	..	..	..	..	1	100	..	100	70	..	60
Latter Day Saints -	1	250	..	250	..	120	296	1	9	..	9	..	..	20
Jews - - -	..	..	..	..	..	..	..	3	180	530	710	131	23	47

LEICESTER.—The number of *attendants* is not given for two places of worship belonging to the ESTABLISHED CHURCH.

LIVERPOOL.—The returns omit to state the number of *sittings* in four places of worship belonging to the ESTABLISHED CHURCH, attended by a maximum number of 1067 persons at a service ; in one place belonging to the WESLEYAN METHODISTS, attended by a maximum number of 15 persons at a service ; in one place belonging to the PRIMITIVE METHODISTS, attended by a maximum number of 30 persons at a service ; in one place belonging to the INDEPENDENT METHODISTS, attended by a maximum number of 30 persons at a service ; in one place belonging to the SANDEMANIANS, attended by a maximum number of 39 persons at a service ; in one place belonging to an ISOLATED CONGREGATION ; and in one place belonging to the ROMAN CATHOLICS, attended by a maximum number of 75 persons at a service.—The number of *attendants* is not given for three places of worship belonging to the ESTABLISHED CHURCH ; for one place belonging to the REFORMED IRISH PRESBYTERIANS ; for one place belonging to the PARTICULAR BAPTISTS ; and for two places belonging to the JEWS.

TABLE F.—*continued.*

RELIGIOUS DENOMINATION.	Number of Places of Worship	Number of Sittings.			Number of Attendants at Public Worship on Sunday, March 30, 1851 [including Sunday Scholars].			Number of Places of Worship	Number of Sittings.			Number of Attendants at Public Worship on Sunday, March 30, 1851 [including Sunday Scholars].		
		Free.	Appropriated.	Total.	Morning.	Afternoon.	Evening.		Free.	Appropriated.	Total.	Morning.	Afternoon.	Evening.
	CITY OF LONDON. *(Municipal Borough.)* Population, 127,869.							MACCLESFIELD. *(Municipal Borough.)* Population, 39,048.						
TOTAL	115	18,387	30,253	67,576	31,575	6724	19,804	27	7164	8742	15,906	7782	3233	6168
PROTESTANT CHURCHES:														
Church of England	73	11,140	16,053	41,199	18,790	6055	10,918	7	3204	4225	7429	3584	2297	1918
United Presby. Church	2	800	1200	3000	955	..	1250	..	..	..	..	..	..	..
Presby. Ch. in England	2	..	530	1180	460	..	370	..	..	..	..	..	..	..
Independents	10	1869	5837	7706	4790	150	3340	3	347	1210	1557	550	36	584
General Baptists	..	..	..	..	..	..	..	1	100	400	500	160	..	200
Particular Baptists	4	737	1195	1932	602	..	854	1	..	..	..	16	24	..
Baptists (*not otherwise defined*)	..	..	..	..	..	..	..	1	100	..	100	62	31	46
Society of Friends	..	..	..	..	..	..	..	1	230	..	230	37	21	..
Unitarians	2	300	620	920	252	..	110	1	100	250	350	150	300	..
Moravians	2	1100	..	1100	246	..	126	..	..	..	..	..	..	..
Wesleyan Methodists	4	386	1246	1632	978	50	1080	4	727	1319	2046	1230	209	1377
Methodist New Connex.	..	..	..	..	..	..	..	3	1300	800	2100	522	165	634
Primitive Methodists	..	..	..	..	..	..	..	2	246	238	484	330	30	241
Wes. Meth. Association	..	..	..	..	..	..	..	1	150	160	310	151	..	136
L'Huntingdon'sConnex.	1	100	720	820	400	..	600	..	..	..	..	..	..	..
Sandemanians	1	200	..	200	200	..	..	..	..	..	..	..	..	..
Isolated Congregations	3	200	345	1345	476	..	143	..	..	..	..	..	..	..
Lutherans	1	120	400	520	90	..	..	..	..	..	..	..	..	..
French Protestants	1	280	..	280	150	..	160	..	..	..	..	..	..	..
Reformed Church in the Netherlands	1	350	..	350	70	..	..	..	..	..	..	..	..	..
OTHER CHRISTIAN CHS.:														
Roman Catholics	1	..	..	2500	1350	..	..	1	660	140	800	990	..	880
Greek Church	1	105	..	105	160	..	..	..	..	..	..	..	..	..
German Catholics	1	100	200	300	500	..	200	..	..	..	..	..	..	..
Latter Day Saints	..	..	..	..	..	..	..	1	..	..	..	..	120	200
Jews	5	600	1887	2487	1104	469	713	..	..	..	..	..	..	..

LONDON.—The returns omit to state the number of *sittings* in one place of worship belonging to the CHURCH OF ENGLAND, attended by a maximum number of 190 persons at a service.—The number of *attendants* is not given for four places of worship belonging to the CHURCH OF ENGLAND, and for one place belonging to the PARTICULAR BAPTISTS.—*Neither sittings nor attendants* are given for one place of worship belonging to the CHURCH OF ENGLAND.

MACCLESFIELD.—The returns omit to state the number of *sittings* in one place of worship belonging to the PARTICULAR BAPTISTS, attended by a maximum number of 24 persons at a service; and in one place belonging to the LATTER DAY SAINTS, attended by a maximum number of 200 persons at a service.

TABLE F.—continued.

RELIGIOUS DENOMINATION.	Number of Places of Worship.	Number of Sittings.			Number of Attendants at Public Worship on Sunday, March 30, 1851 [including Sunday Scholars].			Number of Places of Worship.	Number of Sittings.			Number of Attendants at Public Worship on Sunday, March 30, 1851 [including Sunday Scholars].		
		Free.	Appropriated.	Total.	Morning.	Afternoon.	Evening.		Free.	Appropriated.	Total.	Morning.	Afternoon.	Evening.
	MAIDSTONE. (*Municipal Borough.*) Population, 20,740.							MANCHESTER. (*Municipal Borough.*) Population, 303,382.						
TOTAL	17	3522	6105	10,327	6064	3406	3148	122	33,627	60,892	95,929	64,467	8868	32,048
PROTESTANT CHURCHES:														
Church of England	6	2519	2813	5782	3738	2944	1243	32	14,498	24,622	38,120	20,050	4519	11,375
Church of Scotland	..	..	..	..	..	..	..	2	..	1060	1060	280	100	100
United Presby. Church	..	..	..	..	..	..	..	2	200	800	1000	820	..	350
Presby. Ch. in England	..	..	..	..	..	..	..	4	550	3070	3620	2060	710	1150
Independents	1	200	500	700	377	53	284	19	4306	8392	12,698	6396	210	2664
Particular Baptists	3	225	1002	1227	721	262	682	7	1780	2470	4250	1727	65	1855
Baptists (*not otherwise defined*)	..	..	..	..	..	..	..	1	36	204	240	..	150	200
Society of Friends	1	..	..	250	37	20	..	1	1330	..	1330	453	202	..
Unitarians	1	150	250	400	138	..	50	4	620	2080	2700	1210	160	500
Wesleyan Methodists	1	236	810	1046	488	77	387	17	4789	8184	12,973	6403	781	5683
Methodist New Connex.	..	..	..	..	..	..	..	2	600	550	1150	559	..	191
Primitive Methodists	1	62	130	192	53	50	22	5	715	1141	1856	1143	105	1150
Bible Christians	..	..	..	..	..	..	..	1	150	300	450	157	177	..
Wesleyan Association	..	..	..	..	..	..	..	10	2335	2936	5271	2662	157	1534
Welsh Calvinistic Meth.	..	..	..	..	..	..	..	1	40	260	300	..	150	146
L'Huntingdon's Connex.	1	..	600	600	500	..	450	1	64	513	577	322	..	433
New Church	..	..	..	..	..	..	..	1	250	500	750	350	..	200
Isolated Congregations	2	130	..	130	12	..	50	2	220	..	220	85	..	160
OTHER CHRISTIAN CHS.:														
Roman Catholics	..	..	..	..	..	..	..	7	3400	3450	6850	19,880	1052	3647
Greek Church	..	..	..	..	..	..	..	1	86	..	86	60	..	..
Jews	..	..	..	..	..	..	..	2	68	360	428	150	80	110

* MAIDSTONE.—The number of *attendants* is not given for one place of worship belonging to the CHURCH OF ENGLAND.

MANCHESTER.—The number of *attendants* is not given for five places of worship belonging to the CHURCH OF ENGLAND, and for one place of worship belonging to the INDEPENDENTS.

TABLE F.—continued.

RELIGIOUS DENOMINATION.	Number of Places of Worship	Number of Sittings.			Number of Attendants at Public Worship on Sunday, March 30, 1851 [including Sunday Scholars].			Number of Places of Worship	Number of Sittings.			Number of Attendants at Public Worship on Sunday, March 30, 1851 [including Sunday Scholars].		
		Free.	Appropriated.	Total.	Morning.	Afternoon.	Evening.		Free.	Appropriated.	Total.	Morning.	Afternoon.	Evening.
	MARYLEBONE. (Parliamentary Borough.) Population, 370,957.							MERTHYR TYDFIL. (Parliamentary Borough.) Population, 63,080.						
TOTAL -	126	35,752	59,576	98,753	77,055	13,448	47,175	84	16,767	16,676	34,629	22,706	4966	28,159
PROTESTANT CHURCHES:														
Church of England	55	23,858	36,102	62,085	49,405	13,288	26,301	10	1602	916	3764	1443	76	1837
United Presby. Church	1	80	600	680	210	..	150	..	..	..	..	..	..	..
Presby. Ch. in England	2	782	1900	2682	1775	..	1080	..	..	..	..	..	..	..
Independents -	17	3414	8189	11,603	9205	869	8309	20	2989	5477	8466	7902	889	8336
Particular Baptists	10	1936	4388	6324	3096	690	3262	19	5681	5183	10,864	9041	809	10,664
General Baptists, New Connexion -	2	450	800	1250	1074	..	1098	..	..	..	..	..	..	..
Baptists (not otherwise defined) -	1	100	400	500	200	..	200	..	..	..	..	..	..	..
Unitarians -	1	50	450	500	300	..	200	2	261	200	461	263	..	204
Wesleyan Methodists -	10	1657	3501	5158	3814	..	3010	10	1429	1851	3310	760	176	1619
Primitive Methodists -	3	130	50	180	102	68	201	2	150	310	460	142	80	276
Wesleyan Association -	2	138	60	198	277	..	336	..	..	..	..	..	..	..
Wesleyan Reformers -	1	70	..	70	45	..	60	2	120	..	120	40	..	115
Welsh Calv. Methodists	..	..	..	..	..	..	..	10	2640	2639	5279	1544	1728	3977
L'Huntingdon's Connex.	2	140	766	906	525	..	480	..	..	..	..	..	..	..
New Church -	2	60	..	360	195	..	130	..	..	..	..	..	..	..
Isolated Congregations	5	1040	..	1040	181	52	163	1	265	40	305	226	..	462
OTHER CHRISTIAN CHS.:														
Roman Catholics	6	1394	2070	3464	5693	928	1575	1	300	..	300	600	150	..
Greek Church -	1	100	..	100	20	..	..	..	..	..	..	..	..	..
Catholic and Apostolic Church -	2	1100	..	1100	700	400	450	..	..	..	..	..	..	..
Latter Day Saints -	2	220	..	220	90	120	170	6	1260	..	1260	711	1057	646
Jews -	1	83	300	333	148	..	..	1	10	30	40	34	21	23

MARYLEBONE.—The returns omit to state the number of *sittings* in one place of worship belonging to the ESTABLISHED CHURCH, attended by a maximum number of 600 persons at a service; and in one place belonging to the INDEPENDENTS, attended by a maximum number of 152 persons at a service.—The number of *attendants* is not given for four places of worship belonging to the ESTABLISHED CHURCH; and for one place belonging to the ROMAN CATHOLICS.—*Neither sittings nor attendants* are given for one place of worship belonging to the ESTABLISHED CHURCH.

MERTHYR TYDFIL.—The returns omit to state the number of *sittings* in three places of worship belonging to the INDEPEN- DENTS, attended by a maximum number of 795 persons at a service; in one place belonging to the PARTICULAR BAPTISTS, attended by a maximum number of 200 persons at a service; in one place belonging to the WESLEYAN REFORMERS, attended by a maximum number of 35 persons at a service; and in three places belonging to the LATTER DAY SAINTS, attended by a maximum number of 379 persons at a service.—The number of *attendants* is not given for one place of worship belonging to the ESTABLISHED CHURCH, and for two places belonging to the PARTICULAR BAPTISTS.—*Neither sittings nor attendants* are given for one place of worship belonging to the WESLEYAN METHODISTS.

TABLE F.—continued.

RELIGIOUS DENOMINATION.	Number of Places of Worship.	Number of Sittings.			Number of Attendants at Public Worship on Sunday, March 30, 1851 [including Sunday Scholars].			Number of Places of Worship.	Number of Sittings.			Number of Attendants at Public Worship on Sunday, March 30, 1851 [including Sunday Scholars].		
		Free.	Appropriated.	Total.	Morning.	Afternoon.	Evening.		Free.	Appropriated.	Total.	Morning.	Afternoon.	Evening.
	NEWCASTLE-ON-TYNE. (Municipal Borough.) Population, 87,784.							NEWPORT. (Municipal Borough.) Population, 19,323.						
TOTAL	51	11,165	15,931	23,806	18,710	4640	11,730	21	4635	5383	10,018	5365	646	5424
PROTESTANT CHURCHES:														
Church of England	11	2877	7051	9928	7202	2643	4691	3	905	631	1536	1177	128	820
Church of Scotland	2	500	..	1500	625	..	800	..						
United Presby. Church	3	500	..	1200	1170	225	275	..						
Presby. Ch. in England	2	260	1310	1570	704	..	548	..						
Independents	2	86	950	1036	826	..	518	5	755	1068	1823	873	..	1007
Particular Baptists	5	1548	350	1898	1028	40	698	3	1000	924	1924	912	..	1150
Scotch Baptists	1	250	..	250	44	..	42	..						
Baptists (not otherwise defined)	1	..						..						
Society of Friends	1	512	..	512	217	112	..	..						
Unitarians	2	257	815	1072	461	..	118	..						
Wesleyan Methodists	6	1150	2502	3652	1270	139	1307	2	590	1250	1840	463	..	634
Methodist New Connex.	3	680	782	1472	210	145	280	..						
Primitive Methodists	4	1006	757	1823	806	370	742	..						
Bible Christians	..							1	50	180	230	71	..	84
Wesleyan Association	..							..						
Wesleyan Reformers	2	495	..	495	630	..	780	2	425	250	675	210	..	409
Welsh Calv. Methodists	..							1	150	80	230	260	98	201
New Church	1	350	50	400	70	..	70	..						
Isolated Congregations	2	150	..	150	8	66	57	2	460	..	460	19	20	19
OTHER CHRISTIAN CHS.:														
Roman Catholics	2	410	1334	1744	3389	900	604	1	300	1000	1300	1300	200	700
Latter Day Saints	..							1	..	..	60	200	400	
Jews	1	74	30	104	50	..	..	..						
	NORTHAMPTON. (Municipal Borough.) Population, 26,657.							NORWICH. (Municipal Borough.) Population, 68,195.						
TOTAL	28	5049	7622	14,268	7381	2226	7289	86	9422	10,330	23,834	13,240	10,374	7908
PROTESTANT CHURCHES:														
Church of England	11	2407	3436	6840	2987	1031	2513	41	8966	2533	15,551	6520	6381	2186
Independents	3	339	1467	1806	1518	..	987	3	380	1866	2246	1735	250	989
Particular Baptists	5	580	1241	2121	1545	675	1495	4	699	1748	2447	1639	817	1169
General Baptists, New Connexion	..							1	150	150	300	200	150	150
Baptists (not otherwise defined)	..							3	206	..	256	116	138	182
Society of Friends	1	400	..	400	59	..	450	1	408	..	408	93	41	..
Unitarians	1	95	195	290	230	..	160	1	120	380	500	491	..	136
Wesleyan Methodists	2	465	932	1397	796	388	1236	5	696	1495	2191	494	506	669
Primitive Methodists	1	128	172	300	79	92	128	4	196	858	1054	607	604	788
Wesleyan Association	1	35	179	214	107	..	120	..						
Wesleyan Reformers	..							1	120	450	570	323	117	294
L'Huntingdon'sConnex.	..							1	250	700	950	160	115	80
New Church	..							1	12	120	132	90	..	106
Isolated Congregations	1	200	..	290	30	40	100	11	1740	..	1740	497	974	1035
OTHER CHRISTIAN CHS.:														
Roman Catholics	1	..	..	300	..	..	..	1	..	..	250	..	..	
Latter Day Saints	1	400	..	400	30	..	100	1	400	..	400	..	181	150
Jews	..							1	59	30	89	26	..	24

NEWCASTLE-ON-TYNE.—The returns omit to state the number of *sittings* in one place of worship belonging to the UNITED PRESBYTERIAN CHURCH, attended by a maximum number of 275 persons at a service; and in one place belonging to an ISOLATED CONGREGATION, attended by a maximum number of 30 persons at a service.—The number of *attendants* is not given for one place of worship belonging to the ESTABLISHED CHURCH.—*Neither sittings nor attendants* are given for one place of worship belonging to the ESTABLISHED CHURCH; for one [place belonging to the PARTICULAR BAPTISTS; and for one place belonging to the BAPTISTS, not otherwise defined.

NEWPORT.—The returns omit to state the number of *sittings* in one place of worship belonging to the ESTABLISHED CHURCH, attended by a maximum number of 200 persons at a service; and in one place belonging to the LATTER DAY SAINTS, attended by a maximum number of 400 persons at a service.

NORTHAMPTON.—The number of *attendants* is not given for one place of worship belonging to the ESTABLISHED CHURCH and for one place belonging to the ROMAN CATHOLICS.

NORWICH.—The returns omit to state the number of *sittings* in three places of worship belonging to the ESTABLISHED CHURCH, attended by a maximum number of 360 persons at a service; in one place belonging to the PRIMITIVE METHODISTS, attended by a maximum number of 15 persons at a service; in one place belonging to an ISOLATED CONGREGATION, attended by a maximum number of 59 persons at a service; and in one place belonging to the ROMAN CATHOLICS, attended a maximum number of 250 persons at a service.—The number of *attendants* is not given for one place of worship belonging to the ESTABLISHED CHURCH.—*Neither sittings nor attendants* are given for one place of worship belonging to an ISOLATED CONGREGATION.

TABLE F.—*continued.*

RELIGIOUS DENOMINATION.	Number of Places of Worship.	Number of Sittings.			Number of Attendants at Public Worship on Sunday, March 30, 1851 [including Sunday Scholars].			Number of Places of Worship.	Number of Sittings.			Number of Attendants at Public Worship on Sunday, March 30, 1851 [including Sunday Scholars].		
		Free.	Appropriated.	Total.	Morning.	Afternoon.	Evening.		Free.	Appropriated.	Total.	Morning.	Afternoon.	Evening.
	NOTTINGHAM. (*Municipal Borough.*) Population, 57,407.							OLDHAM. (*Municipal Borough.*) Population, 52,820.						
TOTAL -	37	11,484	14,763	26,947	16,854	1450	14,846	29	7445	8739	16,784	7229	4698	4792
PROTESTANT CHURCHES:														
Church of England	8	3522	2320	7042	5370	508	4124	9	3295	3975	7870	2784	2489	920
Independents	5	1067	2774	3841	2014	277	1345	4	630	1760	2390	1634	757	1642
Particular Baptists	3	1050	1320	2370	1096	50	1225	2	280	490	770	500	102	510
General Baptists, New Connexion	3	426	1705	2131	1231	20	1419	..	..	..	..	..	..	..
Baptists (*not otherwise defined*)	1	100	..	100	30	14	47	..	..	..	..	..	..	..
Society of Friends	1	550	..	550	87	40	..	1	48	140	188	115	88	..
Unitarians	1	60	550	610	606	..	..	1	400	84	484	179	293	185
Moravians	..	..	..	..	..	..	..	1	..	..	..	..	..	..
Wesleyan Methodists	2	1030	2634	3664	1830	45	2250	3	370	1220	1590	779	122	707
Methodist New Connex.	1	132	850	982	734	..	493	1	84	358	442	148	223	146
Primitive Methodists	2	583	1267	1850	1223	..	1900	2	298	484	782	100	150	610
Wesleyan Association	1	140	200	340	165	..	245	2	200	188	388	190	..	360
Independent Methodists	..	..	..	..	..	..	..	2	790	..	790	260	224	252
Wesleyan Reformers	1	600	..	600	500	..	700	..	..	..	..	..	..	..
New Church	1	200	..	200	60	..	100	..	..	..	..	..	..	..
Isolated Congregations	2	770	..	770	176	24	147	2	600	..	600	..	..	60
OTHER CHRISTIAN CHS.:														
Roman Catholics	2	500	623	1123	1420	312	604	1	450	40	490	550	250	..
Cath. and Apos. Church	1	400	..	400	..	..	..	..	..	..	..	..	..	..
Latter Day Saints	1	324	..	324	83	136	233	..	..	..	..	..	..	..
Jews	1	30	20	50	27	15	14	..	..	..	..	..	..	..

RELIGIOUS DENOMINATION.	Number of Places of Worship.	Number of Sittings.			Number of Attendants.			Number of Places of Worship.	Number of Sittings.			Number of Attendants.		
		Free.	Appropriated.	Total.	Morning.	Afternoon.	Evening.		Free.	Appropriated.	Total.	Morning.	Afternoon.	Evening.
	OXFORD. (*Municipal Borough.*) Population, 27,843.							PLYMOUTH. (*Municipal Borough.*) Population, 52,221.						
TOTAL -	32	6650	5413	15,518	8242	2785	5488	38	9258	13,647	23,905	13,176	3056	12,542
PROTESTANT CHURCHES:														
Church of England	19	4171	3445	11,296	5767	2235	3273	10	3891	4624	9615	6086	1642	5074
Independents	3	394	550	944	606	..	..	5	736	2232	2968	1517	62	1440
Particular Baptists	3	1000	450	1525	1053	..	1070	1	329	707	1036	797	114	569
Society of Friends	1	300	250	550	100	..	..	1	400	..	400	60	30	..
Unitarians	..	..	..	..	..	..	..	1	168	506	674	213	..	209
Wesleyan Methodists	1	186	516	702	448	500	400	5	810	1466	2976	1487	78	1363
Primitive Methodists	2	90	156	246	122	50	190	..	..	..	..	..	..	..
Bible Christians	..	..	..	..	..	..	..	1	88	540	628	279	203	401
Wesleyan Association	..	..	..	..	..	..	..	1	136	172	308	77	..	44
Wesleyan Reformers	1	95	..	95	86	..	71	..	..	..	..	..	..	..
New Church	1	50	..	50	..	..	40	..	..	..	..	..	..	..
Isolated Congregations	..	..	..	..	..	..	..	10	2450	3050	5500	2527	853	3342
OTHER CHRISTIAN CHS.:														
Roman Catholics	1	40	40	80	50	..	..	..	..	..	..	..	..	..
Cath. and Apos. Church	..	..	..	..	..	..	..	1	250	..	250	83	50	60
Jews	1	24	6	30	10	..	..	1	..	150	150	50	24	4

NOTTINGHAM.—The number of *attendants* is not given for one place of worship belonging to the CATHOLIC AND APOSTOLIC CHURCH.—*Neither sittings nor attendants* are given for one place of worship belonging to the ROMAN CATHOLICS.

OLDHAM.—The returns omit to state the number of *sittings* in one place of worship belonging to an ISOLATED CONGREGATION, attended by a maximum number of 60 persons at a service.—The number of *attendants* is not given for two places of worship belonging to the ESTABLISHED CHURCH, and for one place belonging to an ISOLATED CONGREGATION.

OXFORD.—The returns omit to state the number of *sittings* in one place of worship belonging to the CHURCH OF ENGLAND, attended by a maximum number of 1000 persons at a service.

TABLE F.—continued.

RELIGIOUS DENOMINATION.	Number of Places of Worship	Number of Sittings.			Number of Attendants at Public Worship, on Sunday, March 30, 1851 [including Sunday Scholars].			Number of Places of Worship	Number of Sittings.			Number of Attendants at Public Worship, on Sunday, March 30, 1851 [including Sunday Scholars].		
		Free.	Appropriated.	Total.	Morning.	Afternoon.	Evening.		Free.	Appropriated.	Total.	Morning.	Afternoon.	Evening.
		PORTSMOUTH. *(Municipal Borough.)* Population, 72,096.							**PRESTON.** *(Municipal Borough.)* Population, 69,542.					
TOTAL	44	9400	14,813	26,013	17,044	6039	13,501	29	9750	14,892	24,642	11,803	1603	4293
PROTESTANT CHURCHES:														
Church of England	12	5708	5027	12,230	7878	4076	4455	10	4900	6900	11,800	2479	951	180
Independents	6	1193	3370	4563	3108	573	3251	2	410	1220	1630	1065	..	750
General Baptists	2	350	900	1250	998	..	985	..	..	..	..	..	..	..
Particular Baptists	7	411	1679	2090	1394	291	1655	2	164	752	916	437	..	282
Scotch Baptists	..	..	..	..	..	..	..	1	60	..	60	23	23	..
Baptists *(not otherwise defined)*	2	130	..	430	30	41	131	..	..	..	..	..	..	..
Society of Friends	..	..	..	..	..	..	..	1	528	..	528	153	69	..
Unitarians	1	80	520	600	144	..	292	1	..	145	145	86	..	40
Wesleyan Methodists	6	735	2166	2901	2325	319	1910	3	726	1487	2213	1505	..	1480
Primitive Methodists	1	73	167	240	115	109	130	1	300	500	800	342	..	345
Bible Christians	2	140	418	558	456	517	552	..	..	..	..	..	..	..
Wesleyan Association	..	..	..	..	..	..	..	1	150	340	490	254	..	328
L'Huntingdon's Connex.	..	..	..	..	..	..	..	1	50	750	800	142	..	..
New Church	..	..	..	..	..	..	..	1	50	200	250	100	60	66
Brethren	1	100	..	100	65	..	..	..	..	..	..	..	..	..
Isolated Congregations	1	40	..	40	40	18	40	1	200	..	200	120	..	80
OTHER CHRISTIAN CHS.:														
Roman Catholics	1	345	256	601	931	..	..	4	2212	2598	4810	5097	500	742
Latter Day Saints	1	100	150	250	30	70	80	..	..	..	..	..	..	..
Jews	1	..	160	160	35	25	20	..	..	..	..	..	..	..

RELIGIOUS DENOMINATION.	Number of Places of Worship	Number of Sittings.			Number of Attendants			Number of Places of Worship	Number of Sittings.			Number of Attendants		
		Free.	Appropriated.	Total.	Morning.	Afternoon.	Evening.		Free.	Appropriated.	Total.	Morning.	Afternoon.	Evening.
		READING. *(Municipal Borough.)* Population, 21,456.							**ROCHDALE.** *(Parliamentary Borough.)* Population, 29,195.					
TOTAL	21	3953	5014	9977	7068	1434	6198	23	5207	7634	12,841	6385	3722	4420
PROTESTANT CHURCHES:														
Church of England	7	2371	2976	5457	3969	500	3130	3	1333	1567	2900	1350	1000	700
Independents	8	895	1320	1715	1497	487	1101	1	240	730	970	740	..	445
Particular Baptists	2	140	560	700	510	290	640	3	570	1400	1970	641	803	472
Baptists *(not otherwise defined)*	1	80	40	120	110	30	130	..	..	..	..	..	..	..
Society of Friends	1	414	..	414	80	..	58	1	400	..	400	60	33	..
Unitarians	..	..	..	..	..	..	..	2	40	380	420	330	330	..
Wesleyan Methodists	3	168	521	689	348	111	343	3	620	1100	1720	596	349	516
Methodist New Connex.	..	..	..	..	..	..	..	1	310	361	671	285	125	163
Primitive Methodists	1	89	531	420	291	..	590	2	346	286	632	220	204	345
Wesleyan Association	..	..	..	..	..	..	..	5	412	1191	1603	910	656	1129
L'Huntingdon's Connex.	..	..	..	..	..	..	..	1	436	564	1000	800	..	650
Isolated Congregations	1	100	..	100	35	..	35	..	..	..	..	..	..	..
OTHER CHRISTIAN CHS.:														
Roman Catholics	1	96	166	262	220	..	140	1	500	55	555	453	222	..
Latter Day Saints	1	100	..	100	8	16	31	..	..	..	..	..	..	..

* PORTSMOUTH.—The returns omit to state the number of *sittings* in one place of worship belonging to the PARTICULAR BAPTISTS, attended by a maximum number of 476 persons at a service.

PRESTON.—The number of *attendants* is not given for seven places of worship belonging to the CHURCH OF ENGLAND and for one place belonging to the ROMAN CATHOLICS.

READING.—The returns omit to state the number of *sittings* in one place of worship belonging to the CHURCH OF ENGLAND, attended by a maximum number of 900 persons at a service; and in one place belonging to the PARTICULAR BAPTISTS, attended by a maximum number of 50 persons at a service.—The number of *attendants* is not given for one place of worship belonging to the ESTABLISHED CHURCH.

* ROCHDALE.—The returns omit to state the number of *sittings* in one place of worship belonging to the WESLEYAN METHODISTS, attended by a maximum number of 101 persons at a service; and in two places belonging to the WESLEYAN ASSOCIATION, attended by a maximum number of 75 persons at a service.—The number of *attendants* is not given for one place of worship belonging to the ESTABLISHED CHURCH.

TABLE F.—*continued*.

RELIGIOUS DENOMINATION.	Number of Places of Worship.	Number of Sittings.			Number of Attendants at Public Worship on Sunday, March 30, 1851 [including Sunday Scholars].			Number of Places of Worship.	Number of Sittings.			Number of Attendants at Public Worship on Sunday, March 30, 1851 [including Sunday Scholars].		
		Free.	Appropriated.	Total.	Morning.	Afternoon.	Evening.		Free.	Appropriated.	Total.	Morning.	Afternoon.	Evening.
	SALFORD. (*Municipal Borough.*) Population, 63,850.							**SHEFFIELD.** (*Municipal Borough.*) Population, 135,310.						
TOTAL -	26	9599	11,373	21,772	12,686	630	10,043	70	14,222	29,513	44,189	20,300	4587	18,534
PROTESTANT CHURCHES:														
Church of England -	8	4006	3970	8776	4691	300	4702	23	6815	11,797	19,562	6291	2934	5656
Church of Scotland -	1	800	..	800	195	..	140	..	..	..	..	..	..	..
Independents -	4	1019	2757	3776	2139	..	1466	10	1112	3974	4486	2283	413	1854
Particular Baptists -	1	300	..	300	250	..	120	2	220	1250	1470	831	..	624
General Baptists, New Connexion -	1	150	50	200	140	300	210	2	250	500	750	362	..	527
Society of Friends -	..	..	..	..	..	..	..	1	800	..	800	136	80	..
Unitarians -	..	..	..	..	..	..	..	1	50	850	900	650	..	350
Wesleyan Methodists -	4	1240	2858	4098	1518	30	1313	16	3067	7412	10,479	5282	966	4319
Methodist New Connex. -	..	..	..	..	..	..	..	5	402	1550	1952	1000	..	1183
Primitive Methodists -	1	390	410	800	159	..	200	1	350	650	1000	977	..	1550
Wesleyan Association -	2	410	466	876	427	..	425	2	90	580	670	241	..	161
Independent Methodists -	1	100	66	166	40	..	60	..	..	..	..	..	..	..
Wesleyan Reformers -	..	..	..	..	..	..	..	2	..	..	..	30	100	..
Welsh Calv. Methodists -	1	284	216	500	130	..	127	..	..	..	..	..	..	..
New Church -	1	..	450	450	306	..	160	..	..	..	..	..	..	..
Isolated Congregations -	..	..	..	..	..	..	..	2	350	..	350	50	..	64
OTHER CHRISTIAN CHS.:														
Roman Catholics -	1	900	130	1030	2500	..	1100	1	..	950	950	2000	..	2000
Cath. and Apos. Church -	..	..	..	..	..	..	..	1	320	..	320	140	100	250
Jews - - -	..	..	..	..	..	..	..	1	500	..	500	27	..	..
	SOUTHAMPTON. (*Municipal Borough.*) Population, 35,305.							**SOUTH SHIELDS.** (*Municipal Borough.*) Population, 28,974.						
TOTAL -	29	6977	10,732	17,959	10,302	2440	8829	30	5058	8920	13,978	4768	2796	5831
PROTESTANT CHURCHES:														
Church of England -	10	3913	6268	10,181	5729	1293	4697	9	2366	2844	5210	1550	695	1960
United Presby. Church -	..	..	..	..	..	..	..	2	50	650	700	335	164	180
Presby. Ch. in England -	..	..	..	..	..	..	..	2	436	660	1096	427	145	230
Independents -	2	815	1743	2558	1909	373	1640	1	..	900	900	352	..	341
Particular Baptists -	3	260	660	920	460	70	387	1	70	..	70	40	40	40
Baptists (*not otherwise defined*) -	..	..	..	..	..	..	..	1	..	420	420	224	..	276
Society of Friends -	1	..	..	250	54	15	..	..	..	..	..	..	..	..
Unitarians -	2	70	400	470	267	..	336	..	..	..	..	..	..	..
Wesleyan Methodists -	1	500	600	1100	635	100	600	5	478	1706	2184	295	112	525
Methodist New Connex. -	..	..	..	..	..	..	..	1	100	400	500	145	266	230
Primitive Methodists -	1	159	114	273	178	208	248	3	600	760	1360	570	727	1240
Bible Christians -	2	190	90	280	154	..	165	..	..	..	..	..	..	..
Wesleyan Association -	..	..	..	..	..	..	..	..	430	450	880	300	370	589
Isolated Congregations -	2	450	500	950	285	..	409	1	210	30	240	89	144	150
French Protestants -	1	250	..	250	..	..	..	..	..	..	..	..	..	..
OTHER CHRISTIAN CHS.:														
Roman Catholics -	1	..	300	300	500	300	..	1	270	100	370	430	110	..
Cath. and Apos. Church -	1	150	..	150	80	60	80	..	..	..	..	..	..	..
Latter Day Saints -	1	200	..	200	30	30	50	1	48	..	48	11	23	..
Jews - - -	1	20	57	77	21	..	17	..	..	..	..	..	..	..

SALFORD.—The number of *attendants* is not given for one place of worship belonging to the ESTABLISHED CHURCH.
SHEFFIELD.—The returns omit to state the number of *sittings* in one place of worship belonging to the ESTABLISHED CHURCH, attended by a maximum number of 70 persons at a service; in one place belonging to the WESLEYAN METHODISTS, attended by a maximum number of 25 persons at a service; in one place belonging to the METHODIST NEW CONNEXION, attended by a maximum number of 42 persons at a service; and in two places belonging to the WESLEYAN REFORMERS, attended by a maximum number of 100 persons at a service.—The number of *attendants* is not given for two places of worship belonging to the ESTABLISHED CHURCH.—*Neither sittings nor attendants* are given for one place of worship belonging to the ESTABLISHED CHURCH.
SOUTHAMPTON.—The number of *attendants* is not given for one place of worship belonging to the FRENCH PROTESTANTS.
SOUTH SHIELDS.—The number of *attendants* is not given for one place of worship belonging to the WESLEYAN METHODISTS.—*Neither sittings nor attendants* are given for one place of worship belonging to the WESLEYAN METHODISTS.

TABLE F.—continued.

SOUTHWARK (Parliamentary Borough.) Population, 172,863. — STOCKPORT (Municipal Borough.) Population, 53,835.

RELIGIOUS DENOMINATION.	Number of Places of Worship.	Number of Sittings.			Number of Attendants at Public Worship on Sunday, March 30, 1851 [including Sunday Scholars].			Number of Places of Worship.	Number of Sittings.			Number of Attendants at Public Worship on Sunday, March 30, 1851 [including Sunday Scholars].		
		Free.	Appropriated.	Total.	Morning.	Afternoon.	Evening.		Free.	Appropriated.	Total.	Morning.	Afternoon.	Evening.
TOTAL	82	19,901	23,706	46,860	31,879	6180	27,066	35	7791	14,177	22,168	12,110	1457	9502
PROTESTANT CHURCHES:														
Church of England	32	12,026	9819	23,588	13,038	4591	11,077	8	3528	5278	8806	4010	1020	3270
Presby. Ch. in England	1	50	850	900	300	..	150	..						
Independents	10	2204	4951	7155	5019	431	5147	5	863	2223	3086	1598	..	1716
General Baptists	1	100	150	250	..	..	40	..						
Particular Baptists	13	1356	4726	6342	4145	20	3938	2	360	510	870	340	..	405
General Baptists, New Connexion	1	700	300	1000	550	..	600	1	150	..	150	30	..	40
Society of Friends	1	500	..	500	75	29	..	..						
Unitarians	1	350	50	400	55	..	120	1	50	400	450	250	..	150
Wesleyan Methodists	7	1457	2206	3663	1070	..	850	9	1910	3021	4931	2600	110	2201
Methodist New Connex.	..							2	340	989	1329	640	..	672
Primitive Methodists	1	100	..	100	51	..	80	2	360	322	682	253	187	480
Wesleyan Association	3	218	484	702	169	95	187	1	100	264	364	250	..	120
Independent Methodists	..							1	130	120	250	50	30	175
Wesleyan Reformers	1	100	70	170	100	..	160	..						
Welsh Calv. Methodists	1	100	..	100	..	100	60	..						
Isolated Congregations	4	220	..	220	57	14	127	1	..	..	200	..	..	173
OTHER CHRISTIAN CHS.:														
Roman Catholics	3	300	20	1570	7200	900	4500	1	..	1050	1050	2000	..	..
Latter Day Saints	..							1	..	..	80	140	160	
Jews	2	120	80	200	50	..	30	..						

STOKE-UPON-TRENT (Parliamentary Borough.) Population, 84,027. — SUNDERLAND (Municipal Borough.) Population, 63,897.

	Number of Places of Worship.	Free.	Appropriated.	Total.	Morning.	Afternoon.	Evening.	Number of Places of Worship.	Free.	Appropriated.	Total.	Morning.	Afternoon.	Evening.
TOTAL	73	17,100	23,113	40,723	15,012	6732	12,609	63	14,395	14,371	30,766	14,096	1942	14,972
PROTESTANT CHURCHES:														
Church of England	18	6269	9374	17,163	5681	2852	2331	9	4190	4533	8723	4461	1061	3526
United Presby. Church	..							4	100	1100	2110	1219	..	1296
Presby. Ch. in England	1	100	350	450	201	..	179	1	21	700	721	456	..	418
Independents	7	966	1854	2890	1135	15	1046	4	962	1486	3448	1387	..	1563
Particular Baptists	3	245	280	525	371	..	209	4	1650	100	1750	814	125	1407
General Baptists, New Connexion	1	80	..	80	71	44	40	..						
Baptists (not otherwise defined)	..							2	..	..	80	..	..	..
Society of Friends	2	400	..	400	52	22	..	1	700	..	700	136	93	..
Unitarians	..							1	250	50	300	20	..	200
Wesleyan Methodists	12	3247	4040	7297	3697	997	3365	15	2125	3531	5656	1350	301	2052
Methodist New Connex.	13	3052	3942	6994	2427	1012	2914	3	234	326	560	328	..	452
Primitive Methodists	7	1143	865	2008	445	1320	1367	6	1360	1240	2600	1510	..	2080
Wesleyan Association	3	1003	628	1631	242	320	783	4	729	1171	1992	637	48	665
Wesleyan Reformers	..							3	1110	70	1180	722	56	1260
New Church	1	35	..	35	30	..	..	..						
Brethren	2	175	..	175	..	..	65	..						
Isolated Congregations	..							3	830	..	830	16	260	20
OTHER CHRISTIAN CHS.:														
Roman Catholics	3	365	780	1145	1260	150	310	1	50	30	80	950	..	..
Jews	..							2	82	34	116	12	..	13

SOUTHWARK.—The returns omit to state the number of sittings in one place of worship belonging to the CHURCH OF ENGLAND, attended by a maximum number of 250 persons at a service ; and in one place belonging to the ROMAN CATHOLICS, attended by a maximum number of 4000 persons at a service. The number of attendants is not given for three places of worship belonging to the CHURCH OF ENGLAND ; for one place belonging to the WESLEYAN METHODISTS ; and for one place belonging to the JEWS.

STOCKPORT.—The returns omit to state the number of sittings in one place of worship belonging to the WESLEYAN METHODISTS, attended by a maximum number of 43 persons at a service ; and in one place belonging to the LATTER DAY SAINTS, attended by a maximum number of 160 persons at a service.

STOKE-UPON-TRENT.—The number of attendants is not given for two places of worship belonging to the CHURCH OF ENGLAND.

SUNDERLAND.—The returns omit to state the number of sittings in one place of worship belonging to the BAPTISTS (not otherwise defined), attended by a maximum number of 80 persons at a service ; and in one place belonging to the METHODIST NEW CONNEXION, attended by a maximum number of 90 persons at a service.—The number of attendants is not given for one place of worship belonging to the JEWS.—Neither sittings nor attendants are given for one place of worship belonging to the BAPTISTS (not otherwise defined).

TABLE F.—continued.

RELIGIOUS DENOMINATION.	Number of Places of Worship	Number of Sittings.			Number of Attendants at Public Worship on Sunday, March 30, 1851 [including Sunday Scholars].			Number of Places of Worship	Number of Sittings.			Number of Attendants at Public Worship on Sunday, March 30, 1851 [including Sunday Scholars].		
		Free.	Appropriated.	Total.	Morning.	Afternoon.	Evening.		Free.	Appropriated.	Total.	Morning.	Afternoon.	Evening.
	SWANSEA. (*Municipal Borough.*) Population, 31,461.							TOWER HAMLETS. (*Parliamentary Borough.*) Population, 539,111.						
TOTAL -	37	7101	10,158	18,239	6835	2042	9491	214	24,299	62,273	120,444	83,532	18,581	63,870
PROTESTANT CHURCHES :														
Church of England	5	1770	3597	5067	1597	673	1175	65	21,063	22,805	67,126	34,724	7632	25,551
Church of Scotland	..	..	..	..	..	..	..	1	150	602	752	505	..	245
Presby. Ch. in England	..	..	..	..	..	..	..	1	50	480	530	370	..	220
Independents	7	1466	2289	3755	1658	109	2466	46	8900	17,379	26,779	18,931	2073	15,994
General Baptists	..	..	..	..	..	..	..	2	350	460	810	694	..	450
Particular Baptists	3	1413	1654	3067	1221	185	2150	22	4412	5975	10,387	6373	1764	6423
Seventh Day Baptists -	..	..	..	..	..	..	..	1	300	..	300	15	40	16
Baptists (*not otherwise defined*)	..	..	..	..	..	..	..	5	440	384	974	690	..	193
Society of Friends	1	240	..	240	22	15	..	1	560	..	560	66	24	..
Unitarians	1	..	400	400	157	..	121	2	270	500	770	298	..	263
Wesleyan Methodists	4	502	914	1416	473	..	769	20	4348	7381	11,729	5851	709	5583
Methodist New Connex.	..	..	..	..	..	..	..	3	290	52	342	111	..	75
Primitive Methodists -	1	140	160	300	150	..	260	4	280	505	785	573	366	724
Bible Christians -	..	..	..	..	..	..	..	1	100	300	400	290	..	200
Wesleyan Association	..	..	..	..	..	..	..	2	200	200	400	310	..	160
Wesleyan Reformers	..	..	..	..	..	..	..	4	186	550	7362	886	..	870
Welsh Calv. Methodist	5	1150	1860	3010	758	863	1450	..	..	..	..	..	..	..
L'Huntingdon's Connex.	1	50	600	650	450	..	600	3	520	2752	3272	1698	..	1787
Brethren	..	..	..	..	..	..	..	2	..	130	130	60	..	45
Isolated Congregations	1	150	..	150	..	130	..	13	817	788	2285	1001	470	1360
Lutherans	..	..	..	..	..	..	..	2	431	321	752	570	100	..
German Pro. Reformers	..	..	..	..	..	..	..	1	140	60	200	120	..	60
OTHER CHRISTIAN CHS. :														
Roman Catholics -	1	200	12	212	300	..	300	6	585	761	2006	8340	..	2300
Cath. and Apos. Church	..	..	..	..	..	..	..	1	700	..	700	400	..	..
Latter Day Saints	1	..	..	..	50	70	200	5	550	18	618	117	253	231
Jews -	1	30	42	72	..	..	..	1	50	..	50	40	40	40

RELIGIOUS DENOMINATION.	Number of Places of Worship	Number of Sittings.			Number of Attendants at Public Worship			Number of Places of Worship	Number of Sittings.			Number of Attendants at Public Worship		
	TYNEMOUTH. (*Municipal Borough.*) Population, 29,170.							WAKEFIELD. (*Municipal Borough.*) Population, 22,065.						
TOTAL -	26	3647	8429	12,086	6288	1787	4784	26	5977	6894	14,821	7900	3257	4540
PROTESTANT CHURCHES :														
Church of England	8	965	3000	3965	2550	950	1500	9	1852	1892	5494	3875	2397	1512
United Presby. Church	1	40	366	406	253	358	..	..	..	..	..	..	..	..
Presby. Ch. in England	1	100	700	800	660	..	..	..	..	..	..	..	..	..
Independents	2	330	955	1285	651	..	534	4	120	2516	2636	1098	369	752
Particular Baptists	1	100	590	690	220	..	260	1	650	..	650	253	..	164
Society of Friends	1	400	..	400	78	..	85	1	500	..	500	66	85	..
Unitarians	..	..	..	..	..	..	..	1	..	500	500	243	..	84
Wesleyan Methodists	4	400	1240	1640	841	70	964	4	605	1766	2371	710	66	491
Methodist New Connex.	3	300	950	1250	630	..	660	1	150	110	260	110	..	100
Primitive Methodists -	1	200	250	450	..	300	350	2	130	460	590	226	150	480
Wesleyan Reformers	2	540	30	570	420	42	404	2	1550	..	1550	1022	85	957
Isolated Congregations	1	100	..	100	15	..	20	..	..	..	..	..	..	..
OTHER CHRISTIAN CHS. :														
Roman Catholics -	1	166	334	500	..	..	..	1	120	150	270	300	160	..
Jews -	1	6	24	30	20	17	17	..	..	..	..	..	..	..

SWANSEA.—The returns omit to state the number of *sittings* in one place of worship belonging to the LATTER DAY SAINTS, attended by a maximum number of 200 persons at a service.—The number of *attendants* is not given for one place of worship belonging to the PARTICULAR BAPTISTS ; nor for one place belonging to the Jews.

TOWER HAMLETS.—The returns omit to state the number of *sittings* in one place of worship belonging to the ESTABLISHED CHURCH, attended by a maximum number of 900 persons at a service ; in four places belonging to the INDEPENDENTS, attended by a maximum number of 2288 persons at a service ; in one place belonging to the PARTICULAR BAPTISTS, attended by a maximum number of 130 persons at a service ; and in one place belonging to the WESLEYAN METHODIST REFORMERS, attended by a maximum number of 150 persons at a service.—The number of *attendants* is not given for six places of worship belonging to the ESTABLISHED CHURCH.

TYNEMOUTH.—The returns omit to state the number of *sittings* in one place of worship belonging to the WESLEYAN METHODISTS, attended by a maximum number of 85 persons at a service ; and in one place belonging to the METHODIST NEW CONNEXION, attended by a maximum number of 30 persons at a service.—The number of *attendants* is not given for one place of worship belonging to the ROMAN CATHOLICS.—Neither *sittings* nor *attendants* are given for one place of worship belonging to the WESLEYAN METHODISTS.

WAKEFIELD.—The number of *sittings* is not given for one place of worship belonging to the CHURCH OF ENGLAND, attended by a maximum number of 400 persons at a service ; and in one place belonging to the INDEPENDENTS, attended by a maximum number of 154 persons at a service.

TABLE F.—continued.

RELIGIOUS DENOMINATION.	Number of Places of Worship	Number of Sittings.			Number of Attendants at Public Worship on Sunday, March 30, 1851 [including Sunday Scholars].			Number of Places of Worship	Number of Sittings.			Number of Attendants at Public Worship on Sunday, March 30, 1851 [including Sunday Scholars].		
		Free.	Appropriated.	Total.	Morning.	Afternoon.	Evening.		Free.	Appropriated.	Total.	Morning.	Afternoon.	Evening.
	WALSALL. (*Municipal Borough.*) Population, 25,680.							WARRINGTON. (*Municipal Borough.*) Population, 22,894.						
TOTAL -	19	4497	5906	10,503	5147	2285	3699	15	3501	6154	9655	6686	2564	4272
PROTESTANT CHURCHES:														
Church of England -	4	1955	2862	4917	2158	1395	1075	4	1811	3199	5010	3235	1911	2218
Independents -	1	200	700	900	598	..	307	1	..	..	..	120	..	150
Particular Baptists -	2	300	520	820	436	22	280	1	120	138	258	150	..	90
General Baptists New Connexion -	1	220	110	330	115	..	170	..	..	..	..	..	..	..
Baptists (*not otherwise defined*) -	1	125	..	125	..	108	..	..	..	..	..	..	..	..
Society of Friends -	..	..	..	..	..	..	..	1	355	..	355	72	28	..
Unitarians -	..	..	..	..	..	..	..	1	250	250	500	196	..	58
Wesleyan Methodists -	5	985	930	1915	865	390	1035	1	450	956	1406	991	..	1000
Primitive Methodists -	3	404	182	586	229	80	162	1	75	194	269	250	..	200
Independent Method. -	..	..	..	..	..	..	..	2	300	250	550	425	375	184
L'Huntingdon'sConnex.	..	..	..	..	..	..	..	1	160	550	710	360	..	350
Isolated Congregations	..	..	..	..	..	..	..	1	80	..	80	15	..	22
OTHER CHRISTIAN CHS.:														
Roman Catholics -	2	308	602	910	946	290	670	1	..	617	617	870	250	..
	WESTMINSTER. (*Parliamentary Borough.*) Population, 241,611.							WIGAN. (*Municipal Borough.*) Population, 31,941.						
TOTAL -	99	24,514	41,092	74,349	49,845	14,582	27,921	15	2920	5579	9449	8687	3194	5102
PROTESTANT CHURCHES:														
Church of England -	59	18,278	25,671	52,142	33,019	13,391	14,823	3	1029	2204	3233	3302	2308	2312
Church of Scotland -	3	354	2160	2514	2250	100	1950	..	..	..	..	..	..	..
United Presby. Church	1	100	500	600	510	..	..	..	..	..	..	..	..	..
Independents -	11	2622	7538	10,160	7022	..	6977	3	500	1120	1620	907	320	696
Particular Baptists -	4	260	1350	1760	749	631	860	2	460	..	460	285	304	..
Society of Friends -	1	..	..	400	106	..	49	..	..	..	..	..	..	..
Wesleyan Methodists -	5	450	1021	1471	827	..	884	1	267	705	972	691	..	478
Primitive Methodists -	1	..	..	..	20	..	58	..	..	..	..	..	..	..
Independent Method. -	..	..	..	..	..	..	..	1	200	150	350	200	212	42
Wesleyan Reformers -	1	120	120	240	212	..	160	..	..	..	..	..	..	..
Welsh Calv. Methodists	2	550	150	700	400	120	130	1	100	..	100	30	50	56
Isolated Congregations	..	..	..	..	..	..	..	1	164	..	164	47	..	46
Lutherans - -	3	380	520	900	300	60	..	..	..	..	..	..	..	..
Italian Reformers -	1	150	..	150	..	20	..	..	..	..	..	..	..	..
OTHER CHRISTIAN CHS.:														
Roman Catholics -	5	1230	1460	2690	4300	610	2000	3	200	1400	2550	3225	..	1570
Jews - - -	2	20	602	622	130	30	30	..	..	..	..	..	..	..

WALSALL. - The number of *attendants* is not given for one place of worship belonging to the PRIMITIVE METHODISTS.
WARRINGTON. The number of *sittings* is not given for one place of worship belonging to the INDEPENDENTS, attended by a maximum number of 150 persons at a service.
WESTMINSTER. The returns omit to state the number of *sittings* in one place of worship belonging to the ESTABLISHED CHURCH, attended by a maximum number of 300 persons at a service ; in one place belonging to the PRIMITIVE METHODISTS ; attended by a maximum number of 58 persons at a service ; in one place belonging to the LUTHERANS, attended by a maximum number of 50 persons at a service ; and in one place belonging to the ROMAN CATHOLICS, attended by a maximum number of 500 persons at a service.—The number of *attendants* is not given in the case of three places of worship belonging to the ESTABLISHED CHURCH ; in one place belonging to the LUTHERANS ; and in one place belonging to the ROMAN CATHOLICS.—*Neither sittings nor attendants* are given for one place of worship belonging to the ESTABLISHED CHURCH.
WIGAN.—The number of *attendants* is not given for one place of worship belonging to the INDEPENDENTS.

TABLE F.—continued.

RELIGIOUS DENOMINATION.	Number of Places of Worship	Number of Sittings.			Number of Attendants at Public Worship on Sunday, March 30, 1851 [including Sunday Scholars].			Number of Places of Worship	Number of Sittings.			Number of Attendants at Public Worship on Sunday, March 30, 1851 [including Sunday Scholars].		
		Free.	Appropriated.	Total.	Morning.	Afternoon.	Evening.		Free.	Appropriated.	Total.	Morning.	Afternoon.	Evening.
	WOLVERHAMPTON. (Parliamentary Borough.) Population, 119,748.							WORCESTER. (Municipal Borough.) Population, 27,528.						
TOTAL -	97	25,363	22,892	48,455	27,015	11,919	24,650	35	6299	8276	15,547	9296	2090	6887
PROTESTANT CHURCHES:														
Church of England	23	11,328	10,735	22,263	11,578	2455	8966	20	3919	4698	9587	6466	1630	4700
Presby. Ch. in England	1	..	100	100	28	..	42	..	..	..	..	..	..	..
Independents -	6	1765	1700	3465	1986	475	1567	1	200	500	700	424	..	356
Particular Baptists -	9	1760	2146	3906	1494	1052	1644	..	..	..	..	..	..	..
Baptists (*not otherwise defined*) -	1	200	..	200	130	..	150	1	252	444	696	441	..	305
Society of Friends	..	..	..	..	..	..	..	1	360	..	360	80	59	..
Unitarians -	2	346	200	546	340	280	58	..	..	..	..	..	..	..
Wesleyan Methodists -	26	4891	4787	9678	7140	3507	7118	4	656	1106	1762	550	69	599
Methodist New Connex.	7	860	1084	1944	1178	1207	1413	..	..	..	..	..	..	..
Primitive Methodists -	14	2661	1086	3747	1481	1697	1967	1	74	176	250	50	60	100
Welsh Calvinistic Meth.	1	180	..	180	..	150	150	..	..	..	..	..	..	..
L'Huntingdon's Connex.	..	..	..	..	..	..	..	3	551	1014	1565	540	72	684
Isolated Congregations	1	350	..	350	..	..	..	2	198	..	198	45	..	84
OTHER CHRISTIAN CHS.:														
Roman Catholics -	4	862	1034	1896	1645	1040	1750	1	89	340	429	500	200	..
Latter Day Saints -	1	150	..	150	..	44	55	1	..	..	..	200	..	..
Jews - -	1	10	20	30	15	12	..	..	..	..	..	..	..	..

RELIGIOUS DENOMINATION.	Number of Places of Worship	Number of Sittings.			Number of Attendants at Public Worship on Sunday, March 30, 1851 [including Sunday Scholars].		
		Free.	Appropriated.	Total.	Morning.	Afternoon.	Evening.
	YORK. (Municipal Borough.) Population, 36,303.						
TOTAL -	40	7922	11,465	23,650	10,675	3452	8488
PROTESTANT CHURCHES:							
Church of England -	24	2362	5056	12,181	4427	2714	2628
Independents -	2	900	1860	2760	1333	80	1018
Society of Friends -	1	1000	..	1000	273	170	..
Unitarians -	1	10	30	40	97	..	60
Wesleyan Methodists -	4	1390	2329	3719	1759	120	1833
Primitive Methodists -	1	120	380	500	141	92	500
Wesleyan Association -	1	100	450	550	187	25	194
Wesleyan Reformers -	2	1150	550	1700	1058	..	1317
New Church -	1	60	..	60	60	..	13
Isolated Congregations	1	150	..	150	80	..	150
OTHER CHRISTIAN CHS.:							
Roman Catholics -	2	180	810	990	1350	251	780

WOLVERHAMPTON.—The number of *attendants* is not given for three places of worship belonging to the ESTABLISHED CHURCH; for one place belonging to the INDEPENDENTS; for one place belonging to the PARTICULAR BAPTISTS; and for one place belonging to an ISOLATED CONGREGATION.

WORCESTER.—The returns omit to state the number of *sittings* in one place of worship belonging to the ESTABLISHED CHURCH, attended by a maximum number of 130 persons at a service; and in one place belonging to the LATTER DAY SAINTS, attended by a maximum number of 200 persons at a service.

YORK.—The number of *attendants* is not given for three places of worship belonging to the ESTABLISHED CHURCH; for one place belonging to the WESLEYAN METHODISTS; and for one place belonging to the WESLEYAN REFORMERS.

TABLE F F.

Accommodation provided by various Religious Bodies in LARGE-TOWN DISTRICTS, as compared with the rest of England.

		Popula- tion, 1851.	Number of Places of Worship provided by							Number of Sittings,* provided by						
			Church of England.	Independents.	Baptists.	Wesleyan Methodists (all sections).	Roman Catholics.	Others.	All Religious Bodies.	Church of England.	Independents.	Baptists.	Wesleyan Methodists (all sections).	Roman Catholics.	Others.	All Religious Bodies.
LARGE-TOWN DISTRICTS:— Districts having Towns with a Population of	10,000 and less than 20,000	91,821	49	14	28	22	8	13	124	29,389	9,008	10,690	8,456	411	8,122	61,078
	20,000 „ 50,000	2,544,704	1504	395	412	1556	96	408	4727	763,511	141,146	120,708	364,155	27,416	107,771	1,534,707
	50,000 „ 100,000	2,332,799	788	230	189	869	69	289	2399	465,703	119,596	76,357	286,581	36,460	101,863	1,085,537
	100,000 and upwards	4,369,796	811	397	214	603	80	331	2336	737,126	184,982	100,258	240,198	51,909	161,449	1,445,922
TOTAL OF LARGE-TOWN DISTRICTS		9,229,120	3457	996	839	3050	268	1036	9586	1,995,729	454,729	318,013	896,372	118,196	344,905	4,127,244
RESIDUE OF THE COUNTRY		8,698,489	10,620	2909	1949	7951	301	1744	24,874	3,522,186	618,031	484,330	1,297,926	67,915	352,411	6,088,799
ENGLAND AND WALES		17,927,609	14,077	3945	2788	11,001	569	2780	34,460	5,517,915	1,067,760	782,343	2,194,298	186,111	697,816	10,216,043

* Including an Estimate for Defective Returns.

Proportions contained in the above Table.

		Number of Sittings to 100 persons, provided by						
		Church of England.	Inde- pendents.	Baptists.	Wesleyan Metho- dists (all sec- tions).	Roman Catholics.	Others.	All Religious Bodies.
LARGE TOWN-DISTRICTS:— Districts having Towns with a Population of	10,000 and less than 20,000	32·0	9·8	11·6	9·2	·5	3·4	66·5
	20,000 „ 50,000	30·0	5·6	5·1	14·3	1·1	4·2	60·3
	50,000 „ 100,000	20·0	5·1	3·3	12·2	1·7	4·4	46·7
	100,000 and upwards	17·3	4·8	2·4	5·6	1·2	3·1	33·9
TOTAL OF LARGE-TOWN DISTRICTS		21·6	4·9	3·5	9·7	1·3	3·7	44·7
RESIDUE OF THE COUNTRY		36·2	7·0	5·0	14·9	·8	4·1	70·0
ENGLAND AND WALES		29·7	6·0	4·3	12·2	1·0	3·9	57·0

TABLE G.

Showing the ACCOMMODATION provided, in each County of England and Wales, by the most numerous Religious Bodies.

TABLE G. • • • • •

Showing the ACCOMMODATION provided, in each COUNTY of England

| COUNTIES. | Number of Places of Worship. | | | | | | | | | Number of | | | |
	Church of England.	Scottish Presbyterians.	Independents.	Baptists.	Wesleyan Methodists.	Calvinistic Methodists.	Roman Catholics.	Others.	TOTAL.	Church of England.	Scottish Presbyterians.	Independents.	Baptists.
ENGLAND AND WALES	14,077	160	3,244	2,789	11,007	937	570	1,683	34,467	5,317,915	86,692	1,067,760	752,343
Bedford	133	..	19	55	96	..	1	23	327	43,842	..	6,155	14,902
Berks	206	..	34	41	125	4	6	19	435	69,868	..	9,596	9,306
Buckingham	226	..	56	72	120	1	4	20	499	67,247	..	11,091	16,796
Cambridge	176	..	38	72	101	1	3	13	404	59,703	..	12,195	18,168
Chester	252	5	66	31	402	12	17	48	833	125,652	2,157	21,909	7,176
Cornwall	265	..	37	25	734	3	7	33	1,104	102,341	..	9,067	5,934
Cumberland	161	17	24	9	186	..	8	34	389	58,688	6,070	7,247	2,296
Derby	250	..	45	39	404	2	8	28	776	89,714	..	13,307	11,477
Devon	549	..	142	112	379	..	8	107	1,297	221,969	..	42,010	25,562
Dorset	304	..	69	15	147	..	7	21	563	94,097	..	19,296	3,814
Durham	169	14	25	21	351	..	20	21	621	68,958	6,550	9,397	5,797
Essex	433	..	134	59	90	2	9	39	766	147,807	..	47,809	16,392
Gloucester	433	..	96	102	214	11	14	58	928	165,003	..	35,439	27,325
Hereford	243	..	20	16	115	5	5	22	426	54,590	..	2,892	3,765
Hertford	162	..	47	44	60	6	4	24	347	55,193	..	13,839	12,611
Huntingdon	96	..	7	30	46	..	..	17	196	25,453	..	2,074	8,375
Kent	479	3	86	107	250	5	13	54	997	213,666	1,776	27,727	27,799
Lancaster	529	22	170	100	521	19	114	152	1,627	389,546	16,715	83,368	35,694
Leicester	289	..	41	85	201	1	12	26	655	88,242	..	12,972	24,814
Lincoln	657	..	38	62	703	1	13	27	1,501	165,087	..	11,508	14,162
Middlesex	419	19	155	102	119	10	32	106	962	352,220	15,535	89,899	39,836
Monmouth	159	..	51	79	100	26	8	11	434	36,131	..	14,911	29,364
Norfolk	719	..	49	91	516	2	6	58	1,441	187,210	..	15,519	21,000
Northampton	292	..	56	87	118	4	6	29	592	92,793	..	17,906	23,471
Northumberland	154	68	14	17	196	..	20	17	488	55,044	32,360	6,060	4,443
Nottingham	248	..	21	54	273	..	5	29	630	76,960	..	8,707	14,421
Oxford	266	..	43	50	116	1	8	20	504	79,270	..	8,369	7,545
Rutland	53	..	6	12	18	..	..	2	91	13,362	..	1,066	1,941
Salop	291	..	59	31	262	11	11	14	679	95,451	..	11,912	5,987
Somerset	553	..	110	89	309	4	8	56	1,129	181,484	..	26,399	22,279
Southampton	389	..	116	69	187	3	13	41	818	150,800	..	32,241	15,135
Stafford	317	4	63	35	377	1	34	32	863	163,856	1,150	21,004	10,599
Suffolk	519	..	90	91	163	..	4	28	895	161,398	..	31,463	26,009
Surrey	262	1	84	68	73	2	14	42	546	151,062	900	31,388	20,054
Sussex	350	..	78	50	80	5	8	46	617	132,327	..	20,739	11,983
Warwick	278	1	64	50	133	3	26	38	593	128,525	700	21,958	15,868
Westmorland	78	1	9	4	59	..	2	12	165	24,788	400	1,800	1,012
Wilts	352	..	76	101	196	2	3	24	754	117,258	..	21,910	24,636
Worcester	244	1	24	46	127	9	12	26	489	88,548	650	7,732	10,220
York (East Riding)	235	1	34	14	362	..	10	14	670	70,921	600	12,009	4,013
„ (City)	24	..	2	8	..	..	2	4	40	12,181	..	2,760	..
„ (North Riding)	301	1	48	13	425	..	22	33	843	86,149	450	12,203	3,357
„ (West Riding)	583	2	158	99	1,060	..	31	123	2,056	288,343	739	74,125	39,738
North Wales	364	..	273	143	324	478	5	27	1,614	115,830	..	52,900	24,194
South Wales	615	..	367	297	209	303	7	65	1,863	148,718	..	121,984	83,077

* Including an Estimate for Defective Returns.

TABLE G.

and Wales, by the most numerous Religious Bodies.

Sittings.*					Proportion per cent. of Sittings to Population.									Population in 1851.
Wesleyan Methodists.	Calvinistic Methodists.	Roman Catholics.	Others.	TOTAL.	Church of England.	Scottish Presbyterians.	Independents.	Baptists.	Wesleyan Methodists.	Calvinistic Methodists.	Roman Catholics.	Others.	TOTAL.	
2,194,298	250,678	186,111	356,766	10,212,563	29·7	·5	6·0	4·2	12·2	1·4	1·0	2·0	57·0	17,927,609
19,226	..	21	5,515	89,661	35·2	..	5·0	12·0	15·4	..	..	4·4	72·0	124,478
17,768	1,089	1,192	2,996	111,817	41·1	..	5·6	5·5	10·4	0·6	0·7	1·8	65·7	170,065
18,400	140	527	2,771	116,972	41·1	..	6·8	10·3	11·2	0·1	0·3	1·7	71·5	163,723
18,299	550	350	2,497	111,762	32·2	..	6·6	9·8	9·9	0·3	0·2	1·3	60·3	185,405
80,524	2,600	6,196	12,176	255,390	27·6	0·5	4·8	1·6	17·7	0·6	1·1	2·7	56·6	455,725
152,905	964	1,445	6,574	279,230	28·8	..	2·6	1·7	43·1	0·3	0·4	1·8	78·7	355,558
26,489	..	2,877	6,707	110,374	30·0	3·1	3·7	1·2	13·6	..	1·5	3·4	56·5	95,472
72,065	430	2,454	5,728	195,195	30·3	..	4·5	3·9	24·4	0·1	0·8	1·9	65·9	296,064
64,613	..	1,250	24,463	379,887	39·1	..	7·4	4·5	11·4	..	0·2	4·3	66·9	567,098
21,197	..	1,752	4,049	144,207	51·1	..	10·5	2·1	11·5	..	0·9	2·2	78·3	184,307
81,501	..	4,816	4,813	181,833	17·6	1·7	2·4	1·5	20·9	..	1·2	1·2	46·5	390,997
15,257	838	2,354	9,407	239,364	40·0	..	13·0	4·5	4·1	0·1	0·6	2·5	64·8	369,318
44,843	4,642	4,109	13,440	294,801	36·0	..	7·7	5·0	9·8	0·8	0·8	2·9	64·2	458,805
10,590	966	900	3,148	76,851	47·3	..	2·5	3·3	9·1	0·8	0·8	2·7	66·5	115,489
9,742	795	455	3,402	96,127	33·0	..	8·2	7·5	5·8	0·5	0·3	2·1	57·4	167,298
7,641	..	..	3,636	47,179	39·7	..	3·2	13·0	11·9	..	..	5·7	73·5	64,183
43,076	2,297	3,651	7,259	327,263	34·7	0·3	4·5	4·5	7·0	0·3	0·6	1·2	53·1	615,766
177,896	10,139	58,747	41,256	813,335	19·1	0·8	4·1	1·8	8·8	0·5	2·9	2·0	40·0	2,031,236
33,441	170	2,537	4,725	166,901	38·3	..	5·6	10·8	14·5	1·1	1·1	2·0	72·4	230,508
118,173	260	2,333	3,521	315,044	40·5	..	2·8	3·5	29·0	0·1	0·6	0·9	77·4	407,222
43,216	6,097	17,846	28,067	592,716	18·7	0·3	4·8	2·1	2·2	0·3	1·0	1·5	31·4	1,886,576
23,457	7,691	2,764	1,890	116,223	22·9	..	9·5	18·6	14·9	4·9	1·8	1·2	73·8	157,418
76,637	1,570	1,456	9,521	312,913	42·3	..	3·5	4·7	17·3	0·4	0·3	2·2	70·7	442,714
21,227	144	705	4,151	160,397	43·7	..	8·4	11·0	10·0	0·1	0·3	2·0	75·5	212,380
41,532	..	4,914	3,890	148,283	18·1	10·6	2·0	1·5	13·7	..	1·6	1·3	48·8	303,568
54,850	..	1,982	6,314	160,234	28·5	..	3·2	5·3	20·2	..	0·7	2·4	60·3	270,427
15,180	230	1,335	3,966	115,895	46·5	..	4·9	4·4	8·9	0·1	0·8	2·3	67·9	170,439
2,051	..	..	90	18,530	58·1	..	4·7	8·5	8·9	..	..	0·4	80·6	22,983
33,267	1,906	1,837	1,993	152,553	41·6	..	5·2	2·6	14·5	0·8	0·8	0·9	66·4	229,341
55,052	1,160	2,382	11,055	301,811	40·9	..	6·4	5·0	12·4	0·2	0·5	2·5	67·9	443,916
30,203	567	2,904	6,430	238,283	37·2	..	8·0	3·7	7·4	0·1	0·7	1·6	58·7	405,370
92,965	180	9,756	4,762	304,292	26·9	0·2	3·5	1·7	15·3	..	1·6	0·8	50·0	608,716
23,886	..	544	6,100	249,340	47·9	..	9·3	7·7	7·1	..	0·1	1·8	73·9	337,215
17,871	600	8,046	7,372	237,896	22·2	0·1	4·6	2·9	2·6	0·1	1·2	1·1	34·8	683,082
12,872	1,963	1,216	9,420	190,522	39·3	..	6·1	3·6	3·8	0·6	0·3	2·8	56·5	336,844
26,843	732	6,891	16,615	218,112	27·5	0·1	4·5	3·3	5·6	0·1	1·4	3·4	45·9	475,013
8,502	..	700	3,037	40,239	42·5	0·7	3·1	1·7	14·6	..	1·2	5·2	69·0	58,287
28,206	340	790	3,458	196,594	46·1	..	8·6	9·7	11·1	..	0·3	1·4	77·3	254,231
28,629	3,354	2,834	5,128	147,095	32·0	0·2	2·8	3·7	10·3	1·2	1·0	1·9	53·1	276,926
63,988	..	2,568	3,604	157,703	32·1	0·3	5·5	1·8	29·0	..	1·1	1·6	71·4	220,963
6,489	..	990	1,250	23,650	33·6	..	7·6	..	17·8	..	2·7	3·4	65·1	36,308
74,441	..	4,016	6,465	187,081	40·0	0·2	5·7	1·6	34·6	..	1·9	3·0	87·0	215,214
278,211	..	8,346	25,774	715,777	21·7	0·1	5·6	3·0	21·0	..	0·7	1·9	54·0	1,325,495
56,800	111,372	885	5,326	367,307	28·1	..	12·8	5·9	13·8	27·0	0·2	1·3	89·1	412,114
44,186	87,392	1,938	12,925	500,118	25·1	..	20·5	14·0	7·4	14·7	0·3	2·2	84·2	593,607

TABLE I.

DISTRICTS with MOST and LEAST ACCOMMODATION respectively.

Districts with most Accommodation.	Population, 1851.	Number of Sittings provided by all Religious Bodies.	Proportion per Cent. of Sittings to Population.	Excess of Sittings above the Number required to provide for 58 per Cent. of the Population.	Districts with least Accommodation.	Population, 1851.	Number of Sittings provided by all Religious Bodies.	Proportion per Cent. of Sittings to Population.	Deficiency of Sittings below the Number required to provide for 58 per Cent. of the Population.
606. Machynlleth	12,116	14,979	123·6	7,952	20. Shoreditch	109,257	19,614	17·9	43,755
300. Camelford	8,448	10,180	120·5	5,280	23. St. Geo. in the East	48,376	10,039	20·8	18,019
111. Catherington	2,493	2,961	119·6	1,535	30. Newington	64,816	15,399	23·7	22,194
617. Dolgelly	12,971	15,048	116·0	7,525	26. St. Saviour, South^k	35,731	8,707	24·4	12,017
410. Billesdon	7,009	8,034	114·7	3,971	15. Clerkenwell	64,778	16,065	24·8	21,506
599. Builth	8,345	9,555	114·5	4,715	439. Radford	26,776	6,608	24·9	8,862
622. Conway	11,650	13,182	113·3	6,437	31. Lambeth	139,325	34,818	25·0	45,991
521. Skirlaugh	9,279	10,492	113·1	5,110	22. Whitechapel	79,759	19,903	25·0	26,237
605. Rhayader	6,796	7,667	112·8	3,725	7. Marylebone	157,696	39,565	25·1	51,551
619. Pwllheli	21,788	24,091	110·6	11,454	25. Poplar	47,162	11,989	25·4	15,365
616. Bala	6,736	7,349	109·1	3,442	24. Stepney	110,775	28,578	25·8	35,672
600. Brecknock	18,174	19,166	105·5	8,625	28. Bermondsey	48,128	12,455	25·8	15,459
609. Llanfyllin	19,538	20,576	105·3	9,244	1. Kensington	120,004	31,556	26·3	38,046
595. Lampeter	9,874	10,360	104·9	4,633	13. Strand	44,460	11,996	27·0	13,794
618. Festiniog	16,182	16,906	104·5	7,520	6. St. James, Westm'	36,406	9,877	27·1	11,218
593. Cardigan	20,186	21,075	104·4	9,367	18. West London	28,790	7,981	27·7	8,723
612. Ruthin	16,853	17,188	102·0	7,413	21. Bethnal Green	90,193	25,744	28·5	26,568
312. Scilly Islands	2,627	2,663	101·4	1,139	2. Chelsea	56,538	16,279	28·8	16,513
418. Melton Mowbray	20,583	20,636	100·5	8,727	16. St. Luke	54,055	15,703	29·0	15,649
597. Aberystwith	23,753	23,865	100·5	10,068	10. Islington	95,329	27,652	29·0	27,639
573. East Ward	13,660	13,706	100·3	5,780	395. Aston	66,852	19,805	29·5	18,966
409. Market Harborough	15,839	15,842	100·0	6,655	12. St. Giles	54,214	16,139	29·8	15,305
255. Marlborough	10,263	10,172	99·1	4,219	33. Camberwell	54,667	16,492	30·2	15,215
504 b. Hemsworth	8,158	8,077	99·0	3,345	393. King's Norton	30,871	9,348	30·3	8,557
594. Newcastle-in-Emlyn	20,173	19,901	98·7	8,201	9. St. Pancras	166,956	51,275	30·7	45,559
299. Stratton	8,580	8,382	97·7	3,406	507. Ecclesall Bierlow	37,914	11,655	30·7	10,335
614. Llanrwst	12,479	12,152	97·4	4,914	54. Rotherhithe	17,805	5,515	31·0	4,812
583. Bridgend	23,422	22,700	96·9	9,115	461. Liverpool	258,236	80,239	31·1	69,541
602. Hay	10,962	10,574	96·5	4,216	394. Birmingham	173,951	54,319	31·2	46,573
596. Aberayron	13,224	12,749	96·4	5,079	3. St. Geo. Hanover Sq.	73,230	23,068	31·5	19,445
117. Whitchurch (Hants)	5,619	5,404	96·2	2,145	472. Salford	87,523	27,775	31·7	22,989
259. Westbury	12,530	11,982	95·6	4,715	471. Chorlton	123,841	39,462	31·9	32,366
516. Pocklington	16,096	15,368	95·5	6,051	14. Holborn	46,621	14,912	32·0	12,128
587. Llandovery	15,055	14,355	95·4	5,623	465. Wigan	77,539	25,661	33·1	19,311
487. Sedbergh	4,574	4,357	95·3	1,704	473. Manchester	228,433	75,817	33·2	56,674
301. Launceston	16,773	15,896	94·8	6,170	475. Oldham	86,788	28,846	33·2	21,491
304. Bodmin	20,493	19,258	94·0	7,372	35. Greenwich	99,365	33,219	33·4	24,413
170. Brixworth	14,771	13,881	94·0	5,314	4. Westminster	65,609	22,279	34·0	15,774
429. Horncastle	25,089	23,569	93·9	9,017	552. Newcastle-on-Tyne	89,156	31,018	34·8	20,692
588. Llandilofawr	17,968	16,871	93·9	6,450	29. St. Geo. Southwark	51,824	18,209	35·1	11,849
615. Corwen	15,418	14,395	93·4	5,453	17. East London	44,406	15,772	35·5	9,983
589. Carmarthen	38,142	35,377	92·2	13,255	548. Chester-le-Street	28,907	7,518	36·0	4,608
521. Patrington	9,407	8,726	92·8	3,270	508. Sheffield	103,626	38,036	36·7	22,067
601. Crickhowell	21,697	20,044	92·4	7,460	96. Portsea Island	72,126	26,608	36·9	15,255
603. Presteigne	15,149	13,977	92·3	5,191	85. Brighton	65,569	24,363	37·2	13,667
524. Bridlington	14,322	13,070	91·3	4,763	379. Wolverhampton	104,158	39,182	37·6	21,280
451. Louth	33,427	30,346	90·8	10,960	468. Bolton	114,712	43,517	37·9	23,015
296. Holsworthy	11,382	10,300	90·5	3,698	462. West Derby	153,279	58,214	38·0	30,688
285. Kingsbridge	21,377	19,197	89·8	6,798	27. St. Olave, South^k	19,375	7,351	38·0	3,887
443. Bingham	16,241	14,558	89·6	5,133	194. West Ham	34,395	13,110	38·1	6,839

* The figures prefixed to each district refer to its number in the topographical arrangement adopted in the DETAILED TABLES appended to the Report.

TABLE K.

COMPARATIVE POSITION of the CHURCH OF ENGLAND and the DISSENTING CHURCHES, in different Parts of the Country.

COUNTIES.	Proportion per cent. of sittings to Population.		Proportion per cent. of sittings to total Number of Sittings.	
	Provided by the Church of England.	Provided by other Churches.	Provided by the Church of England.	Provided by other Churches.
Bedford	35.2	36.8	46.9	51.1
Berks	41.1	24.6	62.6	37.4
Buckingham	41.1	30.4	57.5	42.5
Cambridge	52.2	28.1	53.4	46.6
Chester	27.6	29.0	48.8	51.2
Cornwall	28.8	49.9	36.6	63.4
Cumberland	30.0	26.5	53.1	46.9
Derby	30.3	35.6	46.0	54.0
Devon	59.1	27.8	58.4	41.6
Dorset	51.1	27.2	65.3	34.7
Durham	17.6	28.9	37.8	62.2
Essex	40.0	24.8	61.7	38.3
Gloucester	36.0	28.2	56.1	43.9
Hereford	47.3	19.2	71.1	28.9
Hertford	33.0	24.4	57.5	42.5
Huntingdon	39.7	33.8	54.0	46.0
Kent	34.7	18.4	65.3	34.7
Lancaster	19.1	20.9	47.7	52.3
Leicester	36.3	34.1	52.9	47.1
Lincoln	40.5	36.9	52.3	47.7
Middlesex	18.7	12.7	59.6	40.4
Monmouth	22.9	50.9	31.0	69.0
Norfolk	42.3	28.4	59.8	40.2
Northampton	43.7	31.8	57.9	42.1
Northumberland	18.1	30.7	37.1	62.9
Nottingham	28.5	31.8	47.3	52.7
Oxford	46.5	21.4	68.5	31.5
Rutland	53.1	22.5	72.1	27.9
Salop	41.6	24.8	62.7	37.3
Somerset	40.9	27.0	60.2	39.8
Southampton	37.2	21.5	63.4	36.6
Stafford	26.9	23.1	53.8	46.2
Suffolk	47.9	26.0	64.7	35.8
Surrey	22.2	12.6	63.8	36.2
Sussex	39.3	17.2	69.6	30.4
Warwick	27.5	18.4	60.0	40.0
Westmorland	42.5	26.5	61.6	38.4
Wilts	46.1	31.2	59.6	40.4
Worcester	32.0	21.1	60.3	39.7
York (East Riding)	32.1	39.3	45.0	55.0
" (City)	33.6	31.5	51.6	48.4
" (North Riding)	40.0	47.0	46.0	54.0
" (West Riding)	31.7	32.3	40.2	59.8
North Wales	28.1	61.0	31.5	68.5
South Wales	25.1	59.1	29.8	70.2
ENGLAND AND WALES	29.6	27.4	51.9	48.1

LARGE TOWNS.	Proportion per cent. of sittings to Population.		Proportion per cent. of sittings to total Number of Sittings.	
	Provided by the Church of England.	Provided by other Churches.	Provided by the Church of England.	Provided by other Churches.
Ashton-under-Lyne	13.1	25.5	33.9	66.1
Bath	38.6	22.5	63.2	36.8
Birmingham	18.3	15.4	46.3	53.7
Blackburn	19.1	20.6	47.1	52.9
Bolton	15.7	19.9	44.1	55.9
Bradford	10.0	21.6	31.6	68.4
Brighton	19.4	15.2	56.1	43.9
Bristol	23.5	29.3	44.5	55.5
Bury	17.8	25.2	41.4	58.6
Cheltenham	31.0	25.5	54.9	45.1
Coventry	23.1	19.8	53.9	46.1
Derby	22.0	28.1	43.9	56.1
Devonport	20.8	25.8	44.6	55.4
Dudley	15.0	26.9	35.8	64.2
Exeter	35.3	24.4	59.1	40.9
Great Yarmouth	22.4	23.7	48.6	51.4
Halifax	14.3	16.0	47.2	52.8
Huddersfield	18.8	32.3	36.8	63.2
Hull	16.0	28.2	36.2	63.8
Ipswich	24.8	23.9	50.9	49.1
Leeds	15.0	31.0	32.6	67.4
Leicester	14.6	26.7	35.4	64.6
Liverpool	16.5	14.9	52.5	47.5
London	17.6	12.1	59.3	40.7
Macclesfield	19.0	23.2	45.0	55.0
Manchester	12.6	19.0	39.9	60.1
Merthyr Tydfil	6.0	52.4	10.3	89.7
Newcastle	11.7	22.8	33.9	66.1
Norwich	24.5	20.7	54.2	45.8
Nottingham	12.3	35.2	25.9	74.1
Oldham	14.1	17.7	44.9	55.1
Plymouth	18.4	27.2	40.4	59.6
Portsmouth	17.0	19.9	46.1	53.9
Preston	17.0	18.4	48.0	52.0
Rochdale	9.9	36.5	21.3	78.7
Salford	13.7	25.1	35.3	64.7
Sheffield	15.0	18.9	44.2	55.8
Southampton	28.8	22.1	56.6	43.4
Stockport	16.3	25.7	38.8	61.2
Stoke-upon-Trent	20.4	28.1	42.1	57.9
Sunderland	13.7	35.2	28.0	72.0
Swansea	16.1	42.8	27.3	72.7
Wigan	10.1	20.5	33.0	67.0
Wolverhampton	18.6	21.9	46.0	54.0
Worcester	36.2	22.5	61.7	38.3
TOTAL	17.2	18.8	47.8	52.2

¹ This Table may be read thus:—In Bedfordshire, for every 100 persons, the Church of England affords accommodation for 35, and the other churches for 37; while, in the same county, out of every 100 *sittings* provided by all religious bodies together, 49 belong to the Church of England, and 51 to other churches.

TABLE L.

Showing the NUMBER of SERVICES held by EACH RELIGIOUS BODY at different periods of the Day.

RELIGIOUS DENOMINATIONS.	In Towns.								In Rural Districts.							
	Morning only.	Afternoon only.	Evening only.	Morning and Afternoon.	Morning and Evening.	Afternoon and Evening.	Morning, Afternoon, and Evening.	TOTAL.	Morning only.	Afternoon only.	Evening only.	Morning and Afternoon.	Morning and Evening.	Afternoon and Evening.	Morning, Afternoon, and Evening.	TOTAL.
TOTAL	468	277	277	1077	3048	622	1674	7463	3314	3302	2257	7954	5712	4063	2402	27,004
PROTESTANT CHURCHES:																
Church of England	185	110	43	637	765	7	466	2213	2325	1855	222	6526	604	46	286	11,864
Scottish Presbyterians:																
Church of Scotland	2	..	..	..	8	..	1	11	1	..	1	3	2	..	..	7
United Presbyterian Church	5	..	..	7	19	..	4	35	8	2	7	4	8	..	2	31
Presbyterian Church in England	2	..	..	6	28	..	..	36	11	..	2	13	13	..	1	40
Reformed Irish Presbyterians	..	..	..	1	..	..	..	1	..	..	..	..	..	..	..	..
Independents	31	33	51	36	576	55	237	1019	171	233	330	201	679	231	390	2235
Baptists:																
General	1	1	1	3	6	1	5	18	9	5	8	4	4	38	7	75
Particular	18	15	15	48	329	25	237	687	78	105	107	151	310	126	383	1260
Seventh Day	..	..	..	..	..	..	1	1	1	..	..	..	..	..	..	1
Scotch	..	..	..	3	1	..	1	5	..	..	..	7	..	1	1	10
New Connexion General	2	2	2	3	31	3	13	56	5	20	16	10	32	33	11	126
Undefined	7	6	5	7	46	7	46	124	62	38	23	50	50	61	72	426
Society of Friends	53	1	1	145	13	..	1	214	83	7	..	56	4	..	5	157
Unitarians	41	4	30	26	53	2	1	157	9	2	6	33	5	2	15	72
Moravians	..	..	..	1	6	..	2	9	3	3	..	3	7	1	6	23
Wesleyan Methodists:																
Original Connexion	25	43	49	24	462	193	266	1082	231	526	833	442	1073	1806	581	5497
New Connexion	..	1	5	1	46	18	20	91	8	11	16	24	39	59	50	206
Primitive	17	15	15	13	106	181	129	476	127	235	341	106	255	996	335	2395
Bible Christians	..	3	5	1	19	16	21	65	19	70	43	8	67	142	48	417
Wesleyan Association	4	7	4	..	59	27	19	110	9	37	57	17	65	95	29	309
Independent Methodists	1	1	..	..	1	4	4	11	..	1	2	..	..	4	2	9
Wesleyan Reformers	1	2	7	1	49	9	12	81	5	19	48	22	54	77	33	258
Calvinistic Methodists:																
Welsh	2	8	..	4	59	33	10	116	34	70	43	20	309	176	60	712
Lady Huntingdon's Connexion	3	2	3	3	35	3	3	52	2	8	6	5	22	9	5	57
Sandemanians	1	..	..	2	..	..	..	3	1	..	..	1	..	..	1	3
New Church	4	..	2	5	15	2	2	30	..	..	..	11	6	2	1	20
Brethren	5	..	3	1	34	4	7	54	..	6	6	10	16	12	21	78
Isolated Congregations	17	16	24	11	125	20	44	257	37	34	61	46	40	46	28	292
Lutherans	4	..	..	1	1	..	..	6	..	..	..	..	..	..	..	..
French Protestants	..	1	..	..	2	..	..	3	..	..	..	..	..	..	..	..
Reformed Church of the Netherlands	1	..	..	..	..	..	..	1	..	..	..	..	..	..	..	..
German Protestant Reformers	..	..	..	..	1	..	..	1	..	..	..	..	..	..	..	..
OTHER CHRISTIAN CHS.:																
Roman Catholics	37	4	4	70	100	1	54	270	60	10	5	179	25	4	17	300
Greek Church	2	..	..	..	..	..	..	2	1	..	..	..	..	..	..	1
German Catholics	..	..	..	..	..	..	..	1	..	..	..	..	..	..	..	..
Italian Reformers	..	1	..	..	1	..	..	1	..	..	..	..	..	..	..	..
Catholic and Apostolic Church	..	..	1	6	13	..	8	28	1	1	..	..	..	1	1	4
Latter Day Saints	10	1	7	4	4	21	40	87	11	1	..	2	3	45	73	135
Jews	7	..	..	7	15	..	20	49	..	2	..	..	..	1	1	4

TABLE M.

Comparative view of the frequency with which the various Religious Bodies make use of the Accommodation provided for by them respectively.   (*See Report, page 86.*)*

RELIGIOUS DENOMINATIONS.	Proportion per cent. which the occupied Sittings bear to the total Number of Sittings.				RELIGIOUS DENOMINATIONS.	Proportion per cent. which the occupied Sittings bear to the total Number of Sittings.			
	Morning.	Afternoon.	Evening.	Total.		Morning.	Afternoon.	Evening.	Total.
PROTESTANT CHURCHES:					PROTESTANT CHURCHES—*continued.*				
Church of England	47·8	35·6	16·2	33·2	Calvinistic Methodists:				
					Welsh Calvinistic Methodists	37·6	27·9	50·1	41·5
Scotch Presbyterians:					*Lady Huntingdon's Connexion*	54·5	11·3	49·5	38·4
Church of Scotland	50·4	7·0	27·9	28·4					
United Presbyterian Church	56·5	16·2	28·1	33·6	Sandemanians	45·9	26·8	6·4	26·4
Presbyterian Church in England	55·1	8.2	26·1	29·8	New Church	40·0	19·9	25·6	28·5
Independents	49·1	21·8	42·8	37·9	Brethren	30·8	24·3	39·9	31·6
Baptists:					Isolated Congregations	35·4	23·2	41·6	33·4
General	26·3	39·6	41·7	35·9	Lutherans	44·2	10·1	..	18·1
Particular	50·2	30·1	46·7	42·4	French Protestants	40·2	5·7	26·8	24·1
Seventh-Day	6·9	10·3	4·1	7·1	Reformed Church of the Netherlands	20·0	..	..	6·7
Scotch	25·5	33·7	12·3	25·5	German Protestant Reformers	60·0	..	30·0	30·0
New Connexion, General	45·5	29·9	46·9	40·8					
Undefined	40·9	25·5	41·9	36·1	OTHER CHRISTIAN CHS.:				
Society of Friends	15·1	7·0	1·6	7·9	Roman Catholics	135·8†	29·0	41·3	68·7
Unitarians	41·5	13·0	18·5	24·8	Greek Church	82·5	..	.	27·5
Moravians	53·7	26·5	36·7	38·9	German Catholics	166·7	..	66·7	77·8
Wesleyan Methodists:					Italian Reformers	..	13·3	..	4·4
Original Connexion	34·0	26·5	46·1	35·6	Catholic and Apostolic Church	42·7	22·3	36·4	33·8
New Connexion	38·0	23·3	40·9	34·0	Latter Day Saints	24·4	37·3	54·0	38·6
Primitive	24·2	42·6	56·7	41·2	Jews	34·5	14·2	22·7	23·8
Bible Christians	22·3	36·4	51·8	36·8	TOTAL	45·5	31·2	36·0	35·6
Wesleyan Association	32·7	21·4	41·1	31·7					
Independent Methodists	26·6	57·9	53·4	46·0					
Wesleyan Reformers	44·9	23·7	66·3	45·0					

* This Table may be read thus:—Out of every 100 sittings belonging to the Church of England, there were occupied, by attendants,—in the morning, 47; in the afternoon, 35; and in the evening, 16; while the total number of sittings occupied by attendants in the course of the whole day was 33 per cent. of the number which might have been occupied if all the churches had been open for three services. And so of the other Bodies. In many cases, of course, the sittings were not occupied because the buildings were closed.

† The apparent excess of attendants over sittings in the morning among the Roman Catholics is explained by the fact that they generally have several services, for different persons, at that period of the day.

TABLE N.

Number of Persons present at the most numerously attended Services, on Sunday, March 30, 1851.

IN REGISTRATION COUNTIES AND DIVISIONS.

REGISTRATION DIVISIONS AND COUNTIES.	Population, 1851.	Number of Attendants belonging to				
		Church of England.	Protestant Dissenters.	Roman Catholics.	Other Bodies.	All Denominations.
ENGLAND AND WALES -	17,927,609	2,971,258	3,110,782	249,389	24,796	6,356,222
DIV.						
I. LONDON - - - - - -	2,362,236	276,685	186,321	36,334	5,274	504,514
II. SOUTH-EASTERN COUNTIES -	1,523,386	358,028	205,841	6,929	1,616	583,414
III. SOUTH MIDLAND COUNTIES -	1,234,532	308,787	249,290	3,277	1,191	562,175
IV. EASTERN COUNTIES - - -	1,113,982	277,732	206,830	3,296	768	488,556
V. SOUTH-WESTERN COUNTIES -	1,803,991	407,907	381,501	5,134	1,534	796,076
VI. WEST MIDLAND COUNTIES -	2,132,930	376,844	315,946	28,790	4,041	725,621
VII. NORTH MIDLAND COUNTIES -	1,214,538	215,496	272,395	8,869	1,965	498,697
VIII. NORTH-WESTERN COUNTIES -	2,490,827	284,240	293,977	112,523	2,811	693,551
IX. YORKSHIRE - - - -	1,789,047	216,062	374,890	20,668	1,489	612,089
X. NORTHERN COUNTIES - -	969,126	106,335	141,039	17,951	351	265,676
XI. WELSH COUNTIES - - - -	1,188,914	182,940	481,192	5,688	3,683	623,503
DIVISION I.						
MIDDLESEX (Part of) - - - - -	1,745,661	197,841	187,858	27,619	4,457	867,775
SURREY (Part of) - - - -	482,435	157,789	85,240	7,668	665	101,362
KENT (Part of) - - - -	134,900	21,255	13,223	1,047	252	35,777
DIVISION II.						
SURREY (Extra-Metropolitan) - -	202,521	47,572	15,047	1,033	80	63,682
KENT (Extra-Metropolitan) - -	485,021	106,438	64,368	1,308	632	174,736
SUSSEX - - - - -	339,604	76,381	37,285	785	338	114,929
HAMPSHIRE - - - -	402,918	92,939	63,842	3,179	404	160,364
BERKSHIRE - - - -	199,224	43,198	26,399	694	322	89,273
DIVISION III.						
MIDDLESEX (Extra-Metropolitan) - -	150,606	29,631	14,306	575	72	44,584
HERTFORDSHIRE - - -	173,969	48,195	38,351	355	308	77,109
BUCKINGHAMSHIRE - - -	148,655	37,426	31,691	394	100	69,611
OXFORDSHIRE - - - -	170,947	44,943	25,977	1,018	46	71,984
NORTHAMPTONSHIRE - - -	212,844	56,743	46,478	515	281	104,064
HUNTINGDONSHIRE - - -	60,819	16,469	16,688	. .	67	33,219
BEDFORDSHIRE - - - -	129,805	31,213	42,291	80	227	73,781
CAMBRIDGESHIRE - - -	191,894	49,167	39,248	370	148	88,923
DIVISION IV.						
ESSEX - - - - -	344,130	76,906	68,192	1,404	639	146,233
SUFFOLK - - - - -	336,136	100,854	64,184	336	101	165,475
NORFOLK - - - - -	433,716	100,970	74,454	1,286	438	176,848
DIVISION V.						
WILTSHIRE - - - -	240,966	63,726	57,519	1,005	422	122,672
DORSETSHIRE - - - -	177,095	53,240	28,910	797	176	83,123
DEVONSHIRE - - - -	572,330	129,538	98,516	1,394	461	229,849
CORNWALL - - - -	356,641	44,919	116,042	502	16	181,529
SOMERSETSHIRE - - - -	456,359	116,484	80,514	1,416	439	198,853
DIVISION VI.						
GLOUCESTERSHIRE - - - -	419,514	89,860	76,621	3,799	1,290	170,720
HEREFORDSHIRE - - -	90,120	21,559	9,766	456	81	31,862
SHROPSHIRE - - - -	244,896	55,004	89,008	1,527	202	95,741
STAFFORDSHIRE - - -	630,545	89,960	107,789	14,097	359	201,494
WORCESTERSHIRE - - -	259,786	53,135	28,694	3,401	287	85,517
WARWICKSHIRE - - -	480,120	75,706	54,119	10,510	1,898	142,237
DIVISION VII.						
LEICESTERSHIRE - - -	224,957	50,907	54,236	3,062	895	107,620
RUTLANDSHIRE - - -	24,272	6,838	4,518	. .	30	11,386
LINCOLNSHIRE - - -	400,286	78,434	90,877	3,155	678	168,835
NOTTINGHAMSHIRE - - -	294,399	46,931	63,183	1,291	1,070	112,075
DERBYSHIRE - - - -	360,698	87,398	61,061	2,740	162	101,961
DIVISION VIII.						
CHESHIRE - - - - -	422,536	61,430	68,392	8,221	762	138,805
LANCASHIRE - - - -	2,067,301	222,810	225,585	104,302	2,049	554,746
DIVISION IX.						
WEST RIDING - - - -	1,340,051	132,330	273,290	14,069	1,216	427,901
EAST RIDING (WITH YORK) - -	254,352	55,690	55,702	5,276	273	99,440
NORTH RIDING - - - -	194,644	38,036	45,830	2,323	. .	86,098
DIVISION X.						
DURHAM - - - -	411,679	37,871	65,105	8,542	94	111,912
NORTHUMBERLAND - - -	303,568	29,604	49,107	5,930	120	84,761
CUMBERLAND - - - -	195,492	26,757	20,057	2,779	187	49,780
WESTMORLAND - - -	58,287	12,103	6,770	400	. .	19,273
DIVISION XI.						
MONMOUTHSHIRE - - - -	177,130	28,845	59,818	2,470	865	69,586
SOUTH WALES - - - -	607,456	69,366	253,781	2,456	2,514	328,107
NORTH WALES - - - -	404,328	38,729	172,548	762	814	214,949

The mode of compiling this Table has been, to take for every individual church or chapel the service (whether Morning, Afternoon, or Evening) at which most persons were present, and make an aggregate for each of the bodies above mentioned. In some cases the best attendance would be in the Morning, in others, in the Afternoon, in others, in the Evening. The total thus divided would show the minimum number of persons who attended service on March 30, 1851, if none attended more than one church or chapel. To the extent to which the practice prevails of frequenting more than one place of worship will this inference be liable to modification.

The same consideration will affect the comparative proportions between different Bodies; since no doubt some numbers who attended Dissenters' services in the evening had worshipped with the Church of England in an earlier portion of the day.

CPSIA information can be obtained at www.ICGtesting.com
Printed in the USA
LVOW051410090212

267939LV00003B/27/P